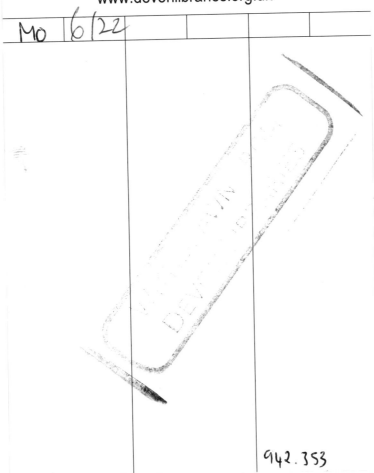

THE BOOK OF
SOUTH TAWTON
AND SOUTH ZEAL

• WITH STICKLEPATH •

THE BOOK OF
SOUTH TAWTON AND SOUTH ZEAL
• WITH *STICKLEPATH* •

A THOUSAND YEARS BENEATH THE BEACON

ROY AND URSULA RADFORD

HALSGROVE

First published in Great Britain in 2000

British Library Cataloguing-in-Publication Data
A CIP record for this title is available from the British Library

ISBN 1 84114 060 0

HALSGROVE
PUBLISHING, MEDIA AND DISTRIBUTION

Halsgrove House
Lower Moor Way
Tiverton, Devon EX16 6SS
Tel: 01884 243242
Fax: 01884 243325
email: sales@halsgrove.com
website: http://www.halsgrove.com

Printed and bound in Great Britain by Bookcraft Ltd, Midsomer Norton.

CONTENTS

Acknowledgments　　　　　　　　　　　　　　　　　　　　　　*7*

CHAPTER 1: SOUTH TAWTON AND ITS MANORS: THE EARLY CENTURIES　　9

CHAPTER 2: STICKLEPATH: CHANTRY CHAPEL AND CHURCHES　　21

CHAPTER 3: SOUTH TAWTON AND SOUTH ZEAL FROM C.1850　　35

CHAPTER 4: THE ONSET OF EDUCATION: 1663-1881　　47

CHAPTER 5: ALMOST A CENTURY AT STICKLEPATH SCHOOL　　59

CHAPTER 6: INDUSTRY IN THE AREA　　73

CHAPTER 7: THE PARISH AND THE CHURCH　　85

CHAPTER 8: THE HELPING HAND　　97

CHAPTER 9: ENTERTAINING OTHERS... AND OURSELVES　　109

CHAPTER 10: THE WAY IT WAS　　121

CHAPTER 11: GLEANINGS FROM A RICH HISTORY　　135

CHAPTER 12: CONVERSATIONS ON...　　143

Glossary　　　　　　　　　　　　　　　　　　　　　　*155*
Bibliography and *References*　　　　　　　　　　　　*156*
Subscribers　　　　　　　　　　　　　　　　　　　　*157*

Acknowledgements

In compiling this book we have greatly appreciated the tremendous help given to us by local people throughout the area and, equally, we value the help given to us by those that lived in the district in the past or who visit the area and who went out of their way to assist us. Our sincere thanks for helping make this publication a community project go to each and every one, wherever they live, including;

Bill Adams, Matthew Appleton and The National Trust, Dr Nick Atkinson and Dartmoor National Park staff, Michael and Sally Bailey, Gerald Bastable, Shirley Bazeley, Nora Bertram, Eileen Birch, Caroline and Michael Boother, Roger Bowden, Elspeth Brint, Jenny and Peter Brotherton, Joyce Cann, William and Christine Cann, John and Theresa Christian, Tony Clarke, Rosemary and Ted Coombes, Faith Crocker, Joan and Charlie Curtis, John Darch, Dave and Shirley Denford, Jan Easterbrook, Diana and David England, Muriel Finnucane, Pauline Fletcher, Hilary Gillespie, Jim Goodwin, Bert and Evelyn Gregory, Janice and Paul Grey, Elizabeth Hampton, Mike Hawkins, Jim Holman, Olive Hooper, Frances and Edgar Hucker, Joan Hutchinson, Wendy Kitchen, Violet Littlejohns, Irene and Arthur Madders, Christine McPhee, Members of South Zeal Women's Institute, Members of Sticklepath Women's Institute, Jon Padfield, David Patmore, Jill Pendleton, Wendy and Keith Redstone, Winnie Roberts, Graham Scott, Barbara and Patrick Shaw, Ian Snell, Ray Souness, Bobby Sutton (Headmistress), teachers and pupils of South Tawton County Primary School, Dr Andrew Stainer-Smith, Bert Stead, Robin Tilley, Brenda and Barry Tombs, Dorothy Vanstone, Ida Wonnacott, Dawn Watkins, Mike Watson, Andrew and Tracy White, Clarence and Pamela White, Clifford and Vera White, Martin and Jane White, Meg Wolton, Leslie and Valerie Wonnacott, Nick Wonnacott, Revd Barry Woods, Albert and Marion Woods, Joyce and Bill Worthington, Wendy Wyburn, and Rose Young.

Our special thanks go to Ann Bowden and Victor Hutchinson for their assistance in providing material on Sticklepath village, and Sticklepath School. The co-operation of the editors of the *Exeter Express and Echo*, the *Okehampton Times*, and the *Western Morning News*, in permitting the use of photos and reports is appreciated. We also received valued help from Devon County Council Libraries, the West Country Studies Library and, especially, by the Senior Librarian and staff at Okehampton Library.

In dealing here with a rural area so rich in a history, filled throughout the ages with characters and stories, we are but opening the door. Our hope is that others, especially the young, will enjoy a glimpse of the past we can all be proud of, explore and reveal it further, and build the future upon their inheritance.

ROY AND URSULA RADFORD
SEPTEMBER 2000

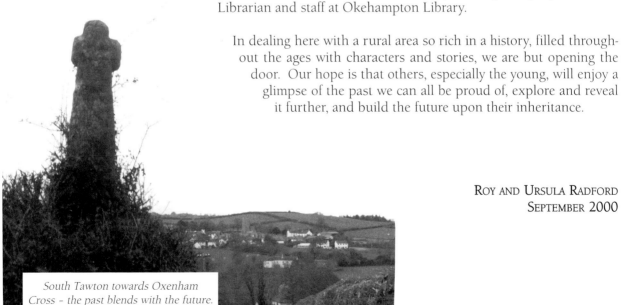

South Tawton towards Oxenham Cross - the past blends with the future.

7

Left: *With war over, in the 1950s, South Tawton parishioners enjoyed the revival of the Beating the Bounds and welcomed the off-ration ram roast. Will Wedlake carving – Ron Cox assisting. Also already identified in the picture on the left are: Mr and Mrs Beazley, Mrs Gillard, Eric Redstone, George Hocking, Tom Wright, Sid Cooper, Johnny Gillard, Mrs Bourke, Joan and Charlie Curtis, Mrs Dyment (née Tucker), Monica Hill, George Hooper, Derek Hooper, Mr and Mrs Trott, Mr Kelly, Mrs Wakley, Mrs Meardon, Jennifer Hooper, Mrs V. Knapman, Mrs B. Pethybridge, Lily Vigers, Wendy Rogers, Peggy Wooland, Mr Wooland, Rosemary Drew, Frances Hucker née Wonnacott, Mr and Mrs John Hooper Joyce Worthington with Billy, Bill Worthington, Frank Hudson, Percy and Betty Aggett, Joan Wonnacott, Tilly Kelly, Marion Lentern, Kath Letheren, Miss Madders, Jack Wonnacott, Mrs Winterbourne, Margaret Tucker, Bill Cann Snr., Mrs F. Ward, Mrs Watkins, Jock Souness and Violet Moore*

Right and centre: *Cosdon Hill stone rows and Throwleigh boundary marker.* Below: *Taking a well-earned rest during beating the bounds, Sticklepath 1951.*

Chapter 1
South Tawton and Its Manors:
The Early Centuries

In the Geld Roll of 1083 Tauetona alone is mentioned but, in the 1086 Domesday survey records two areas are referred to as Tauetona. This seemingly differentiates South Tawton from North Tawton while the survey also more clearly confirms that the King then held a 'Manor Tauetona', which paid tax on three hides and a virgate. This was a manor which before the Conquest had been part of the dowry of Queen Gytha, mother of King Harold; land that she held under King Edward the Confessor despite continuing antagonism between them that eventually led to Gytha being sent into exile across the Channel.

The survey's more detailed information on the 'Manor Tauetona', records that:

> Thirty ploughs can plough it. In demesne the King has a half hide and 8 ploughs. The villeins have 2½ hides and 36 ploughs. The King has there, 50 villeins, 30 Bordars, 12 serfs, 10 head of cattle, 400 sheep, 70 goats, a wood, 2 leugas long and 2 ferlings wide, 60 acres of meadow, 4 long (leugas) and 4 wide, of pasture. The Manor pays 48 pounds by weight, and paid the same when the King took it.

To the 'Manor Tautona' was added another, smaller, manor, named as Aissa that paid tax on land sufficient only for three ploughs to plough it. There the King had six villeins with three ploughs a serf, ten acres of meadow, and eight acres of pasture, and in total was worth thirty shillings.

Before the Battle of Hastings, and during the reign in King Edward the Confessor, this sub-manor, Aissa (Ash), was recorded as being held by a noble Saxon named Ulric, one of the higher or baronial thanes. Some suggest that it was from this Saxon, Ulric, that the Northmore family descended; and it is a family long connected with the area we now know as East Ash.

The Domesday survey refers to Gytha's dowry area as being a King's manor, not an ancient 'crown-lordship,' so it was clearly an area distinctly set apart to provide support to an earl, or to some member of the royal family.

In 1086 William the Conqueror's interest in the sub-manor is recorded as the possession there of six villeins, one serf, and three ploughs, but, soon afterwards, the royal manor of East Ayshe, Cheverston in Kenton, and also Wray in Moretonhampstead, all became the possessions of William de Wygornia.

In addition to its sub-manor of Ayshe, South Tawton also included the sub-manor of Itton and on the death of William Rufus, in 1100, the manor of South Tawton passed into the hands of Henry I who seized the throne. Henry, the fourth son of William the Conqueror, promised a return to good government and, having been born in the country, this promise found favour in England. His popularity grew when he turned his attention to the conquest of

Horses being used for the harvest.

❧ A Parish ❧ Under Plough

The land around the parish has been utilised to provide food, shelter and fuel for over 1000 years, with many working methods remaining relatively unchanged for centuries.

Top: *Looking across the fields towards Cawsand from South Tawton.*

Above right: *Blackhall Farm, South Tawton, c.1906.*

Above: *Wheat reed cutting, Blackhall, 1957.*

Below: *Haymaking at North Wyke.*

Above: *Reed cutters at Blackhall, including Clifford White.*

Far left: *Peat cutting, c.1916.*

Left: *William Webber ploughing with shire horses.*

Normandy, which he completed at Tenchebral. His subsequent triumph over French and Angevin opposition by a combination of war and diplomacy ensured his popularity with his people at home and, with some, that friendship had long been maintained in the bedchamber.

Elizabeth de Bellemonte, the daughter of Richard de Bellemonte or Beaumont, Earl of Leicester, was mother to Constance, and the fifth sidewind daughter of King Henry. The illegitimate offspring of such relationships were usually 'cared for' wherever possible, if not openly acknowledged. Henry lost no time in seeking to secure the future of the child born of his relationship with Elizabeth and c.1130 he gave Ailrichescot, now called Addiscot, in South Tawton, to his sidewind daughter. Constance, albeit born on the wrong side of the sheets, came from an influential family and, with her dowry confirmed by the King, was to become the bride of Roscelin de Bellamonte, Sheriff of Beaumont in Mayne, part of the Duchy of Normandy. On the death of Constance in or around 1157 the grant was continued to her son, Richard de Bellamonte, or Beaumont. Richard had no son to follow him but he paid honour to his mother by naming his daughter after her and in 1199 granted Ailrichescot, together with his daughter Constance, in free marriage, to Roger de Tony.

That recited grant that Constance took with her includes, possibly, the first reference made to a parish in the area, the 'paroch de Suthawthune,' not overlooking that 'Sud Tauetona' was mentioned as 'a hundred' in Pipe Rolls of 1189.

Parishes as we know them were 13th century creations but prior to 1200, as in this instance, the 'paroch' was becoming a legally recognisable district. King John re-affirmed the grant and confirmed the new arrangement, for a fee, since each king on succession renewed or confirmed his predecessor's grants in return for payment. Succession payment for the new grant, it seems, was simply an early form of death duty; but was not a 'tax' that affected the local people. Before the disafforestation of Devon by King John (1204), the manor must have been within the Royal Forest of Dartmoor and its close proximity to the tin-mining area of the region provided the majority of its inhabitants with work. More importantly, as Stannators, they were permitted to benefit from the remission of some taxes and other advantages, including venville common rights, indicating that the local population was not reliant upon agriculture.

Until 1211 Roger de Tony was in possession of Ailrichescot and his widow retained it thereafter until 1214 when the payment of succession grant fell upon Ralph de Tony as son of Constance and Roger de Tony and inheritor of the manor. On Ralf's death in 1239, his son, another Roger de Tony, succeeded him

and remained 'Patron' of South Tawton for almost a quarter of a century. Prior to his death he made over the courthouse of Blackhall and the lordship of the land to Alured de Porta, elsewhere called de Tauntifer (or Tantifer), Mayor of Exeter, who was later to be tried and executed for felony in connection with the death of a local canon, Walter de Lechlade, murdered on 5 November 1283. At the time of his own death in 1263 though, Roger de Tony was not only lord of Ailrichescot, but of the whole of the Hundred of South Tawton, including the borough of Zeal. The records show clearly that he died seized of 'Sutauton Maner and De La Sale Terra' (South Tawton Manor and land of the Hall). In some recent lists South Tawton appears as included in Wonford Hundred but it is described in 'Ancient Petitions' and 'Lay Subsidies' as an 'Ancient Demesne', and while the accuracy of the description is sometimes disputed, records from 1243, 1269, and from later centuries, all indicate that South Tawton was a hundred in itself, and a tithing.

To legally rank as an 'ancient demesne', a manor must have been in the hands of both Edward the Confessor and William the Conqueror. There is ample evidence that in earlier times South Tawton, like Winkleigh, formed a hundred by itself, and was then known as the crown lordship of Southteign or Southing. In the few places where South Tawton or any estate belonging to South Tawton is mentioned in the great Survey, it appears early in the list of hundreds, and never among estates belonging to Wonford Hundred, which comes somewhat low down on the list.

It appears from the Inquest on Roger de Tony in 1263 that at that date there were several sub-manors held in South Tawton. William le Pruz, lord of Gidleigh, held certain lands by charter for which he paid 50 shillings yearly, 'subject to relief when it befalls'. From a document some six years later in date this land was stated to be Coleton; worth £4 a year. Richard de Poltimore held land identified with the manor of Ash to the value of £12.5s.6d. by the service of one fortieth knight's fee, subject to relief and wardship. Henry de Horton held 100 shillings' worth of unidentified land by service of one fortieth fee, also subject to relief and wardship.

This estate, on Henry's death without issue, passed to his sister, Petronilla, wife of Robert Knoel, who on 23 February 1270 conveyed it to Richard Tantifer to hold of the said Petronilla and her heirs at a yearly rent of 50 shillings in place of the 100 shillings previously paid. Richard de Moun secured £10.12s.0d. worth of land in free marriage with Juliana de Vernun, apparently granted before 1240, and considered to be the present manor of Itton or Yedeton.

On the eve of the Feast of St Peter ad Vincula, in the 48th year of the reign of Henry III, 1264, a

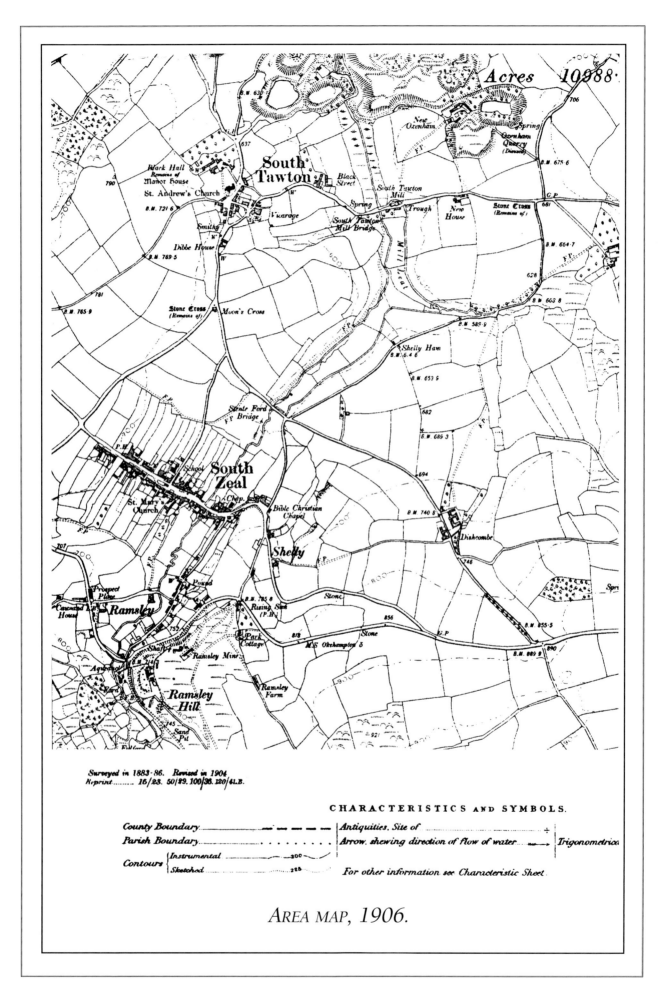

AREA MAP, 1906.

valuation of the manor of Suthtauton was conducted by Jacobû Freysell, for or on behalf of Roger de Tony; or possibly for the King, with succession payments in mind. The detail of the valuation was confirmed under oath by 12 signatories:

Robertû de Stoddon	Will. Chartrey
Henr de Hause	Will. de Colketrywe
Joh de Wyke	Joh. Tollay
Rog de Wyke	Rici de Woneston
Rad de Goseford	Joh. Burnel
Humff de la Sele	Rogi de Logues

It is said here that Roger de Tony holds the 'Manor in Chief of the King', but they 'know not by what service he does so'; that the lord is the patron of the Church of Sutauton, worth 50 shillings per annum; that Aluredus de la Porte holds the Court with Gardens and all its appurtenances paying 1d. per annum for all services; by charter that he holds also all the demesne ('dominicum') and one Water Mill, paying 1d. yearly, at the feast of St Michael for all services (and he holds, or receives, 30 shillings (£1.50) annual rent. Possibly for 'divers lands' which Roger de Wyke used to pay yearly). The valuer says that Will. la Prus holds certain lands by charter of the lord, paying yearly 50 shillings (£2.50), and that he owes relief when it becomes due; Ricard de Poltimor holds (to the value of) £12.5s.6d. of the lord, by the service of one fortieth part of a knight's fee, and owes relief and ward. Henri de Horton holds 100 shillings (£5) [worth] of land of the lord by the service of one fortieth fee, and owes relief and ward; Will. de Mohun holds £10.12s.0d. worth of land of the lord in free marriage with Juliana de Vernun.

This survey provides possibly the first record referring to the existence of burgage plots in Sele since their creation. It shows the lord of Tawton profiting from some revenue from a court at Sele villata and from 31s.2d. derived from 62½ acres used by 42 tenants. Each of the tenants held land varying in plot size, from half an acre to five acres, at a rental of 6d. per acre. They included:

Wiilmo de Poleslond	1 acre	@	6d.
Dionisia scissor	1 acre	@	6d.
Willo Chace	3 acres	@	18d.
Serlone de Wyke	1 acre	@	6d.
Rico le paum	1½ acres	@	9d.
Rici brigge	½ acre	@	3d.
Johe goseling	3 acres	@	18d.
Walter by water	4½ acres	@	2s.3d.
Humfrido le fulur	5 acres	@	2s.6d.
Hugo tayl	1½ acres	@	9d.

Johe Goseling and Willo Chace also paid an additional 1d. each for the use of 'a certain place (placia) of land and while that 2d. was within the rents charged, in total, there were other charges levied. The two entries in the rental are shown 'pro quadam placia terrae' which clearly suggests that a residence of some kind was also associated with each piece of land.

The village we now know was beginning to take shape as Humfrid de la sele, probably reluctantly, was finding 2s.6d. annually to pay for the right to use water at his mill. Rico le belde and Mabilla bugge paid 12d. per annum, possibly for wood, since there was also an 'item' noted of 6d. being paid from pannage of wood (pannage bosci). It was recorded that the lord received 'singulis annis' one third of the value of the market of Northtauton valued at four shillings per annum and from the township, 'villata,' of Sele he received two shillings per annum from 'perquisites'.

Named in recognition of his grandfather, Ralph de Tony succeeded the living as the decades of conflict between Henry III and his barons were coming to a head and taking the country towards civil war. Henry, who came to the throne aged nine, was continually influenced by foreigners throughout his reign. Marriage to Eleanor of Provence in 1253 did little to convince his barons that influence from Poitou, Provence and Savoy would be reduced and the barons continued pressing for direct involvement in government and in appointing royal councillors and ministers. Nothing was achieved until 1258 when Henry's need for funds forced him to accede to the united barons and accept reforms set out in the Provisions of Oxford. Three years later Henry repudiated the Provisions and removed officials appointed with baronial approval. As Ralph de Tony was succeeding to his inheritance of Suthtauton however, determined reformers, joined by lesser gentry and townsmen, rallied behind Simon de Montfort. Success in forcing Henry to return to the Provisions was short lived and when Louis IX, called upon to arbitrate, declared against the Provisions in 1264, civil war became inevitable.

South Zeal - King's Arms and village lane.

Gidleigh held by William le Prouz in c.1274 when it was known as Gyddeleigh.

South Tawton Church House.

War dragged on for three years, through the battle of Evesham in which de Montfort was defeated and killed, until a negotiated settlement was reached through the statute of Marlborough in 1267. Embittered rebels saw their lands confiscated and distributed among royalists but when Edward I came to the throne, in 1272, Ralph de Tony was still in possession of Suthtauton and, like his predecessor, held the gallows rights, and assize of, the right to test bread and beer.

The jurors of the Hundred court c.1274 make note of William le Prouz as the holder of Gyddeleigh, from the king in chief by ancient fee farm, paying £3.12s.1d. yearly, and homage, to the king. They appear also to refer to South Tawton manor as having been given by the Conqueror to Roscelin de Beaumont, but in this they are clearly wrong for as late as 1280 Ralf de Tony's right to the Hundred manor was challenged by the Crown. Any challenge was obviously overcome since Ralph de Tony continued to benefit from the living for at least another 14 or 15 years and is reported to have died in Gascony on the Friday in the week of Pentecost, in 1294 or 1295, but the news didn't reach his Executors in England until the quinzaine of St John, the 15 day after the saint's festival. The Eascheator probably did not hear of Ralph's death for, perhaps, another week or so.

Under feudal law, estates in England held by a noble tenant as reward for service to a superior lord, or king, were estates, or a fief, that could be inherited by the noble's kin, but ownership remained with the superior lord or, as in this case, the king. During his lifetime, Ralph had benefited from the income derived from the estates he held, and his heir would similarly benefit, when he came of age. However, when a tenant died intestate without an heir the fief returned to the owner and the Escheator was empowered to ensure that the reversion terms were enforced. As soon as he was aware of Ralph's death the Escheator descended upon Suthtauton to recover monies from the manor, for the king; and the reversion applied from the date of Ralph's death.

That was late in May, but there were two festivals celebrated for St John, the first towards the end of June for his birth and the second at the end August for his death, so it could have been as late as mid September before the Executors heard of Ralph's demise. It was even later before the Escheator came seeking the king's dues.

South Tawton and Cawsand from the quarries.

Since Ralph's death, however, attorneys following his original instructions had continued to pay creditors and deal with his financial affairs. When the Escheator arrived, expecting to receive the manorial income accrued since May, there was little or no money to receive. The executors petitioned King Edward, pleading that they should not be charged for the period prior to the arrival of the Escheator, during which time they had only been performing their duties on behalf of Ralph, not knowing that he was dead and that the law of revision was in operation. Ralph had estates, lands, and castles in Wales, for which the executors, seemingly, were also responsible. In their petition they reminded the King Edward of the support that Ralph had given to him during his conquest of that country, and emphasised the continuing expenditure borne by Ralph in defending those lands, for the King, thereafter.

The under-age heir, Robert de Tony, who was now a 'ward' of King Edward, added his own request that he should 'soon' have the lands held in custody by the King, which would eventually be his on his coming of age. He admitted that he had already 'granted' parts of these lands to others. He added that, as his father had leased or farmed out a manor, for a term of three years, for the services of the King of Gascony, and the manor was now seized in Edward's hands because of his father's death he, as with the Executors, should not be charged for dues relating to that manor.

The Executors' petition, including Robert de Tony's personal plea, appears to have been kindly considered by the King because, four years later, Robert had inherited Suthtauton and obtained a Charter in 1299 permitting him to hold a weekly market each Thursday, in Zele Tony - he had previously been entitled to one-third of North Tawton market.

Zele Tony, or Tony's Hall was the name given to describe the village of South Zeal within the manor. Robert leased areas of land within Suthtauton to others, some of whom, it appears, rode roughshod over the rights of their tenants and caused continuing conflict. Around the turn of the century the tenants of the 'Ancient demise of Suthtauton' were hard pressed enough to petition the King to request that he confirm to them the customs and rights that had been theirs when the manor had been held by the him, and previous kings. It seems that one

Above and left: *The 700th Charter Anniversary celebrations.*

Richard de Pultemor, a lessee of land at the time, was demanding more of his tenants than they considered his right. Such lessees, including William Prouz of Gyddeligh, could expect individual tenants to undertake the duties of a provost, (bailiff) or disenier (tithing collector) on their behalf and were not averse to demanding increased numbers of such servants from among the tenants. The amount of time devoted to such service or a reduced access to wood, fowl, stone, or even water, would swiftly cause conflict that fostered unrest. The record of the grants, dues and rights given by previous kings and re-affirmed on succession, albeit for the appropriate fee, provided a reliable reference from which petitioners could expect the present monarch to decide the issue and, as in this instance, confirm their rights. For another 700 years the system of 'ancient rights' served the population well; until this inheritance was removed in the last century when the rights were lost to the many, but retained by a few.

Like those who leased the land, the king's own bailiffs in Dartmoor were not averse to a little extortion. The tenants' petition included complaints about a bailiff by the name Suesey as one who treated them badly. From the common pasture of Dartmoor, they claimed, Suesey had taken three of their horses and was holding them until the tenants paid eight shillings rent to him, for having pastured the horses on the moor. The people of Suthtauton had their ancient rights of grazing, knew their ancient rights, and the King, once again, ensured they retained their rights.

During the early years of the 14th century, Edward made peace with France, turned his attention once again on Scotland, and earned himself the reputation of being 'The Hammer of the Scots'. Robert de Tony, by then holding Suthtauton from the King by the service of one knight's fee, was more aware than most of the tide of the times.

There is great debate over the knight's introduction into England, but he was probably a Norman innovation. In return for field service for a stated period, garrison duty, payment of feudal incidents, and a general obligation to give counsel and aid to his lord a knight received land – the 'fee'. Knights, at first, were relatively humble professional fighting men holding only one or two fees, but their status rose as they were called upon to serve in local and central government. In 1301, with his inheritance including land and castles in Wales it is certain that Robert de Tony and his wife Matilda would have welcomed the news of the King's son, also Edward, being created the first English Prince of Wales – but after the death the death of Edward I in 1307 Robert was to enjoy his income from Suthtauton, and his market for only a few more years. At his death in 1309, being without issue, it was his sister Alice who succeeded him. Alice married twice, first to Thomas de Leyburne and, after his death, she married Guy de Beauchamp, Earl of Warwick. In doing so she took with her into the family of the Beauchamps the inheritances of Sele, Southtauton, Ailrichescot, et al. to become an intended possession for succeeding Earls of Warwick. Those possessions were soon back in the hands of Edward II after Guy died in 1315 and Thomas Beauchamp succeeded him as the next Earl of Warwick at the tender age of two.

One area within the inheritance of the young Earl had obviously grown considerably over the past half-century since the income being enjoyed from Sele, alone, was 35s.4d.; and it's populace included 20 burgesses. Despite this, Sele does not appear in the list of townships compiled in 1316 in which it is recorded that in the Hundred of South Tawton, 'there is no (royal) borough and only one single township called South Tawton, the lord of which is... the King.'

The year 1334 brought a dispute between the now adult Thomas de Beauchamp, Kt, Earl of Warwick claimant, and John de Melbourne and Roger de Ledebury, clerk, deforciant, regarding a number of manors, including that of South Tawton. The deforciants, Melbourne and Ledebury, were, according to the Earl wrongfully keeping him from possessing his estate, which should eventually be inherited by his son Thomas. The ownership of estates was rarely if ever disputed, but the 'rights' to gain benefit from them were a regular source of contention. The complexities of ownership, leases, and tenancies, obviously kept those in the legal profession as occupied in the 14th century as they do in the 21st.

After the felonious Mayor of Exeter had been hanged on the Feast of St Stephen, 1285, the courthouse of Blackhall and the lordship of the land seemingly passed to his brother, Walter de Tantifer; who apparently prospered considerably. When his daughter, Joan, married Richard Cheseldon in 1347 she carried the lease of the whole manor and hundred with her to her husband. Richard, with his wife, then held possession and while their family was to retain the holding for over 80 years, the couple had first to fight to establish their inheritance. In 1347 there was a dispute between Ralph son of Thomas de Shyllingford, John Stone of Honiton, Willm, de Chesewege, and Richd Att Well, the claimants, and Richd de Chuselden and Johanna his wife, deforciants, regarding the manors of Penne in Somerset and South Tawton and Rewe in Devon.

The dispute related to many things; the manors with their appurtenances, the advowson of the church of the manor of Rewe, 36 messuages, 12 shops, 2 mills, 8 plough-lands, 22 acres of land, other fields, more acres of bush, £11.2s.2d. rent, and the pasturing for beasts on moorland. The Devon 'interests' were situated in the suburbs of Exon, Silpherton, Aunk (in Clyst Hydon), Nethereaynekesdon (in Ilsington), Wygleigh (in Sampford Courtenay), Sprayton, and North Tawton as well as South. The conflicts of interest in Somerset increased the complexity of the claims laid before the court. The outcome appears equally complex:

Richd de Chuselden and his wife acknowledge the rights of the s'd John Stone. And for the sd manor of Rewe, Penne, ¾ mess, shops, etc, the sd John, Ralph, Will and Rich. Attewelle pay rent in the same court; And the sd Richd de Cheseldon and Johanna convey and grant for themselves and their heirs, to the sd John the aforesaid manor of South Tawton with appurtenances, which Richard de Lamburne held for term of his life; and that 1 messuage, 1 ploughland of arable, and 3 acres brushwood, with appurtenances in the aforesaid township of North Tawton, which Simon atte Pitte held for the term of Henry Goodman's life, and that 1 messuage, 1 mill, 1 ploughland of arable with appurtenances in Sampford Courtenay, which John de Ponton held for term of his life, of the heir of the foresaid Joanna, on the day on which this concord was made; all which, after the decease of the sd Rich de Lambourne, Henr. and Joh. Ponton, ought to revert to the sd Rich. de Chuseldon and Joanna and to the sd Joanna's heirs, and shall, after the decease of the s'd Rich. de Lamburne, Henr. and John Ponton, remain in their entirety to the s'd Ralph, John Stone, Willm, and Richd Attewelle, and the heirs of the sd John, to be held upon the same terms as the aforesaid manors, lands, pasture and advowson, which remain to them by virtue of the sd. fine.

Edward III died amidst an atmosphere of demoralisation and dissension throughout his kingdom in 1377, the same year that the people of South Tawton made their protest against the Stannators. It was a time when the impact of the Black Death was being decisively re-inforced by subsequent outbreaks of plague, the virtual slavery of villeinage was the curse of rural life and, after a quarter of century of wages being fixed at pre-plague rates (Statute of Labour, 1351), the workers were in a mind for revolution.

When, as a boy king, aged ten, Richard II ascended the throne, he was not held responsible for the failings of his government but the imposition of an unjust Poll Tax in 1380 was the last straw. A year later the Peasants' Revolt was short lived, after Richard agreed to abolish serfdom; but later revoked his concession. In South Tawton probably half the population suffered serfdom, or villeinage, the legal condition of personal servitude; as did others in the

Sampford Courtenay Church and village.

South Zeal looking towards St Mary's, c.1908.

Above and left: *Wood c.1906 and one of the parish boundary stones.*

rest of rural England. Serf (Latin servus) and 'villein' were equivalent terms, and only service limitations imposed by law or custom distinguished villeins from slaves. Villeins were 'attached' to the soil, were transferred with the lord's land when it passed to another owner, and in return for rent and services were permitted a small holding. Serfdom, it seems, has never actually been abolished in Britain.

Thomas Beauchamp, Earl of Warwick, and holder of the manor of South Tawton in 1387, was one of the 'Appellants' who lodged an 'appeal' of treason against a group of Richard's friends in the November of that year. The following month, together with his fellow 'Appellants,' the Duke of Gloucester and the Earl of Arundel, Thomas joined forces with the Earl of Nottingham, and Henry Bolingbroke, who later became Henry IV, to defeat a Royalist force at Radcot Bridge. In February 1388, with dubious legality, they steered the 'Merciless' parliament to execute a number of Richard's supporters for treason, imprisoned others, and established controls over the King and his household. Richard regained control the next year but, counselled by his uncle, John of Gaunt, pursued a policy of moderation, until 1397 when he embarked on a period of tyranny; which increased his growing unpopularity.

The name of Thomas, Earl of Warwick, appears again in 1397, not in circles of royal intrigue, but in Okehampton. It was in court there that Matt Chuseman, Willlm Weke, John Northmore, John at Hill, Rich Oxenham, Willm Touwe, Matth. Yeo, Richd Willman, Willm Deyman, Willm Baronn and Rich Wolston were all engaged in determining where and to whom certain 'rights' and 'values' associated with the manor and hundred of South Tawton and the borough of Sele, should be applied.

The Earl of Warwick had held those properties of the King, by military service. The property was reward, obviously, for providing military support to the King but since Warwick had long since ceased to support Richard, it can be surmised that the Okehampton inquiry was dealing with the removal of Earl's 'rights.' In doing so, the hearing confirmed the details of some of the Earl's local agreements and some property values. A year earlier, on 28 June 1396, the Earl had enfeofed John Denham, Chivaler, Ric Bromley, and Thos Aldebury, and others, from the manor and hundred, to his own use... his own military use perhaps as Denham was a knight. It was he whom the men claimed benefited from £12 rent in the manor, approved by the Earl in return for military service. John Webber similarly held lands and rent, in the manor, by military service. This – 1397 – was also the year in which Thomas, Earl of Warwick died.

At the King's command a valuation of the manor of South Tawton was taken at Sele, around 15 November 1398, by Robert Markeley and Thomas Caldwell, among others, at which it was assessed that the manor, with the borough of Sele, was worth £10.2s.9d. yearly, in fixed rents. There was also a 'Fullinge Mill' which was worth six shillings yearly and a certain 'moor' which the two men agreed was worth ¾d. per annum. They found that court payments amounted to 40 shillings each year, over and above the seneschal's fee and the pannage of brushwood from 40 acres of forestation was worth ten shillings a year. Messrs Markeley and Caldwell departed Sele, to report to the King that the manor of South Tawton and the borough of Sele could definitely be regarded as possessing a value of not less than £13.2s.1d. per annum.

Beating the Bounds picnic at Taw Marsh, 1987 and the marker stone is marked again.

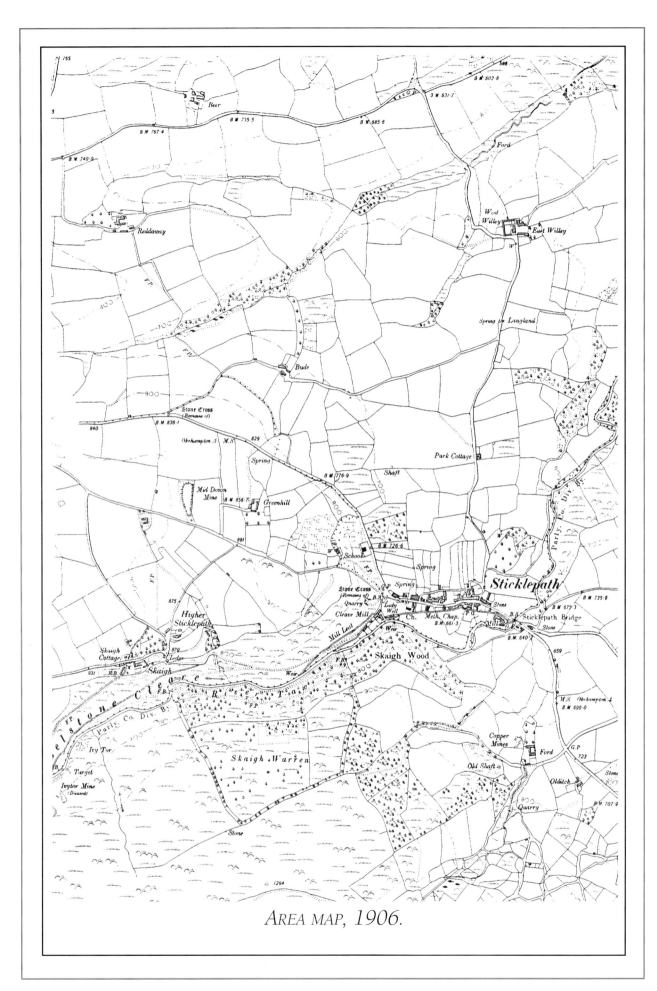

AREA MAP, 1906.

Chapter 2
Sticklepath: Chantry Chapel and Churches

When the first farming tribes felt secure enough to come down from Cosdon, the area of that we know as Sticklepath was as inviting to them as the valley that was to accommodate South Zeal. A track between settlements in both valleys provided a route that was to become part of the 'road' that eventually linked London with the western extremities.

Long before the Romans came, the need for salt assisted the establishment of a west-ward way with a route that has changed very little during the past two millennia. Tin, trade and shipping were sufficient to ensure the route became the main 'road' to the west. Alongside that road the valley residents watched the flow of history and, like their neighbours, let much of it slip past.

Old Sticklepath.

On Saxton's Map of Devon, published in 1575, while Sticklepath is marked only by four green bushes and two brown mole-heaps representing the Dartmoor hills this belies the previous 500 years of its history. The single village street of today, some recent excavation seems to indicate, may once have been a water-way, an earlier course of the nearby river perhaps, and the lane to the north, 'Back Lane' may well be the original valley track-route, or close to it. To the north of Back Lane, even the present-day field patterns still clearly reflect in their size, shapes and arrangement, the Common Field strip cultivation. On maps as recent as those used when a bypass was proposed to run close to the village, or on old tithe maps, the similarity to South Zeal's retained burgage plots is clear. It is, however, to the south side of the present village street where our trip through much of the last 1000 years must begin. Changes to a land-scape can come quickly and perhaps only three gen-erations have passed since the Skaigh Valley was open, clear and farmed. Abandoned to nature its fate reflects the demise of a building that once stood close by, but even its remains were not observed by Saxton when he came this way, map-making.

The origins of Sticklepath's first church are shrouded in mystery but the early historical setting for the village can be readily traced through chaplains appointed to serve the community. Their original religious sanctuary was endowed as a Chantry Chapel, and throughout much of its existence the leading local landowners, the Courtenays, held the advowson and appointed chaplains to say mass there for the souls of their family and others. Local lore suggests that Jane, or Joan, Courtenay established the Chantry Chapel in 1146 in recognition of help given by Sticklepath people to her hus-band, wounded upon the road in a shooting affray.

However, the Courtenays only came over from France in 1152 with Eleanor of Aquitaine, Queen of Henry II, while the Chapel was mentioned in Patent Rolls five years prior to the family's arrival in the country. Their arrival itself was long before they became associated with Sampford Courtenay so the local legend is, perhaps, more picturesque than reliable; even though the early Courtenay association is mentioned by William Crossing in his *Guide to Dartmoor*.

The second mystery surrounds a Robert Fitzroy, one of the illegitimate sons of Henry I and provider of the Chantry land. The pre-fix 'Fitz' is often indica-tive of illegitimate birth and does not always simply infer 'son of' as is often presumed. Henry acknowl-edged some 20 bastard children, including a Robert Fitzhenry, and a Robert Fitzroy who became Earl of Gloucester; one of the richest landowners in England and patron of Geoffrey of Monmouth and William of Malmsbury (two of the greatest historians of the 12th century). But was he the only Robert Fitzroy? Some historians claim, without giving clear reason, that the Robert donating land for Sticklepath's Chantry was not the Earl. It was, however, a Robert Fitzroy, with his wife Matilda d'Avranches, who provided land for the building of a chapel and land for use by a chaplain in his manor of Sampford in 1147 to Bricus, chaplain of the Empress Maud. Robert was half brother to Empress Maud, or Matilda, an illegitimate daughter of Henry I. At eleven years of age, Matilda

Taw Valley at the turn of the 19th century.

Sticklepath - as viewed by Arthur Madders on his 50th birthday balloon trip.

had gained her title, 'Empress,' after marrying the Holy Roman Emperor, Henry V, in January 1114 and, despite not receiving an imperial crown from the hands of the Pope, it is certainly she that is the 'Empress' featured in local lore relating to the Chantry Chapel. Widowed in 1125 when she was 23, Matilda returned to England and two years later the Anglo-Norman barons swore to accept her as their ruler if Henry had no legitimate son and heir. Believing that controlling Norman lords was no job for a woman, Henry hastily married off Matilda to Geoffrey Plantagenet, the powerful Count of Anjou, in 1128. When Stephen succeeded Henry I, with the acquiescence of the Anglo-Norman barons, Matilda, strongly supported by none other than Robert Fitzroy, Earl of Gloucester, began a fight for her rights. This lasted for almost a decade during which time Matilda's authority in England remained restricted to the West Country; her illegitimate half-brother's power base also.

Memories of Matilda may have dimmed, but the Chantry Chapel which her half-brother dedicated to her survived to bring the light of religion into Sticklepath unopposed for many centuries. The Patent Rolls 1414 recite the chantry grant and its confirmation, adding that the endowment was £9.10s.8d., and that it was at Sticklepath. William de Esse, 'De Okehamptone' is mentioned as being chapel chaplain on 8 July 1280. The Advowson for the Rectors of Sampford Courtenay has, since the Conquest, been closely connected with the manor, Sandford, the original name for the village and, until recent times, Sticklepath. At the time of the Conquest the manor was connected with the Honour of Okehampton, granted to Baldwin Fitz-Gilbert, Sheriff of Devon.

Hawisse, Baldwin's great-great-granddaughter and heiress, married Reginald de Courtney, who was Baron of Okehampton, juxta uxoris (through his wife), and died 1195. Reginald came to England in the train of Eleanor of Aquitaine, and was of a family that, in the 12th century, gave counts to Edessa, kings to Jerusalem and emperors to Constantinople.

The Courtenay connection with Sticklepath's chapel was first noted in 1282 when, according to the Episcopal Registers of the See of Exeter, Sir Hugh Courtenay presented Robert de Esse of Okehampton as priest to the 'Perpetua Cantaria Beate Marie de Stikelpethe'. In 1309 another Sir Hugh, son of the former and Baron of Okehampton, provided 'a messuage and one carucate of land', as endowment for the benefit of chaplains celebrating divine service daily in the chapel.

The manor and advowson were by now well and truly in Courtenay hands. The family continued to appoint many of the succeeding chaplains until the

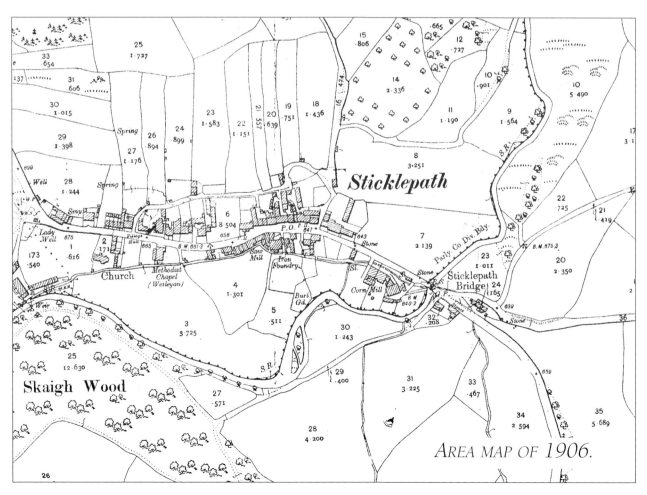

AREA MAP OF 1906.

An early Sticklepath picture, thought to date from 1900.

A Sampford Courtenay scene with village children, early 1900s.

Sticklepath early in the 20th century.

The Devonshire Inn, with Sticklepath children in the street, c.1909.

Sticklepath's famed 'Incised Stone' - and William Tucker (Aubrey's son).

Child at Lady Well - and another child that couldn't wait for the photographer to finish!

Main picture: *The Lady of Skaigh - natural beauty everywhere!*
Inset: *A gentleman at Lady Well early in the 19th century.*

Huntsman and hounds at Sticklepath Post Office - the postcard is postmarked 1954.

☞ Sticklepath ☜ Church and Chapel

Left and below left: *Sticklepath Chapel and interior.*

Below: *Sticklepath church area with Cleave Mill in the foreground.*

Right: *Sticklepath Church interior shown on a 1920s postcard.*

Below: *Billy May cutting grass in Sticklepath churchyard.*

Sunday School commemoration - possibly the 1913 centenary celebrations.

fortune of their family changed dramatically a century and a half later. We include the following list of chaplains not just for information but because in a few lines it reveals a number of questions that cry out for investigation by anyone interested in local history. How did Bishop Grandison come to be one chaplain's patron? Why did three of the chaplains resign in a five year period? Why did two more resign in the same year? What role, if any, did a rector of Throwleigh play in all this?

RICHARD PREDOME. Instituted 12 June 1330. Died: 1342. Patron: Hugh Courtney, 1st Earl of Devon.
WALTER DE TRENDLEBEARE. Instituted 7 February, 1342/3. Died 1351. Same Patron.
(Around this time the Courtenay household numbered 135 persons and included 61 servants, 41 esquires, 14 lawyers, 8 knights, 8 clergymen, and 3 damsels. The esquires were of gentle birth attending the needs of the knights or were of the higher order of English gentry, ranking immediately below the knight. The three damsels would probably be daughters within the family whose unmarried status was regarded as precious, as of yet not being in need of a dowry.)

JOHN CADY. 28 September, 1351. Vacated 1361. Patron Bishop Grandisson
THOMAS COKE. Instituted 26 January, 1361/2. Resigned 1367. Patron: Hugh, 2nd Earl of Devon.
JOHN SMYTH. Instituted 21 April, 1368. Resigned 1370. Same Patron.
JOHN ELYOT. Presented 1370. Resigned 1372. Same Patron. William Byre, Principal Official of the Bishop, reported the presentation was in order (Brant. Regs., p.141).
HUGH GILBERT. Rector of Throuley 'in commendam', 25 May, 1372.
JOHN NEEL. Instituted 25 August, 1372. Resigned 1373. Patron Bishop by lapse.
HENRY LEGGE. Instituted 1372. Resigned 1373. Patron Edward, 3rd Earl of Devon.
WALTER DOLBEARE. Instituted 20 December, 1373. Resigned 1391. Same Patron.
NICHOLAS BUBBEWYTHE. Instituted 16 March, 1391/2. Resigned 1396. Same Patron. Canon Exeter 1403.
PATRICK WODE. Instituted 27 September, 1396. Resigned 1396/7. Same Patron.
HENRY PEKE. Instituted 21 May, 1397. Died 1436. Same Patron. Penetencer, Okehampton Deanery on four occasions.
(During the Wars of the Roses, 1455-87, the Courtenays supported the Lancastrian cause but defeat on the battlefield at Towton on 29 March, 1461 brought with it the downfall of the family. Edward IV granted Sampford Courtney to Thomas, Lord Stafford, who was executed 1470, and then to John, Earl of Northumberland, who was killed at Barnet, 1471.)

JOHN PAYNE. Instituted 20 May, 1436. Died 1475. Patron John Bortieux, husband of Anne, Dowager Countess of Devon.
RICHARD LUKY. Instituted 20 May, 1475. Vacancy unrecorded. Patron: George Plantagenet, Duke of Clarence (executed 1478).
THOMAS RYDYND. Institution and Patron unrecorded. Resigned 1479.
RICHARD LEGHE. Instituted 24 December, 1479. Vacancy unrecorded. Patron: John, Lord Dynham.
(One decisive battle had lost the Courtenays their estates, but the battle at Bosworth Field. 28th August 1485, saw Lord Dynham dispossessed of them also when the Courtenays returned to favour. Edward Courtenay, not only received a knighthood that day from Henry VII, but also had the family estates restored to him, including the Barony of Okehampton and advowson of the Sticklepath Chantry. Edward, Lord Devon, held the advowson until he died in 1509.)

PETER CRECHE. Institution and Patron unrecorded. Died 1515.
(Lord Devon's son, Sir Edward Courtney, had married Katherine, daughter of Edward IV, sister to Margaret, Queen of Henry VII. He was too near the throne for the king's liking and was never allowed to assume the earldom, but on his death in 1515 he was granted an Earl's funeral, and his widow the status of a Countess.)

JAMES TRECETHAN. Instituted 24 September, 1515 Res. 1528. Patron: Katherine, Countess of Devon.
(Her son, Henry Courtenay, 19th Earl of Devon, born c.1498, became the 1st Marquess of Exeter in 1525 but his Plantagenet descent and West Country power earned the suspicion of Henry VIII. Despite supporting the king's divorce Henry's complicity with the opponents of Thomas Cromwell led to his execution in 1539. Sticklepath Chantry valuation 1535, Valor Eccl., £8.4s.7d.; Inquiry Post Mortem Henry, Marquess of Exeter 1539, £2.0s.0d. The Courtenay estates were again confiscated and the advowson of the Chapel passed to Henry's latest Queen, Catherine Howard; but only for three years. Catherine's own execution in 1542 saw the advowson passed on to her successor Katherine Parr whom, with Henry's death pre-dating hers, held it until the Dissolution finally removed its relevance.)

WILLIAM DISCOMBE, OR DISCOURT. Instituted 1528. Ejected 1549. Patron the same. Rector of Belstone 12 March, 1528.
(In 1536 Discourt received £8.4s.7d. added to his annual Belstone stipend of £9.0s.2d. for ministering to the 'Cantaria de Stikylpath'. In 1549 the office of chaplain ceased. The Chantry being eventually suppressed as result of Dissolution Acts that had started to be applied in 1536 was given to Sir William Archer.)

In the Chantry Rolls of Edward VI there is mention of finding a priest 'to mynystre in the Chauntrye distant from ye parish churche of Sampforde Courtenay a myle or more'. (A priest attracted at the time by a 'Situation Vacant' advert would soon find the mileage claim to be far from accurate since in a walk from one to the other they would cover five miles or more.) At the same date, the value of the Chantry's 'landes and possessions' were quoted as being £11.10s.8d. (hopefully, for the potential incumbent, an accurate assessment). The advowson associated with Sticklepath's chapel was removed from the possession of individuals in 1570 when Queen Elizabeth allowed Lord Buckhurst to exchange the manor of Sampford Courtenay with the Provost and Fellows, of King's College, Cambridge. After some delays the agreement became effective in 1601, since which date the College have been Patrons. By 1620, when the historian, Risdon, wrote of the village, it was being referred to as 'Sticklepath in which some time there was a Chantry'. Risdon does not refer to the building having a different use, so can it reasonably be assumed that since the ejection of preacher William Discombe the chapel had been destroyed? If so, then could Dissolution eventually arriving in Sticklepath in 1549 have brought with it the destruction of the chapel? This would certainly help explain Saxton's omission of Sticklepath from his map in 1575 if is there was no Chantry Chapel to note when he was surveying Devon's villages and churches. But, did he, somehow, bypass Sticklepath perhaps and not even see it at all?

In 1649, a Survey of Benefices initiated by Oliver Cromwell containing information on Sampford Courtenay, advises that it 'hath a Chappell called Sticklepath and this within its lymetts we can see fitte to be united to the parishe of Belstone as before'. Whether or not the reference to once again becoming 'united to the parish of Belstone' recognises the connection established earlier by William Discombe in 1528 or to some other an unification must remain a mystery; until some other investigator probes further into this most intriguing diversion. Whatever the reality is behind the mystery, it cannot be doubted that the comments of Cromwell's surveyors indicate religious services were being conducted in a chapel of some sort. A building of cob and thatch is easily destroyed and, with community will, relatively easily replaced. The destruction of one such chapel by fire, sometime in the mid-19th century, was recorded by the Revd Baring Gould in his *Book of Dartmoor*, in which he comments that:

At Sticklepath was a curious old cob thatched chapel, but this was unnecessarily destroyed, and a modern erection of no interest or beauty has taken its place.

Churchwardens' accounts confirm the purchase of 'nitches of reed' to repair the Chantry Chapel thatch as late as the middle of the century and, obviously, prior to the 'unnecessary' destruction.

As early as 1822 it is recorded that that services were rarely held, with the Sacrament administered only on the Sundays after Easter and Michaelmas.

Another version of events around this time suggests that only a single service was held annually 'when the Rector of Sampford Courtenay came collecting. It was said that he read 'prayers in the Chantry before dining with farmers at the Inn and receiving the tithes.' His prayers were certainly said in a chapel that was known to have been destroyed by flames, but we may never know what caused the fire which consumed the aging, decaying building before it became a costly liability to the community.

It was Leicestershire shoemaker that next had a religious influence on the area; George Fox, born in Fenny Drayton in 1624 was 19 years old when he felt the divine call and, bible in hand, began to wander the country arguing against the formalism of the established Church and all social conventions. Journeys to the West Country for the founder of the Religious Society of Friends were seemingly regular, since supporters were to be found in Exeter (where

Sticklepath procession of the Society of Friends.

Above and left: *The Devonshire Inn and the village's popular Crimean War veteran, William Middle.*

many were jailed), North Tawton, South Tawton, Okehampton, and Launceston (where Fox was himself imprisoned for some time). His support in Sticklepath was considerable and it is claimed that the village was home to several hundred Friends. Like others throughout the country they adopted the term Quakers first bestowed upon them derisively by Justice Bennet of Derby. Fox noted in 1650 that this was because they bid people, 'quake at the word of God'.

Land purchased by the Friends near the river became their burial ground. Here still, behind the National Trust Museum, once Finch Foundry, are the gravestones of local families, the Holes, Cooks, Hoopers, Osbornes, Bennetts and Yeos. William Middle, a Crimean veteran lies nearby and, before *his* time, John Langmead, the last of the Sticklepath Quakers, was buried here in 1818 by Thomas Pearse. In South Zeal a 20th-century connection with the Quakers ended only recently when the Friends ceased to use Church House as a regular meeting place.

While area links with the Friends diminished a longstanding relationship developed with the coming of Methodism that continues in both South Zeal

and Sticklepath to this day. Like Fox before him, John Wesley took the main road to Cornwall down which he travelled regularly, carrying the message of the gospel, and in his journal in 1743 he first mentions Sticklepath as the place in which he was welcomed by Quakers inviting him to address them. The friendship and mutual admiration was immediate and Wesley made at least four more references to stops he made in the village during other journeys.

In 1744, according to his journal, he preached to villagers during a heavy storm one day in the open air but was invited indoors that evening to address a congregation gathered in the home of Simon Frewins, a local miller and Quaker. Sticklepath's 'White Rock' is now traditionally regarded as the place from which John Wesley addressed villagers during the storm and the rock continues to attract the attention of visitors, and the warm hands of friendship extended by local people in keeping it 'white.'

The presence of Bible Christians and Wesleyans is recorded throughout the entire region with meeting houses being built by them or premises used in even the smallest villages. By 1816 Sticklepath was opening its own Wesleyan Chapel and the Pearse family, owners of Cleave Woollen Factory, added their immense influence to the growing movement as their factory became a centre for the cause; Thomas Pearse, Thomas Searle his factory manager, and most of the employees were Wesleyans. One of those employees, Thomas Seacombe, became a preacher before he was 20 and ministered to his flock for over 70 years; walking from chapel to chapel each Sunday to ensure that his horse enjoyed its rest on the Sabbath.

The Chapel continues to serve the village but numbers attending services have declined to a point where sometimes only two or three 'gather in His name' although the spirit remains strong. The premises also serve the community as an exhibition centre and meeting place for social events. The chapel room with its bell-turret was added in 1866 to commemorate the Chapel Jubilee; ringing a bell to summon the congregation is very unusual in Methodism.

In South Zeal, where two factions each had their own chapel, the Methodist Church continues to enjoy a larger attendance but, like all churches, the diminishing congregation is all too apparent. Led by local preacher, Edgar Hucker, the word is still available each week for all those who would share the inheritance of the Gospel that was brought westward by Fox and Wesley, and those local people that sometimes suffered to ensure its continuing presence.

Revd Baring Gould considered the Sticklepath Church that we know today as being one 'of no interest or beauty,' yet, built, it is said, on the foundations of the fire-stricken chapel. It has served the community well since 1875 and its plain values, recognised by generations, needed no ornamentation to be appreciated. Its building cost of £700 came in part from subscriptions and in part from a benefactor, John Cook, farmer, butcher, and licensee of the Cornish Inn whose parents' are commemorated by one of the church's two stained-glass windows. A pewter flagon of 1795 was one of the oldest possessions of the church but a small, mutilated, blue-robed figure taking refuge in a wall recess to the left of the altar probably depicted the Virgin Mary, to whom the church was dedicated and was considered by many to have once been a resident in the ancient Chantry Chapel.

In 1951 when alterations were in progress at 'Staplers', old home of both Quakers and woolstaplers, the boards of a partition were removed. On the back of one was the painted representation of a saint, Considered now to be St Jerome, and dating from the early-15th century. This may possibly have been taken from the Chantry and hidden at the time of the Dissolution or, alternatively, bought among 'junk' material when the old building was pulled down. It can now be seen in the church

The union with Belstone that Cromwell's Surveyors had 'seen fit' in 1649 was not actually achieved until almost three centuries later. Through the 1930s and until 1982, Belstone's rectors were responsible for Sticklepath, at which time the livings of Belstone and South Tawton merged and four churches within the benefice began to share church services while retaining their individual identity. The

following notes, drawn from research conducted and published by Sticklepath Women's Institute in 1953, revised in 1993 was provided to us by Mrs Anne Bowden. Reproduced, with minimal amendment, they provide further information into the setting and background of Chantry Endowments:

We have no records of the exact location of the 'landes and possessions' with which the early Chantry Chapel was endowed, but from existing

Top: *Gwen Murrin at Farley Cottage, one of Sticklepath's historic homes, pictured before the church railings disappeared during road widening in the 1960s.*
Centre: *Sticklepath Post Office with the* Western Morning News *on sale.*
Bottom: *Mill – certainly, Toll House – probably, and as such, possibly part of the Uncle Tom Cobley mystery.*

For over 80 years the Women's Institute has had a profound influence on life in Devon. Before numbers grew there was but one Institute in the area, shared by South Zeal and Sticklepath, now there are two, although members still enjoy close links with one another. This photograph is thought to have been taken during Sticklepath WI's inaugural year, 1924.

names we can form some opinion as to their whereabouts.

The 'messuage' or dwelling house and ground, given by Sir Hugh Courtenay II, in 1309 may well have been on the exact site and foundation of the present 'Chantry's Cottage'. This picturesque cob and thatch cottage stands beside the road opposite the Devonshire Inn car-park. When Robert, Henry I's son, appointed Bricus as chaplain, he also made him a gift of 'a certain ferling of land' in the manor of Sampford Courtenay 'to be held free of all secular service' and of 'my wood of Stickilapa as bounded by the grass road to a stream and from the stream to in tau' (Taw?). Here, unfortunately, is some clerical error. But at the back of Sticklepath, behind Steddaford, a little rough lane, known as Woody Park, follows the course of the River Taw. Among the small enclosures carved from its wooded banks, is 'Chantry's Meadow', still an appendage of Chantry's Cottage. This may have been part of Robert's 'wood of Stickilapa', or the granted 'ferling' may have lain nearer to the priest's other 'possessions' and have been part of a stretch of brushy copseland from which the remaining piece of common, 'Wooders', derives its name.

Opposite the church to-day stands Cleave House, built about 1856 upon ground formerly called 'Chauntrey's' – a pretty clear indication. At the back, and adjoining it is Alder Meadow or Allermead, often pronounced Hallermead. This variation arouses interesting speculation. It is the field in which the Ladywell spring rises, and one wonders whether Hallermead is merely a case of a misplaced aspirate; or was this enclosure where the 'holy' spring emerged, the Hallow-mead, later becoming Allermead and finally translated into the modern Alder Meadow? Although the field is marshy and willows grow there, alders do not.

Also rather uncertain is the meaning lying behind the name 'Sentry Head' – a 'standing stone' on the open moor just beyond the boundary wall of Skaigh Warren, on the south bank of the Taw. 'Sentry' is a common corruption of 'sanctuary', and old men speak of a one-time enclosure there, now long since merged with the wild common. Name and circumstances suggest that here perhaps, may once have been a rough 'intake' allotted to the Chantry chaplain for the grazing of his cattle. Whatever meaning lies behind this etymology, it seems that the first historical nucleus developed at the western end of Sticklepath. Here was the Chantry Chapel with some of its 'landes and possessions'; the chaplain's own 'messuage', and the spring from which he drew water for sacred and domestic use – the source of the present Ladywell.

Towards St Mary's in South Zeal.

The chapel that existed before Victory Hall was erected and which filled an educational gap.

Chapter 3
South Tawton and South Zeal
from c.1850

Acentury and half ago, South Tawton was described in records in a way that is still readily recognised and which remains to this day:

... a compact village, pleasantly situated on the banks of the small river Taw, on the north edge of Dartmoor, 4 miles East by South of Okehampton, and 18 miles West of Exeter.

The parish then covered around 6097 acres of land, including 86 acres of woods, 79 acres of orchards, and 1574 acres of open pasture and forest. In 1844, an apportionment of rent charges in lieu of tithes in the hamlet of Taw Green showed that for a little more that 62 acres of land a charge was made of, '£5.14s.10d., including right on Taw Green Common Meadow.' The landowner was Sir Peregrine Acland, Bart and the occupier of his land was John Finch.

Within the parish boundaries also lay the hamlets of Itton, Taw Green, Whyddon Down, Gooseford, Week, Fulford, Ramsley, Dishcombe, and South-Zeal, 'extending from two miles South to three North by East of the church.'

From its two main centres of population through to the furthest of its scattered farmhouses, the parish provided homes for 1871 inhabitants in a beautiful area of the county picturesquely broken into hill and dale rising impressively on the south-west to the heights of Dartmoor, where the Taw and other rivulets have their sources. H.A. Hoare Esq. is the lord of the manor of Blackhall; G. S. Fursdon Esq., is the lord of South Zeal; and William Damarel Esq., is lord of Itton manor; but here are several smaller manors and estates belonging to various owners. Oxenham, the property and occasional seat of H.A. Hoare Esq., belonged to the Oxenham family from the reign of Henry III, till 1814.

Local farmer, Sam Warren (sitting) with enthusiastic holidaymaker Mr Mercer who, in everyday life, was a train driver. Photograph, early 1920s.

These reliable records from the middle of the 19th century provide almost a snapshot of the South Zeal village that can be readily recognised 150 years later. The road through the straggling village at that time was, correctly, considered to be the 'high road', as it had been for centuries. That road still straggles through the village, but it is now a village that has been by-passed three times since those stagecoach-ending, steam-approaching, pre-car, days of 1850. The railway boom brought trains only as close to South Zeal as the stations at Sampford Courtenay and Okehampton and two succeeding local 'high' roads, each needed in their day to reduce traffic troubles, have taken their own place in history.

Mid-way through the 1800s there is confirmation that, of the market and two fairs originally granted at the end of the 13th century to Robert de Tony, then lord of the manor, the village was still sufficiently active in farming affairs to warrant one annual cattle fair; which took place on the Tuesday of the week after the 7 July, the festival of St Thomas Á Beckett.

The ancient chapel in the centre of the village is, at the same time, recorded as having long been used as a school, 'where 60 children are educated at the expense of H.A. Hoare Esq.'. Mr Hoare, the records added, had greatly improved the condition of the poor parishioners.

For almost 200 years the parish has had three almshouses for poor widows, founded by Robert Burgoyne in 1656 and endowed with 1½ acres of land, worth £5 a year. The vicarage of the parish church (St Andrew), valued in K.B. at £10, and in 1831 at £150, was in the patronage of the Dean and Canons of Windsor. The vicar, Revd Thomas Birkett, was responsible for the spiritual welfare and guidance of parishioners, resided in a neat thatched residence, and benefited from 34 acres, 3 rods and 21

Top: *South Tawton before the lych gate was installed, c.1902.*

Above: *Cattle meander through the lanes of South Zeal.*

perches of glebe. It was also noted that the Dean and Canons of Windsor were also appropriators of the great tithes, then leased to H.A. Hoare Esq. and that the area of land known as Itton, or Itton Moor, had been enclosed in 1849, as the tides of time swept past. The tithes, a later report noted, had been commuted in 1844 for £709 and 44 acres of rectorial glebe. It is this information which gives rise to the question, in our minds at least, 'why, six years later, did the Revd Birkett only benefit from 34 acres, 3 rods and 21 perches of glebe?'

If we put that mystery to one side for future consideration we can return to the present day and consider the parish we know at the end of the millennium, and compare it with the parish that thrived one hundred and fifty years ago; and thrive is the word.

The occupations of parishioners in 2000 are certainly diverse but relatively few are employed solely within the parish. In 1850, unlike our own era, employment within or nearby to the parish itself sustained the diverse trades and occupations of many parishioners, including a few ladies. Commuting to Exeter and beyond for work, or even going into Okehampton for it, was something hardly even considered at the time by those whose names have a familiar ring, unsurprisingly since many are still found in local families. Not unexpectedly, farming was the mainstay of the population with over fifty farmers, their families and labourers living, or surviving, through their work on the land. Today, the land remains, but the industry has been decimated with only a handful of farms surviving to continue the work of their predecessors. The 1866 *Kelly's Directory* provides the following list of farmers in the locality:

Arnold, John, owner/farmer	Northwick
Ash, Robert, farmer	Northwick
Ash, William, farmer	Cullaford
Bawden, Thomas, farmer	West Nymph
Bolt, Thomas, farmer	Great Collibeer
Brooks, John, farmer	South Tawton
Cann, George, owner/farmer	Dishcombe
Cann, George, farmer	Lovaton
Cann, Mark, farmer	Taw Green
Cann, Philip, farmer	Nymph
Cooper, James, farmer/carrier	South Zeal
Counter, Richard, farmer	Oxenham Quarry
Counter, Robert, farmer	Allensdown
Crocker, Samuel, farmer	Addiscott
Curson, William, farmer	South Zeal
Dunning, Richard, own./farm.	Lovaton
Dunning, Richard, farmer	Week
Finch, John, farmer	Taw Green
Gidley, James, farmer/carrier	South Zeal
Gillard, John, farmer	Woodland
Harvey, Humphrey, farmer	West Week
Haydon, William, farmer	Taw Green
Hellyer, Joseph, farmer	Blackhall
Hern, Frances, (Mrs) farmer	Lovaton
Hole, John, farmer	Cullaford
Hole, Matthias, farmer	Torhill
Isaac, John, farmer	Yeolden
Jackman, Samuel, farmer	Oxenham
Jackman, William, farmer	Wickington
Knapman, Edward, farmer	Addiscott
Knapman, George, farmer	Addiscott
Knapman, Edward & John, farmers	Ash
Knapman, Edward, farmer	Wood
Lee, John & B. Thomas, farmers	Gooseford
Leonard, Samuel, farmer	Endacott
Moore, Andrew, farmer	Whiddon
Moore, James, farmer	Week
Moore, John, farmer	Ash
Moore, Joseph, farmer	Gooseford
Powlesland Geo., farmer,	Coursebeer
Powlesland, George, farmer	Ford
Powlesland, John, farmer,	Trundlebeer
Powlesland, Thomas, farmer	Powlesland
Raymont, William, farmer	Blackstreet
Rice, Richard, farmer	Collibeer
Sampson, Caleb, farmer	Sessland
Stanbury, Richard, farmer	Great Cocktree
Thorne, Thomas, farmer	Itton

Right: *Ida Wonnacott.*

Below: *Ida Wonnacott's wedding at Addiscott.*

Bottom main picture: *Land's End to the left, South Zeal centre, and London off to the right.*

Insets: *Two boys in a field, Maurice & David Wonnacott, who later became farmers in the field!*

These were major employers in 1866 when farming, quite naturally, also provided work within the area for many others associated with rural crafts or skills, and created an employment chain that bound the parish and its people into a community. The services of blacksmiths and wheelwrights were regularly required, and the inclusion of only one blacksmith with the farmers, James Curson, and one wheel-wright, John Ward, both in South Zeal, highlights the doubtful reliability of directories and records. Similar records, a few years previously, revealed that six people had been engaged in these professions, with enough to keep them busy in the area. Emmanuel Tucker in South Zeal had been recorded as being both a wheelwright and a carpenter; and was still gainfully employed in the profession years later. Blacksmiths may also have been wheelwrights and two blacksmiths, John Beer and Isaac Finch, had been working in the village. Another pair, John Finch and James Gove, each had their smithy at Whyddon Down, while William Knapman was on hand in South Tawton (Richard Knapman had taken over from him there by 1866).

Three corn mills were sustained by local output and needs, with millers William Brely at Taw-Green Mill, John Browning at Frog Mill, and James Yeo being the corn-miller at the Tawton Mill in Dishcombe. The occupation of three village traders is recorded around this time as being that of a 'huckster,' in addition to other work, and while the word perhaps lends itself towards a mercenary person today – or one that haggles – the age-old traditional hawker, pedlar, broker or middleman might have been more appropriate in 1850 when James Cooper proclaimed himself as 'huckster and carrier of South Zeal'. And in South Tawton George Powlesland and George Westaway each had their own businesses as hucksters and carriers.

Charles Arscott, John Glanfield and William Northcott were three carpenters carrying out their trade in South Zeal, but work for the stonemason was obviously more available since George Counter, James Counter, William Counter, Thomas Crocker, James Glanville and William Pearse were all engaged in that business in the village.

Not dissimilar to more recent years, father and son teams operated in the area, and the introduction of mechanization into farming had provided Curson & Sons with the opportunity to establish themselves as 'agricultural machinists & millwrights' in South Zeal. Bearing in mind that few parishioners travelled very far it was probably not competition but necessity that brought six shoemakers to the area. While the turnpikes had brought about some improvements in roads, the village lane would still have had the appearance of a stony, muddy, track, while off this highway the situation would have been far worse.

John Counter, James Crocker, Andrew Jope, George Jope, and George Oades were all very much needed as providers of the essential services of shoemakers in South Zeal, as was William Rogers who added his services in South Tawton. The needs of the community as a whole kept them all busy, when their services could be afforded. Those wealthy enough to own many pairs of boots and shoes were their first source of income. Workers that needed footwear of necessity came to the shoemakers' door next, but beyond that and into the younger age groups, precious boots or shoes for the younger children came by way of hand-me-downs if they came at all. Rough clogs, or wood slats, wrapped around with rags were as much as many could expect. This mode of footwear prevailed until well after the Second World War, if indeed it has fully died out, and it applied its visible divisions in society through clothes as much as shoes. While many grew to adulthood before ever knowing what new boots, shoes, or clothes were even like to wear, South Tawton still provided the district with three tailors, John Cann, Charles Finch and William Madders, each having premises there. Thomas Endacott provided his tailoring services in South Zeal where, also, the local ladies enjoyed the services of Mrs Elizabeth Crocker, dressmaker.

However, not everyone could afford tailors and dressmakers when, so recently, the Old Poor Law had crumbled in the south-western counties in the face of growing poverty. The 1834 Amendment Act, often hailed as important social legislation was, in reality, designed to discipline an 'irresponsible' and fast growing population and moderate the cost of Poor Relief – which continued for another century – harshly administered to, mainly, the aged, sick, and orphans.

The (American) potato blight that had arrived in 1845 brought widespread suffering throughout Europe, a famine that devastated Ireland, and was another problem endured by local people. Clearly, the parish of South Tawton in the 1850s–60s was a well populated, busy place but it was a far cry from the one we know today since real poverty existed hand in glove with on-the-spot employment and the availability of many services; far more so than is the case today.

That 'on-the-spot employment' no longer relied on farming. It was now offered below ground. The South Tawton Copper Mine had been advertised for sale in the *Exeter Flying Post* on 1 June 1826. The Fursdon Mining Company was working it in 1866 with John Collins of South Tawton employed as the company's resident manager. Also in the village lived Joseph Gilbert Martien, resident agent for the Taw River Copper Mine, and Robert Brooks, who was resident manager for the South Zeal Consols Copper Mine.

An Irish connection was being established, with an influx of miners, while the butcher, the baker and the candlestick maker were certainly all part of the everyday scene in South Zeal, if two reference to a William Arscott are correct. He is found first, recorded as being a butcher in South Zeal, but later goes on to better things.

There is no doubt about Robert Holman being the village baker though, nor of John Arscott being the local tallow chandler. His wide-wicked, green tallow candles, sold in bunches of 30, were being used underground by the miners who carried them to their perilous work, stuck in clay and stuck to their hats. William Perkins also had a profession in which he, like the poetic trio, seems to have suffered no competition. He was the rope and twine maker, working in South Tawton or South Zeal, whichever record you refer to (or perhaps he moved from one to the other).

Two people who did not move from South Zeal were John and Richard Aggett, both of whom were thatchers, serving the area for many years. The work of the plumber was not yet required in the district but while the ladies were visiting their dressmaker, in South Zeal, they could also benefit from the trader no one could do without, Mr George Curson, draper, who was astute enough to combine his business with that of providing them with groceries. Having said that, one of the tailors in South Tawton, Charles Finch, was also a general shopkeeper. Then again, so was Mrs Mary Perkins in South Zeal, who had the advantage of having the butchers' nearby but who also competed for clients with Arthur Wedlake, shopkeeper, and carrier to boot.

In addition to Mr Wedlake, two other carriers traded on the Exeter route each Tuesday; James Cooper from South Zeal was also a farmer but James Hooper, also based in South Zeal, appears to have followed only the one occupation. George Holman conducted his carrier business from his London Inn, with his cart setting out for Plymouth each Wednesday and returning on the following Friday. Farmers, George Powlesland and James Gidley, dealt for their carrier trade with business opportunities open to them on the route to Torquay to which their cart or carts traveled each Monday and returned the following day. There was also the more local business with North Tawton and Chagford on a daily basis and, perhaps more significantly, the stations on the North Devon Railway at North Tawton, Belstone Corner, or Copplestone. Carriers, in those days, in addition to carting goods around the area, to and from market or in general delivery, were also providing public transport, of a kind. South Zeal may well have been on the main road to the west, or the east depending upon your destination, but coach travel was beyond the means of most county people. The

walk to Okehampton might not be too much but long-distance travel to Exeter, Torquay, Plymouth or elsewhere in foreign parts could best be endured by ambling along beside a carrier's waggon; or, if luck held out, precariously perching on its tarpaulin covered contents and holding on for dear life. What luxury a farthing or halfpenny could bring for those with money to spare.

Where competition did run riot around 150 years ago was in the catering trade, or 'victualing' provision. South Tawton and South Zeal boasted at least eight public houses c.1850-1870. There was also a beerhouse at Whyddon Down run by John Powlesland. The records generally ignore the houses that provided cider, or gin, or the normal backyard brewed ale, but there are local families that have admitted to the knowledge of their ancestors' trade; but who also asked for confidentiality to be respected. Inn-keeping was certainly big business around the mid-19th century and competition was fierce in the district. With South Zeal having a coaching trade it could be thought that the village had the edge on

Top: *The Seven Stars at South Tawton.*
Above: *The internationally known Oxenham Arms.*
Inset: *Almost every year for the past 25 years Boyd Templeton from San Francisco has visited the Oxenham Arms. Here with Wanda Hinkle and Jan Butdorf from Florida.*

❧ The Working ❧ Community

THIS PAGE

Left: *Okehampton Market where much local produce went.*

Below: *Charles Finch, tailor of South Tawton, caught on camera c.1895.*

Below left: *One of the South Tawton shops and its customers - probably with Miss Finch.*

Bottom right: *Willy May delivering coal.*

FACING PAGE

Top: *Potato picking at Ford. A.G. Finch is in the centre.*

Centre left: *Traditional haymaking.*

Centre right: *Vera White with the important things in her life, including a thatched rick.*

Bottom left: *Throwleigh smithy, c.1912.*

Bottom right: *Ramsley's master craftsman of metal, Dave Denford, continues the trade and preserves tradition.*

Main picture: *Summer festivities at Wood.*
Inset: *An introduction to traditional English morris dancing at the Kings Arms for Michael and Jacqueline Wright, visitors from the Cayman Islands.*

Gertie's hayfield tea as recorded by Ruth St Leger Gordon in the 1950s.

South Tawton for business opportunity but at the Seven Stars, where William John Upjohn Hill was victualler, there was a regular local clientele and with larger premises the landlord was able to provide catering services for business and private parties, weddings and social events. In their time, James Moore had been master of the Lamb Inn, which is Clarence and Pam White's farmhouse now, and John Arscott had been running the Victoria, in the front room of what was to become Patrick and Barbara Shaw's home, Yellands. Sadly, the Rising Sun, on the outskirts of the village, recently ceased serving the public after travellers were speedily diverted down new roads. The old inn then lost much of its role as a resting and refreshment place for weary travellers that it had sustained for centuries.

In 1866, run by John Lethbridge, the inn set upon its seemingly lonely moorland position, seen in the light of day by miners emerging from beneath the ground, would have been a welcoming beacon, beckoning them to its doors and offering a just reward for their back-breaking toil. In the valley below, the inns in South Zeal were vying for trade from coaches that came clattering into the village. It was in the level square, close by the Oxenham, that speculate coaches stopped to allow passengers to alight or enter.

The elite, full-fare-paying passengers found their presence appreciated and catered for by William Arscott at the ancient, but never monastic, Oxenham Arms. William Arscott, previously listed as the local butcher, and the farmer/owner of the Oxenham Arms, seems likely to have been one and the same, listed at differing times during a successful career.

At the London Inn, a few paces down the road George Holman, who was in business as yet another carrier, catered for those who paid a little extra to travel on a seat near the driver, or at least a safe one to the rear of the coach. At the White Horse, on the corner of Ramsley lane, passengers that scrambled off the top of the coach, or out of its luggage compartment, might sample the fare offered by mine host, James Trace, who also employed several ostlers.

Westbound coaches, after crossing Whyddon moor, possibly needed fresh, or additional horses more likely, when facing the awaiting hills. The Oxenham Arms certainly possessed stabling sufficient to house the horses required, but in serving 'society' its ostlers would almost certainly devote their attention mainly to the private coaches and traps of the local nobility. The London Inn, with lesser facilities might be expected to cater more for the individual rider while the White Horse could comfortably cope with carrier waggons and carts as well as coaches. South Zeal was not a place for major team-changes but the need for additional horses was ever present throughout the coaching period. William Knapman, host at the Kings Arms, half way

up, or down, the hill is least likely to have concerned himself with the coach trade, apart from providing additional brake horses when the weather made this necessary. Harnessed to the rear of the eastbound coach they would ensure passenger safety as the coachman coaxed his team to descend what can still be a treacherous hill when icy conditions prevail. Homecoming miners, farmers, and local labourers enjoyed the hospitality of Mr Knapman, whose family, if not the same person, was associated with the inn from 1841 - 1878.

In the chapel of St Mary's in South Zeal (see page 34), the business of providing education to children was being conducted by Mr William Grimsher Pym during the week while an infant class was held in the church of St Andrew, superintended by the curate the Revd William Watson English; who also provided Sunday School tuition there. His living at that time was the Vicarage with an annual value of £150, with residence, in the gift of the Deans and Canons of Windsor, and held by the Revd Thomas Collingwood Hughes BA, of Downing College Cambridge.

William Madders, the South Tawton tailor whose additional occupation is listed as Parish Clerk, played a prominent role in the community at a time when parochial self-government continued under the jurisdiction of the Manor Court and of the Vestry. Many of their functions were not superseded for another two or three decades until the Local Government Acts in 1888 and 1894, which set up the County, District, and Parish Councils. Even then the ancient 'borough' of Zeal still appointed the traditional portreeve, reeve, constable, pound-keeper and ale-taster, sworn in triennially, with due ceremony, by the lord of the manor, George Fursdon, or his representative. For the 1500 or so parishioners, 700 of whom lived in Zeal, of the two fairs given by Robert de Tony in 1298, one remained, mainly for the sale of cattle, and took place on the first Tuesday after 9 July; such traditions were to continue well into the 20th century

William White's *Gazetteer* for 1890 attributed South Tawton parish with having had 1254 inhabitants in 1881, and described it as containing 10879 acres of land, including the hamlets of Itton, Taw Green, Whiddon Down, Gooseford, Week, Fulford, Ramsley, Dishcombe, Addiscott, and South Zeal. It had a rateable value of £6803. As the last decade of the century approached, we find that the representatives of the late H.A. Hoare Esq. are now lords of the manor of Blackhall; G. S. Fursdon Esq. had appointed his last ale-taster, died, and now his representatives are lords of the manor of South Zeal. William Damarel Esq., is lord of Itton manor. There were several smaller manors and estates belonging to several owners and George Cann Esq. of Dishcombe, had now become the principal resident landowner.

Above: *Dishcombe before 1922.*

Left: *Postman Perry Vallance collects and delivers mail nowadays.*

With South Zeal school having been removed to new buildings, erected by the School Board, St Mary's chapel underwent thorough restoration at a cost of about £500, defrayed by the munificence of William Lethbridge Esq. whose family has been connected with the parish for some centuries. On Christmas-eve 1870, the Revd Thomas Collingwood Hughes' Vicarage house was almost entirely destroyed by fire but was later rebuilt on a larger scale, at a cost of £1600, mostly at the expense of his successor, the Revd John Bliss, vicar of the parish from 1872–80.

A School Board was formed on 1 August 1872. New school buildings, with teacher's residence, were erected at South Zeal at a cost of £1700 to accommodate about 200 children. Further accommodation was provided for children in the Whiddon Down district, in conjunction with the Drewsteignton School Board, and there was a third school in the outlying district called Lang Down.

The church of St Andrew was completely restored in 1881. In the north aisle there was now a stained-glass window, given by the parishioners in memory of Revd John Bliss, and his widow also erected a very handsome reredos. The Revd John Foulkes Clarke, BA, had by then been vicar for a year and was to serve for a further 27. The Bible Christians had their chapel in South Zeal near the White Horse, and the Wesleyans their own chapel at Shelly.

In 1833 Post from Exeter and Okehampton arrived daily. Letters by footpost being received at 8.00a.m., and despatched around 5.00p.m., via Okehampton; which was the nearest Money Order Office. The letterbox at South Tawton was cleared at 5.00pm weekdays only.

Richard Aggett continued to thatch the roofs around the parish, but no longer with John. While most of the established families remained, a new generation of farmers was beginning to emerge. Sylvanus Bawden now farmed at West Nymph, George Moore had taken over at Week, but Joseph Moore was still farming at Gooseford. Samuel Sampson (who had taken over from William Raymont as farmer at Blackstreet), John Powlesland (farmer at Trundlebeer), and John Sampson (who inherited the Sessland farm from Caleb) were among the first members of the South Tawton Parish Council.

Wives, following in the footsteps of Mrs Hern who had farmed at Lovaton, were taking up the traces from husbands who had devoted their lives to the land or who had provided a service in the community. Mrs Mary Ash had taken over from her husband as farmer at Cullaford, Mrs Mary Ann Holman was now carrier and victualler at the London Inn, South Zeal, and also continued her husband's former business as a carrier. Widowed, Ann Trace now had the responsibility as victualler at the White Horse, Walter Aggett at the Rising Sun, Thomas Lang at the Seven Stars, Jacob Wright at the King's Arms, and John Warne was victualler at the Oxenham Arms.

Of the three corn mills that dealt with local output in 1833, miller William Woolaway was looking forward to retirement at Taw-Green Mill, John Browning remained at work in Frog Mill but his colleague, James Yeo, had been replaced by Richard Williams at the Tawton mill. Charles Arscott continued to ply his trade as a carpenter, as did the stonemasons George Counter and James Glanville. Robert Holman was still busy baking bread before sunrise in South Zeal.

George Oades, the boot and shoemaker, added another string to his bow, and was now also postmaster in South Zeal.

Carriers, some from the past, some inheriting the business, continued to provide their services to the community. James Cooper, James Hooper and James Westaway to Exeter on Tuesdays; George Powlesland and George Wedlake taking the Torquay route on Mondays; John Wright and Mrs M.A. Holman making their way to Newton Abbot on Wednesdays.

Richard Knapman, blacksmith still in South Tawton, William Knapman, draper, grocer and seedman, in South Zeal, James Stanley, wheelwright and carpenter nearby Mrs Hill, shopkeeper in South Tawton, and Mr Finch trading there too – all are among the trades and businesspeople that were busy in a parish that was growing confident of its future as the new century drew near.

Between 1887–89 the tower of St Andrew's was repaired at a cost of about £900, and by 1893 the church contained a clock, presented by the late William Lethbridge Esq. Visitors to the parish at this time found in the church that a chancel screen had

North Wyke East, c.1912 and the entrance hall as shown on an early postcard.

been erected, in 1904, to the memory of William Lethbridge, a beautiful window in the south aisle had been erected in memory of George D. Cann Esq. M.A., LL.M. Cantab. (d.1921) by his wife and, in the north aisle, they now could pause and give a silent prayer perhaps while considering the oak tablet placed there in memory of the men connected with the parish who gave their lives in the Great War.

At this date the living was now a Vicarage, with the chapelry of South Zeal annexed, joint net yearly value £300, including residence and nine acres of glebe, held since 1916 by the Revd Edward Foley Ball M.A. of Jesus College, Cambridge, Hon. C.F., and rural dean of Okehampton.

The Ecclesiastical Commissioners were the impropriators of the great tithes, amounting to £700 a year. Church house was used as a Sunday School, and for parochial purposes, and at Taw Green there was the Baptist Chapel with a classroom attached. The local charities now had a yearly value of £75, of which £28 was derived from Northmore's Okehampton charity.

The principal landowners were Henry Christopher Kingsford-Lethbridge Esq. at Wood, Mrs G.D. Cann, and the trustees of the late Mrs Wykes Finch. The trustees of the late R.L. Kingsford-Lethbridge Esq. are lords of the manor of Blackhall; and Messrs John Endacott and Frank May, joint lords of the manor of Ash.

The copper mines and the limestone quarry in the parish were by now all now disused. The parish had apparently been extended by 81 acres since its area was now recorded as 10 960 acres of land, of which 2836 was unenclosed and common, and 28 of water. The rateable value had increased though, and had risen to £7347; the population in 1921 was 1154. Motor mail from Okehampton now brought letters direct to Sticklepath, but pedal power took its on to South Zeal to Miss Mary N. Crocker, sub-post-mistress.

The trustees of the late Charles Fursdon Esq. (d.1912) were lords of the manor of South Zeal at this time but the village still had a portreeve, reeve, poundkeeper and ale-taster, sworn in triennially. The granite built Victory Hall had been in use for some years, having been erected in 1922 at a cost of about £2000, in memory of the men of South Tawton parish who fell in the Great War.

The extent of change in the parish over the previous 60 years had been quite small. Farming was still a major source of employment. Jn. Pinney Hocking at Oxenham manor declared himself a 'yeoman,' farming in excess of 150 acres, while further down the scale Jn. Gillard at Woodland, Fredk. Jn. Howes at Gooseford, Arthur B. Johns at Blackstreet, Thomas H. Letheren at Hillstead and Herbert Madders at Newtake, all declared themselves to be smallholders.

FARMERS AT THE TIME
(those working 150 acres or more marked*),
WERE LISTED AS:

Baker Wm. & Son *
Branton Thos. Tor Hill, Throwleigh
Buckingham, Frederick Robert, Dishcombe *
Burgoyne Bros, Taw Green
Clarke, Wm., Collibeer *
Cooper, John, Spitlar
Crocker, Jas. Thos., South Zeal
Darch, Bessie (Mrs) & Sons, Lovaton *
Dart, George, Itton Manor *
Dennis, Albt., Sessland *
Dennis, Jn. 1ssac, Wickington *
Endacott, Alfd. E., West Gooseford & Fairhaven *
Finch Brothers, Ford
Friend, Hy., Great Youlden *
Hill, William, West Week, South Zeal
Hill, William, East Week, South Zeal
John, Thos., Cullaford *
Jones, Bros., West Nymph *
Kelly, Herbt., Trundlebeer *
Knapman, Jn., Addiscott *
Knapman, Jn., Thorn, Throwleigh *
Letheren, Fredk., Middle Gooseford, South Zeal
Lott, Ernest Jn., Collibeer *
Madge Bros., Great Cocktree *
Maynard, Stephen J. East Week, South Zeal
Moore, John, Higher Gooseford
Ould, Geo. Colestone, Throwleigh
Palk, Chas. Yendacott
Ponsford, Henry, Moorside, South Zeal
Powlesland Bros., Coursebeer & Powlesland *
Putt, Jn., Cullaford
Rowell, Donald M., East Ash manor, South Zeal *
Sampson, Aaron Knapman, East Ash, S. Zeal
Sampson, Rd., Addiscott
Stanbury, Edwin, Northwyke *
Stanbury, Ernest Jeffry, Taw mill *
Stanbury, Jn., Blackhall *
Tucker, Jn., Livaton
Tucker, Wm. Thos., Oxenham quarry *
Vigers, Edwin, Dibbehouse
Warren, Samuel, Addiscott
Williams, Geo., poultry farmer, Ramsley *
Wilmington, Ray, Taw Green *
White Thos. & Chas. South Zeal
White Ernest, South Zeal
Wright Thomas, South Zeal

Note: Walter Brown, at Cocktree, reckoned himself to be a 'cowkeeper'.

The five licensed houses continued to trade with the People's Refreshment House Association Ltd. making full benefit of being based at the Seven Stars Inn. Walter Aggett kept the Rising Sun Inn, Thomas Holman the King's Arms, William Lentern the Cawsand Beacon and George Millington the Oxenham Arms Hotel. In South Zeal it was possible to choose between the services offered by two banks; Lloyds Bank Ltd and National Provincial Bank which continued the service well into the 1980s in the front room of a house. Most needs were provided for by an army of local traders few of whom would survive the cataclysm of change that was already on the horizon:

Aggett, Walter, carpenter
Bennett, Edwd. C., hand-loom weaver
Brimblecombe, Elias, carpenter, East Week
Brock, Alfred, carpenter, Whiddon Down
Clements, Catherine L. (Mrs), music teacher,
       Blackstreet
Counter, Jas. & Wm, masons
Counter, William & Sons, builders and general
       contractors, Moorlands
Counter, Alfd. J., bldr
Day, Frederick George, cycle &. motor cycle agent,
       accessories, repairs, petrol & oils
Endacott, Louisa (Mrs), shopkeeper
Endacott, William Thomas, baker
Finch, George, blacksmith, Taw green
Gratton, Bertram, granite merchant &
       monumental & stone mason
Hill, Eliz. (Miss), shopkeeper
Holman, John & Sons, bakers
Holman, Saml. & Jas. fishmongers
Holman, Geo. poulterer.
Knapman, Wm R. blacksmith
Madders, Jas. stone mason
Madders, Wm. boot & shoe repairs
Potter, Alfred threshing machine owner
Redstone, William & Sons, carpenters, Woodball Cot.
Vigers, Edwin, tailor
Wedlake, William Glanfield & Son,
       poulterers, Cawsand view.
Westaway, James, jun. carrier
Westaway, Susan (Mrs), shopkeeper
White, Jas. miller (water), Tawton mill
White, Susan (Mrs), fishmonger
Willcocks & Bennett, hand-loom weavers, Little
       Down
Wonnacott, Alfred, butcher
Wonnacott, James, boot maker
Wonnacott, James, shopkeeper
Wonnacott, Samuel, hawker
Woods, Edwd. Jn. mason
Wright, Eliz. (Mrs), shopkeeper
Yeo, Jas. assistant overseer & clerk to
       the Parish Council

Chapter 4
The Onset of Education:
1663–1881

According to Restoration period Diocesan Records, in 1663 James Dyham petitioned for a licence to teach on the basis that, 'our parish hath been long destitute of a teacher.' Since this could indicate previous teachers being licensed, he cannot be confirmed as initiating education in the parish. William Bawden of Whitstone, Cornwall, petitioned for licence in 1664, but letters originating around 1700 show that one Henry Hutchings, the Parish Clerk, received consent, probably from the clergy, to keep a reading and writing school, 'there being no schoolmaster in the parish.'

Hutchings fell foul of the clergy when the vicar wanted 'a groom to keep his horses for him and to ride with him to Exeter and other journeys.' Hutchings declined the duties, on the basis that he could not undertake them, 'in regard of his inability of body and because it would impede his care of his said school.' The vicar dismissed him, and substituted Richard Markes, 'a tailor and an alehouse keeper, who hath lost his custom as a tailor by his alehouse keeping and cannot read the lessons or write legibly.'

Hutchings was later restored as Clerk and schoolmaster. Richard Burll, a former Exciseman discharged from the service, is also mentioned in correspondence as being accepted on probation as schoolmaster and as applying for licence. The vicar commented, 'I do not approve the man, and the little school he has speaks this to be the opinion of many others.'

In 1736, John Hill from Drewsteignton was licensed for reading, writing, and arithmetic. In his petition he declared that there was no licensed schoolmaster nearer than Okehampton, and that the parishioners had given their consent for a school in the chapel in South Zeal, where he had taught for some time. The 18th-century Visitation Query Returns - perhaps unreliably - indicate no school operating in 1744, a public school without endowment in 1764, and 'no public school' in 1779. In 1778, when John Gillard was Surveyor, the chapel was being maintained, as this extract from an 'Account of Disbursements on the road in the boro' of Zeale confirms.

Children at Victory Hall - the occasion is unknown.

Paid

for a lock to the chapel door	*2s.6d.*
To Wm Curson for timber and labour on the	
chapel	*1s.4d.*
To Wm Bevens for painting chapel window	
	11d.
to lime about the chapel that the Helyars made use	
of – Mr Routley bargained with for repairing	
clock	*2s.0d.*
Joseph Drew, Helyar, for work & creses to	
chapel	*2s.3d.*
ditto, for carriage of stones to foot the chapel	
	2s.6d.
Lintels over the chapel window	*6s.0d.*
To Wm Lang for righting the hammer	
and spring of the clock	*1s.2d.*

The village school was obviously operational in 1781 however, because the parish then appointed a man named Langmead as schoolmaster and made St Mary's Chapel over to him as a combined residence and schoolroom. Later, his services proved unsatisfactory, his presence became a problem to the community and in 1795 the parish sought legal advice in a letter to the Counsel dated 1795:

In the Borough of South Zele in the p'sh of S. Tawton is a very ancient messuage, formerly a chapel. It is of such antiquity that no one of the boro. recollects the building of it. This chapel as appears from the way-rate book has from time to time been repaired by & out of the monies collected by the inhabitants for the repairs of their road, within the said boro. so that it is conceived that the freehold is vested in them.

That Duty was done in this chapel about 20 or 30 years since on every Good Friday, but the same being from that time discontinued, and rather than it should remain useless, the inhabitants converted it into a school-house, – and school-masters have been put by them in possession of this house, gratis, for the purpose of teaching school there. That about 12 or 14 years since a Vestry was held in the school-house for the purpose of electing and choosing a school-master.

When Langmead was approved of by the inhabitants of the said boro' to teach school – who has ever since occupied this house by virtue of his office. But Langmead through his ill conduct & very bad behaviour has gained the ill-will of almost all those who were once his friends & has totally neglected his school, so much so that several of the parents have taken off their children, & the new school is now reduced almost to nothing. The inhabitants are willing to procure a proper person to teach school there after the present occupant is turned out of possession., they would wish to be

advised how possession is to be obtained in a legal manner - if it be necessary to give him notice to quit previous to the bringing of an ejectment, and by whom & in whose name must such an ejectment be brought ? Or may they not unroof the house & leave it in that state till he is out of possession ? It is understood that Langmead is not a licenced school-master.

There are one or two inhabitants who seem to sanction him in his present situation; will this avail anything in his favour, as a considerable majority is totally against his keeping school there upon any account whatever, or must they all be unanimous before any proceedings can take place ?

An extract of the several items which relate to the repairs of the chapel, & which were taken from the way-rate book, is here inserted, but you will observe that they are of rather a recent date owing to the old way-rate book being lost, in which were mentioned several articles concerning the chapel many years antecedent to this.

The Counsel replied as below and it is assumed that the advice given was followed:

I am afraid that if Langmead is obstinate his possession will protect him from being turned out of his school-house, there being no better title in any person to enable them to resist him. If the repairs to the chapel had been done by an individual or by a corporation such repairs would have afforded good evidence that the freehold was in the person or body corporate who paid for them. But inhabitants paying highway rates are not such a Body as can take an estate in real property. Though I would not advise the inhabitants to be at any expense in legal proceedings against him I yet think it would not be improper to convene a vestry and upon some evidence of Langmead's ill conduct pass a resolution to turn him out, which should be communicated to him, & notice given him to quit the chapel, signed by the inhabitants present at such vestry. Perhaps this may alarm him and induce him to quit upon sane terms, but should he disregard this notice, & set the inhabitants at defiance, I think they cannot compel him to quit, & therefore I cannot advise them to put themselves to any expense in a litigation in which I do not think they will succeed.

M. Dampier Holt Sept. 10th '95.

By 1798 local children had the benefit of 'several reading and writing schools.' Subscribers listed in the 1809 Churchwardens' Accounts paid a total of five guineas towards the salary of the master at the main school; to which it is thought was added money

Above: *Pupils in South Tawton.*

Right: *South Zeal Chapel and cottages – the cottages were demolished in 1877.*

from the local Rate to provide him with a generous, £25, annual income. The Parliamentary Returns show that in 1818 there were several day schools in the village, catering for about 150 children. The master of the 'principal' school, presumably in the chapel, was paid £20–£30 from the Poor Rate and received subscriptions for educating 20-30 children. By 1833 the chapel school had 80 children attending it and another four schools, including two for the 'very young', had 71 children attending 'at parents' expense.' In 1850 the ancient chapel accommodated 60 children being educated by schoolmaster, James Yeo, who seven years later was teaching 110.

James Janes was appointed in 1859 as the school's first 'certificated' master, and the 1866 *Kelly's Directory* mentions, in addition to his parochial school, an 'Infant and Sunday School held at the church.' This was probably held in the Church House, South Tawton, which was used for general parish purposes. James Janes was followed by the equally qualified Ebenezer W. Spiller in 1868 but the Parochial School in the chapel was only first put on the grant list a year later when William Hancox was appointed. His first HM Inspector's report stated that Mr Hancox had found the school 'in a very low condition', and that it had not been possible 'to make much impression upon it'. In the single room, thought to have been 37 by 14 feet, Hancox, assisted only by some unpaid 'weekly monitors', coped with week averages of over 70 pupils. Despite this, the Inspector gave him a good report in his second and final year. On leaving, for unknown reasons, he observed that his time in South Zeal had been:

... the happiest two years of my life hitherto which is principally owing to the extremely good conduct of the children, the great kindness and consideration of the Vicar, and the good treatment of the parishioners generally.

In 1870 the village was credited with possessing its Parochial School, a Nonconformist School and two others (both of these refusing to provide returns). One was presumably the infant school being run in Church House, beside the Parish Church, by Mrs Holloway, and which the School Management Committee took over immediately before the formation of the School Board.

George Honey was appointed Master of the Chapel School in 1872. A 'School Board' was imminent and a Vestry meeting in June voted for its establishment. Uncontested, the previous Management Committee was 'elected' in August as the 'School Board' but this voluntarily act was an exception to the rule in Devon: most parishes waited for a Board to be forced upon them. Under the new system a mortgage could be raised from the Public Works Loan Board for a new school; the Board's, and Honey's, ambitions would be realised within three years.

Carnival and Fayre

Top left: *The carnival of 1955 attracted a good attendance.*

Centre left: *In 1938 Clifford White was already on the way to becoming a farmer!*

Left: *Rosemary Wonnacott is crowned 'Carnival Queen'.*

Above: *Zale Fayre 2000 and post-race 'duck' recovery is conducted with military precision by Tony Clarke, with the help of a willing platoon.*

Above right: *Jessica Jeffery – Miss Zale Fayre 2000.*

Right: *At Zale Fayre 2000 it was Chagford's team that won the Football Trophy.*

SOUTH TAWTON AND SOUTH ZEAL WITH STICKLEPATH

EXTRACTS FROM THE SCHOOL LOGBOOK, 1872
SOUTH TAWTON INFANT SCHOOL;
ELIZABETH HOLLOWAY CERTIFIED TEACHER.

July 8th. This being Zeal Fair week, a very thin attendance. [Such annual events invariably provided children with an extra holiday; sometimes even given with approval.]

August 16. Holidays for harvest commenced today. [Those five words separate town and country. Town children took holidays, but few found their time consumed like that of their country cousins. The over-riding needs of farming and labouring families at harvest time was for every pair of hands to be available.]

October 8th. The Revd J. Bliss called, and stayed some time. [Such visits, associated with the running the school, are often recorded. Regular notes confirm that School Board Members examined the work and performance of children many times throughout the year and Members obviously took their responsibilities in these matters very seriously.]

October 25th. Part of apparatus arrived – 1 dozen 1 Standard reading books, one box of slates, pencils, 4 dozen cases, and one box of chalk.

November 6 The Rev J. Bliss visited the school. Some more apparatus today – a box of letters with alphabet card and 1 dozen of easy reading books, also case for reading cards. The prints which are much-needed are not yet come.

November 13th. Gave the children permission for an holiday to morrow, it being the South Tawton Ploughing Match. [The holiday confirms the importance of the annual rural event but not all pupils came from farming families and special arrangements were necessary for some.]

November 18th. Admitted for children as half timers from the Ramsley Copper Mine. It is proposed for them to attend school every alternate week by arrangement with the School Board. Three of the children from the mine cannot say any portions or knew a letter of the alphabet. I am prohibited by the School board admitting any children over 7 years. Get several applications, but am obliged to refuse.

1873 ON MARCH 3RD THE MISTRESS RECEIVED
1 DOZEN SLATES.

March 8th. Noticed an improvement in the writing of Standard 1.

March 29th. Sent home a dirty child to be cleaned. [Not all the teacher's problems were confined to education.]

May 25th. A very thin attendance to day in consequence of there being a Public Tea. [She seemed strangely unaware that free food and fun have always been a priority for children.]

June 25th. Major lists of the following songs sung by the scholars. 1 'The song of the grass'. 2 'The months'. 3 'The north wind doth blow'. 4 'Wildwood Flowers'. 5 'The Father's return'. 6 'The little dog'. 7 'The little doll'. 8 'Bread making'. 9 'Little drops of rain'. 10 'When the morning light'. 11 'The pony'. 12 'Hot Cross Buns'. [From the titles, educational values can be gleaned and the relevance to everyday life in the countryside is equally apparent.]

The future for many children lay in the land or, later, beneath it in the mines.

Schoolchildren at Throwleigh Cross.

South Tawton scholars, c.1931.

The younger children here are fairly taught, though more might be done with them, if the school were properly supplied with apparatus, and the Mistress were more energetic, and earnest in her work. The presence of children other than infants ought not to be allowed.

The Logbook continues:

October 10th. Friday: Punished several children for coming late by keeping them in. Those from Dishcombe and Ramsley are often later than any others attending the school.

October 17th. Friday: Sent home some dirty children to be cleaned.

October 23rd. A supply and coal arrived to day.

October 24. Friday: Owing to the stove being out of order fire could not be lit - though some of the little ones appeared to be suffering from the cold. Obliged to send home several children for their school fees this afternoon. Thomas Wonnacott returned with 1 penny for two weeks.

December 5th. Friday. There has been a decrease in the average attendance this I think owing to cold weather. Several of the younger children are removed by their parents during the winter.

December 24th. This closes the second quarter of the school year. Sent in today my resignation to the Members of the South Tawton School Board. E. Holloway (mistress.) [The South Tawton School Board members to whom her resignation was addressed were; Revd John Bliss M.A. (chairman) George Cann - farmer and landowner - Dishcombe, William Brely - miller - Taw Green, George Grendon - farmer - Oxenham, and John Knapman - farmer - Ash.]

1874

February 6th. Friday: Average attendance 39. Samuel Wonnacott and Mary Wonnacott absence in consequence of chilblains. Their Mother called at the school today, and said they would come next week if possible.

Mr Honey, an efficient teacher, was considered by some to be a rather devious man. For some time he was Clerk to both his School Board and the Throwleigh Board, until that body rebelled against both him and its Rector/Chairman over malpractice; a lengthy story to be found fully documented in the Throwleigh records. Honey's own records in 1874 are revealing:

February: Desk accommodation is very limited, there being room for 40 children only in the desks,

and during the past week 81 children have been in the school. [The need for the new school could hardly be more clear.]

March 30th. Mistress sent in a requisition to the Members of the School Board to be allowed to conduct the school until after the visit of HM inspectors. [Her request was accepted.]

April 27th. Monday: Several children absent to day planting potatoes.

May 27th. Friday: This week closes the school year. Finished up the year with an average attendance of 43.2. [Miss Holloway resigned her charge of the school on 3 July].

Mr Honey, Clerk to the School Board and also Master at the main school was well aware of problems and wrote in his own School Log in July: 'Of the 113 children in the school during the year, only 48 made the 250 or more attendances" (necessary to qualify for Grant Examination). On Monday 27 July Miss Eleanor Walsh re-opened the Infants School as Mistress, with 28 children present, and soon noted a reason for absence, as if previously unaware that: 'some of the children are employed in the harvest fields.' This was not the only reason though, for on 16 September the following was noted: 'Received a note from Mr Honey saying that Board had granted a holiday next Monday in consequence of the bazaar at Belstone'. The school conditions endured by the children during the winter months were never more distressingly revealed in the Infant School Logbook than in the following entries:

November 13th. Friday: Miserably cold. Attendance as usual

November 23rd. Monday: Very cold. No fire. Attendance last week rather better, not so many today.

November 30th. Monday: Very cold, no fire.

December 3rd. Thursday: Very cold, - not many children.

December 7th. Monday: Very cold - the snow - many children ill.

December 15th. Tuesday: Miserably cold - smoke - very little fire - few children.

December 21st. Monday: Cold - smoke - very few children - many of them absent from illness.

December 24th. Thursday: very few children, many have whooping cough and scarletina - close school for two weeks. Xmas holidays.

1875

January 11th. Monday: reopened school after two weeks holidays - very few children - many sick - no fires.

January 20th. Very few children - no fire - weather cold and wet. Many children ill.

January 26th. Still in the old school - no fire -very cold. Very few children

And so it went on. It was not until 8 March that the mistress noted that the weather had become milder.

The Board's new school was at last ready for occupation and four years later the Board would also open a small school at Langdown. Mr Honey's new South Zeal school, which included infants in a separate department, brought some relief from over-crowding but with it came an immediate rise in the fee rate, to 3d. per week for those over nine. Parents objected, sometimes forcibly, and for some time nothing was done to enforce attendance.

On Thursday 25 March, Lady Day once again, Mr Honey called upon Miss Walsh to tell her that she could open her school in the new building on the fol-lowing Monday. The new school could not overcome illness problems though, nor offer greater attraction than the annual village fair:

May 14th. Friday: Closed school for the Whitsuntide holidays. Several children are ill with measles.

May 23rd. Monday: Reopened school - only 12 children present - all ill with measles.

July 12th. Monday - Attendance poor - owing partly to the weather, chiefly to Zeal Fair. There seems to be always something to interfere with the regular attendance of the children which has only been 45 per cent the last year.

July 14th. Wednesday. Close school for two days in consequence of the Fair.

August 5th. Thursday: - The Mistress sent her res-ignation to the Board.

August 19th. Thursday - Closed school for three weeks, being Harvest Holidays.

Miss Walsh made her last entry in the Log in 1875 on 22 September, noting good attendance, and visits made to the school by the Revd Bliss and Revd Newman. The next entry, undated, is another 'Summary of the Inspector's Report':

This school is very low in attainment and though the change of premises may have done something to hinder its efficient working, there is no excuse for the ignorance of the first-class in Reading and Numbers. Annual admission register is required. Ventilation requires attention.
Emma Trace was noted as Pupil Teacher of the First Year.

Following that criticism, Miss Walsh retired from the office of mistress on 29 September. The school was placed in the temporary charge of Mrs Jones of South Zeal, who carried out the duties of mistress and maintained the register until Christmas. (The former British school house in South Zeal was acquired by the Wesleyans for use as their chapel in 1875.)

On 10 January 1876 the school reopened with 34 children present to meet their new mistress, Elizabeth Jane Ryder, a former student of the Truro Training College. The Log continued:

Revd J. Bliss called this afternoon and asked the Mistress about it; the door was closed, not locked. The children could not have tried much to open the door, or they would have been heard.

Under the guidance of 'Bessie' Ryder, improvements in school standards were soon noticed by the Inspector who reported that the school was 'much improved since last Inspection in order and attain-ments... '. Emma Trace was then noted as a 'Pupil Teacher of the Second Year' whom, having been dili-gent in her work had succeeded in passing her own examinations 'fairly well'. Elisabeth Ryder also impressed the master and was soon to become Mrs Elizabeth Jane Honey.

On Thursday 19 October the children enjoyed a day off school 'in consequence of the annual South Tawton Ploughing Match,' but on Tuesday 31 October 31 it was noted that a great many children were absent because they had gone to 'help dig potatoes'. School fees, and absence, continued to be a problem. On Monday 27 November Edith Willis came to school the week ending 10 November, one day only, and brought no money. The next week she came and brought twopence, which was one week's fee. She was told that she had not brought any money the week before. The mistress sent a note to the mother, and the answer was that she knew noth-ing about it. The child said that as she had only been to school one day and that her mother did not intend to pay for it.

1877
***23rd February.** Friday - Class 1 appear very stu-pid over their arithmetic. They cannot remember their numbers. A few can get on, but the rest are very backward, although the teacher has been working very hard with them. I think it is owing to the very irregular attendance of children.*

Edith Willis was soon in trouble again: 'Sent a letter to the school board, acquainted them of the non-payment of school fees by Edith Willis, who was 4d. in arrears.'

In his annual report that year the Inspector acknowledged that the school was doing well but noted that its ventilation ought to be attended to. He also noted that Emma Trace, 'Pupil Teacher of the Third Year', had passed 'fairly' and was to attend to

Grammar and Geography. Mrs Honey was ensuring that others attended to their letters, but in a manner that didn't always receive parental approval.

On Monday 20 August it was noted that several children in the class did not know their letters, although they were five years old. They were to be kept in every day for a quarter of an hour to learn them. Mrs Gillard, the mother of one of the above-mentioned children, came to the school and spoke to the mistress about keeping the child in. The mistress told her that the arrangements which she had made were to be abided by. The following day Revd Bliss, Chairman of the School Board, called and informed the mistress that Mrs Gillard had been to see him that morning. After it had been explained to him, he agreed that the mistress should abide by her arrangement. On 7 September the children were very troublesome, and were kept in standing still for ten minutes. While Mrs Gillard had not wanted her child 'kept in' for extra tuition, other parents had other ideas. On 13 November Mrs Wedlake brought her son Thomas to school and 'wished the mistress to keep him in after four o'clock for playing truant in the morning' - this was done.

On 7 January 1878 there were 64 children present in the morning. Mary Jane and Richard Mott though over eight years of age did not know the alphabet. Nor did Eli Osborne who was six and, although he could read fairly well, was backward in arithmetic. There was swift justice awaiting those who could not 'tell' their alphabet:

January 25th. Friday. Examined Class III in the alphabet, and found that nearly all could tell them, put the rest that could not tell them with the babies until they can say them.

January 29th. Tuesday. Teacher told Frank Hellier to bring his money in the afternoon, as he had been to school six weeks without bringing his Fees. His mother sent to say she would not neglect to pay it on Friday.

February 1st. Frank Hellier has not been at school yesterday or today, therefore the school fees not paid as promised.

February 15th. Friday children are unable to get their boots on because of chilblains. Frank Hellier came to school Monday morning bringing a penny for fees, teacher sent a note to his mother, he has not been to school since.

A particularly sad note on 21 March recorded that one pupil's name was to be removed from the register as he had been killed 'by a cart-wheel breaking his neck'. Lacking explanation, does the note imply that the tragedy occurred at work? Mrs Honey favoured the name and shame method of dealing with pupils that didn't reach her expectations:

April 1st. Examined Class II. Twenty present, 8 failed in Arithmetic, viz Thomas Wedlake, William Harvey, Mary Gillard, Annie Cooper, Ellen Westaway, Edward Knapman, John Powlesland, John White. 5 failed in Writing, the first by the failed in Arithmetic. 3 failed in Writing, viz, Thomas Wedlake, Mary Gillard, Annie Cooper.

Poor results were attributed to poor attendance. The Board now began to prosecute parents whose children were regularly absent; producing an influx of pupils and a week average of 113 in the mixed department, with 153 on the roll. The Inspector's comments in his report the previous year also achieved a result; 'May 27th. Ventilation of the school much better since the new window has been in.' On 21 June, Alberta Knapman, having passed the Fourth Standard, was appointed as permanent monitress by Mrs Honey, who viewed her as a future Pupil Teacher and potential certificated teacher. Such appointments, while assisting many a career, ensured that the Mistress had unpaid helpers in the classroom and a flow of pupil teachers to act as assistants. The yearly report has a 20th-century familiarity about it:

This department is in very good order and the children are on the whole well taught. The want of a Class room is already beginning to be felt and will be more so as the attendance increases. The managers would do wisely to supplying one with as little delay as possible.

Mrs Honey's attention though was, yet again, taken with finances. On 19 August she sent home James Wright and Frank Hellier for their school fees which were in arrears, and they stayed at home all day. She also sent home Albert and James Wonnacott and James Hortop for the same reason. James Hortop came with only a halfpenny when he ought to have brought a penny. She sometimes enjoyed success, and made much of it when she did, as, on 20 August, when 'Frank Hellier and James Wright came to school... and brought their fees.' But the problem was not one that could easily be resolved:

December 13th. The Gentleman of the School Board have issued an order to the effect, 'that if children come to school without their fees they are to be sent home for them.' On this order, I sent home three children viz. Thomas Wonnacott, George Counter, Frank Hellier. Only one (Thomas Wonnacott) returned and brought his fees.

Magistrates proved reluctant to impose fines on those who failed to pay their children's fees.

❧ School ❧ Groups of the 1930s

Above: *Miss Westaway and pupils, 1930.*

Right: *South Tawton Mixed School 1934 – including two future shopkeepers, Rosemary Wonnacott and Bill Holman.*

Below: *South Tawton mixed school, 1935.*

Above: *South Tawton Junior Mixed School, 1939.*

Right: *Young and eager pupils, including Perce Aggett it is said, c.1931.*

Below: *Facing an uncertain future - South Tawton Mixed School, 1940.*

On 20 January the following was recorded:

Monday   It having come to my knowledge that Emma Trace had, during the holidays, gone to a dance at two public houses, I called her attention to the fact that it was no fit place for her to go, and that it became her as a Pupil Teacher to set a better example. She said she did not think it's a wrong place to go to, or she should not have gone, that she agrees with me now that it was a wrong place to go to, and she will not go again. Alberta Knapman, monitress also went, and I spoke to her about it.

March 11th. Tuesday. Mistress gave a 'lesson' on 'Tobacco.'

March 21st. Friday. Average attendance this week 72. The want of a class room is much felt, now the attendance is greater.

April 29th. E. Trace gave a lesson on 'Pearl'. This lesson was not given at all well. Emma's future is far from clear, but Mrs Honey has other worries:

May 9th. I am obliged to keep one class in lavatory as I have not a Class room.

May 30th. Tuesday. 97 children present this afternoon, I am obliged to use the lavatory as a class room.

Meanwhile an extract from the Inspector's report read: 'This department continues to be conducted with order and success.' Prospects for Emma Trace were brighter after she attended a meeting of the School Board in 1880 and was appointed as an assistant in the school at the salary of £20 a year.

Alberta Knapman, the monitress, was by now giving 'object' lessons to the children on various things including, the Saucepan, Barley, the Pear, Briar Rose, and a Chair. Such lessons may seem rather odd and outdated, but are they? Leap forward to our own times for a moment:

May 16th 2000. Tuesday. Results of the British Potato Council Study, carried out in schools across the country, reported in the Daily Mail: 'Half the youngsters aged six to nine questioned in a survey said that they believed that potatoes grow on trees.' 'Fifty-four percent of children have no concept of what a new potato is...'.

The worried council commissioned an educational bus to travel around schools! In 1881 and the week ending 25 March it was recorded in the Log:

Took the 3rd class to see how many of the names of the fruits that they had learnt the week before and found, with a few exceptions, they had all forgotten them, so I taught them the names of four of the fruits.

The Potato Council might note that the names of more fruits were included in lessons each week and that by 6 May the mistress had confirmed that all but three or four pupils knew their fruits, without an educational bus in sight.

On 23 December the Christmas holidays began for three weeks and the mistress gave up charge of the school. George and Elizabeth Honey departed their posts in December 1881. Through their work, and the work of the other teachers and pupil teachers, the foundation for education in South Zeal had been made secure in less than a decade.

Miss Warnock and class, 1970s.

Chapter 5
Almost a Century at Sticklepath School

In 1979, to celebrate the centenary of the building of the village school, then known as Sticklepath (Okehampton) County Primary School, the Headmaster, Mr V.W. Hutchinson published a chronicle of its history which he had compiled. We are privileged that Mr Hutchinson has not only given his approval for this chapter to be based upon his work, which includes the reminiscences of previous pupils, but that he has also provided previously unpublished notes and correspondence that carry the school story forward to its closure in 1984. It was totally co-incidental, but very convenient, that Mr Hutchinson's research begins in the same decade in which we ended our own early history of the South Zeal Schools.

Mr Hutchinson and pupils celebrating Sticklepath School's Centenary, 1879-1979.

This was the period in which the outcome of the Forster Education Act of 1870 were felt in the area which was, like the entire country, divided into districts, each of which was obliged to set up a School Board. Parliament had taken an interest in education and had allocated money regularly to existing schools since 1833, but schools still continued to depend on local people for most of their financial requirements, resulting in the poorer areas having fewer schools. The new Boards could now raise money to build necessary schools, to be called Elementary Schools, but as well as the local people contributing by means of a 'rate,' parents, other than the poorest, had to pay ninepence a week for each child attending.

Kelly's Directory records that 'a School Board, of five members, was formed in 1874 for the united district of Sampford Courtenay and Honeychurch with Belstone contributory with two members.' Although Sticklepath was at that time within the parish of Sampford Courtenay the School Board decided that Sampford Courtenay and Sticklepath should each have a school.

The conveyance of the site for the Sticklepath School is dated 18 April 1878 and signed by George Underhill Wills, lord of the manor of Sticklepath. A year later a school was built that could accommodate 80 children, summoned to it by a big brass bell that not even the sleepiest of heads could suggest would not be heard at the other end of the village. The main building that was erected to introduce children to their education consisted of one long room, 36 feet by 16 feet. Access to the school was from a roadside entrance, the nearest water supply was Lady Well, and sanitation came in the form of bucket lavatories. The collection of rainwater in a tank did help during the following 70 years or so.

The year after the school was built saw the passing of the Mundella Education Act, which made it compulsory for children to attend school from the age of five years although they could leave after their tenth birthday if their work was of a certain standard.

Unfortunately there appear to be no other recorded details of the early years except for the names of some headteachers. John Arbory was appointed to the school in 1883 and remained in charge until 1889 when William Avery was appointed. It was in this year that the school was enlarged to accommodate 100 pupils; but the extension could hardly be termed generous in proportion. It was during his term of office, in 1891, that school fees were abolished and Elementary School education became free.

The next headmaster was short lived in his position. William Richard Hoile stayed for only one year, 1893-94, before Mr Ernest William Pym then assumed command of the children's education in the village and stayed in the post until 1897. The following year, Mr Frank Richards entered the school in January as its headmaster. He was to remain there for almost four decades.

Main: *The beauties of Taw Valley and Belstone which surrounded the pupils at Sticklepath School.*
Inset: Right: *Even visiting Canadian schoolchildren find our moorland 'cool' - Shannon and Leah Hardy and their father, from Ontario.*

Above: *Sticklepath School and the quarry, c.1910.*
Left: *A School for Sundays - Sticklepath church in the 1920s.*

Around 1900 the amount of money granted to a school was based on what was said in the Inspector's report and the grant was the only source of income for the whole of that particular year. The bare details of the grant for several years at the turn of the century are recorded. Although there is no explanation of the itemised amounts, it is quite clear that the most important factor was the average daily attendance. The number on roll in 1900 reached 83 but, as was usually the case at that time, attendance was far from good. Epidemics of measles, German measles, diphtheria, whooping cough, influenza, mumps and chicken pox occurred fairly regularly; weather conditions often prevented children from the 'country' attending; some children were frequently kept at home to work, particularly at harvest time and for picking whortleberries. The average daily attendance in the final year of the 19th century was 55 and it is not really surprising, therefore, that the allocation of money to the school was based on the attendance figure rather than the number on roll. The sum payable was arrived at in the following manner:

Principal Grant	14s.0d.
Discipline and Organisation	1s.6d.
Singing by Ear	6d.
Elementary Science and History	2s.0d.
Geography	2s.0d.
Total	20s.0d.
Grant on Total Average Attendance	20s.0d. x 55
	= £55.0s.0d.
Grant on Drawing (34 boys)	1s.9d. x 34
	= £2.19s.6d.
Grant on Needlework (21 girls)	1s.0d. x 21
	= £1.1s.0d.
Amount of Grant	£59.0s.6d.
Additional 'Payment of Fee Grant'	£7.12s.6d.
Total Sum claimable	£66.13s.0d.
Deduction of Teachers' Superannuation	
Contributions	£3.10s.0d.
NET SUM PAYABLE	£63.3s.0d.

Top: *Collecting water from Lady Well c.1910.*
Above: *Sticklepath pupils c.1909.*

Even as the headmaster worked within these figures the school leaving age for his pupils was being raised to 14 years but even this was not compulsory since able pupils could leave earlier. He also dealt with temporary, local, absence also. For example: 'July 9th. Number present 42 out of 82. Many are gone picking whortleberries and others are busy haymaking.' Many similar entries confirm that children, instead of being at school were, as was to be expected, often engaged in 'family' work gathering mushrooms, picking fruits in season, digging potatoes, helping with the harvest and, through these rural activities, often reducing total attendance down to one-third. On 5 December in 1900. a 'very wet day', only 38 out of a possible 83 attended.

Newspapers of the period confirm in their reports that the start of the new millennium was quite correctly celebrated in this Victorian age as the

Above: *Pupils in 1920, with Mr Richards.*

Left: *Mr Richards, a very popular teacher, held in high esteem by the community.*

last day of 1900 departed. For the children, there was even more to celebrate as school did not start again until 7 January. When they did return on that day, they found the chill of winter had penetrated the school. Two windows, having been broken by stones during the holiday had reduced the temperature in classroom to 39°F.

It was not only the children that had priorities such as whortleberry picking that kept them from school; the teachers had theirs also and if teachers didn't always have priorities, they sometimes had unusual problems:

May 5th   School opened at 1.30 this afternoon to enable the master to attend a rifle shoot at the range.
October 23rd   School closed on account of the illness of the master, suffering from 'Congestion of the Brain'.
December 16th   A very rough morning. Three children came wet through and had to return home.

Such wet weather problems as this were repeatedly recorded in the Log and on one occasion 24 children were sent home.

The Fisher Education Act of 1902 now made the leaving age of 14 compulsory, but this was only a minor part of an Act which completely re-organised education. The School Boards system was ended and the counties and county boroughs were made responsible for educational provision, each one forming its own Local Education Authority. One effect of this was that Sampford Courtenay Sticklepath Board School became Sampford Courtenay Sticklepath Council School.

On 1 September, the Log records: 'The Sunday School scholars having gone to Bude today for their annual outing, the school was not opened.' Those who recall such outings in the 1920s and '30s expressed happy memories of times when the traditional treat was not just welcomed by many children as a day out, but as a day off work. After school, or instead of it, at the weekends, and in the early hours of each day many children had work to do. On 25 April 1904 we read that 'School closed for the afternoon in consequence of a Band of Hope tea being held at Belstone' (an event which happened on a number of occasions). George Mortimer, during the dinner-time, was knocked over by a cyclist and sustained a slight sprain in the leg. He was sent home in

SIMMONS PARK, OKEHAMPTON

a passing cart under the charge of his older sister. On 22 August George attended for the first time since his accident.

With over 90 children on the school Roll in 1905, Frank Richards then had 67 of them under his control, in the main room. On 22 August 1906 Miss Bolt was late to school in the morning, arriving at 10 o'clock because of a puncture in the tyre of her bicycle. On 8 July 1907 the whole district had something to celebrate; the opening of Simmon's Park in Okehampton. The school closed for the afternoon to allow children to attend the ceremony. Another 'treat,' one that continued for many years and is still remembered, was recorded in the Log on 16 October: 'Extremely wet morning. 8 children came wet and as no fires had been lit, they were sent to the foundry to dry.' The following year on 22 November 'Mima Cook, who [had] been absent for 12 weeks with Whooping Cough, returned [to school].' There is no doubt whatsoever that illness in these days, and later, reached epidemic proportions, spreading through schools from child to child and then onwards to rage throughout the communities. It is far from unusual to read in Logbooks of teachers being instructed to close their schools. On 15 July 1910, it was recorded that 'School closed for the Summer Holiday, the whortleberries being now ripe.' Whortleberry picking was an important source of income for many families and this simple entry does appear to indicate that the annual holiday, whether taken slightly early or somewhat late, was determined by the readiness of the berry.

LUGG & SONS, PHOTOGRAPHERS, OKEHAMPTON.

Above: *Simmon's Park, Okehampton, as the children knew it c.1905.*

Left: *Albany George Finch, daughter Jessie Emma, and son Alfred, photographed c.1900 by Lugg & Sons, Okehampton.*

Right: *Ann Finch, shopkeeper, with Jessie and Florrie Bovey (Bovery) from White Rock View, later part of White Rock Cottage.*

a Regimental Sergeant Major and kept his cane up his sleeve, whipping it out like lightning to cut across the legs of misbehaving pupils.' Although the highest recorded number on roll is 103, Mr Brooks was certain that it reached 120 at the time he used to call the register for Mr Richards. Many years after he left the school, Percy Brooks returned to serve it, 'unrecognised' as Father Christmas (every year from 1967 to 1976) and, according to many, he made a 'proper job' of it. Mr George Hellier, a fellow pupil of Percy's from 1914-21, remembered:

> *Mr Richards, the master, [left] to go into the Army in 1916, that he served in India, and... one of his temporary replacements was young Mr Carlile, who was a keen sportsman and played cricket with the boys.*

The playground, extending to the road, was uneven and rough, and Mr Hellier recalled it being altered to prevent pupils falling over the low railings on to the main road, an event whcih, he recalled, 'sometimes happened when we were chasing each other while at play.' And 'with the motor car coming into use, the Managers thought there might be a number of accidents.' When the playground surface was smoothed, marbles and spin tops became popular. Marbles was also played in the street in Sticklepath, even by the men and when a car came along the marbles were

The following miscellaneous entries provide a fascinating, and sometimes amusing insight into daily life at the school:

> *1911 January 12th   School closed for a fortnight - 50 cases of Whooping Cough.*
> *1912 August 11th   Cyril Taylor, having put a small bead up his nose, has been sent down to the nurse [above] for her to get it down again. Returned later, having had it removed.*
> *September 17th   Willie Bennett... ditto.*

During the First World War, the children, and the adult parishioners, were encouraged to participate in many savings or fund-raising schemes and in April 1915 the schoolchildren were given a lesson one morning, in the scripture time, on 'Kindness to others weaker than ourselves.' This was introductory to instituting a movement for children to bring eggs for wounded soldiers. These eggs were to be dispatched to the hospitals weekly.

During Mr Richards' wartime service in the Army, from June 1916-February 1919, six different teachers were placed in charge of his school. These included; Mrs Mercer, Mr Carlile, Mr Shapcott, Mr Luxton and Miss Saunders. A pupil at school from 1912-22, Percy Brooks, of South Tawton, remembered that: 'one of the masters who took Mr Richards' place during the First War, a Mr Carlile, was just like

Top: *Nurse Rowe, the village's first District Nurse, who began to help the community in 1912.*

Above: *A football team at Sticklepath School, 1920s.*

Right: *At Cleave Mill, the Littlejohns' lorry had iron wheels.*

hastily removed or left to chance.' Hoops, and the metal crooks used to drive and control them, were made just down the road at the foundry – at a cost of about sixpence. Mr Hellier also remembered that the girls used wooden hoops and skipping ropes whilst on the playground the boys played cricket and football using a tennis ball, which was often lost over the wall among the brambles and ferns. This was a continuing problem experienced by pupils in succeeding generations. Mr Hellier pointed out that 'playing football was rather dangerous as they all wore hob-nail boots which could cause a lot of cuts and bruises.' He remembered that their first real football was given by Miss Shaw, who later became Mrs Ralph Finch, and that they used this ball on Sticklepath Moor. Two other playground games remembered were called Prisoners Base and Hat Ball, and there was one occasional visitor to the school that made his mark in Mr Hellier's memory: 'I remember Mr. Cook, always known as Butcher Cook, coming to school annually to present those who had attended regularly with a shilling, also certificates. He was of portly build and always wore a silk top hat.'

Ceremony at White Rock.

On 24 August 1921 'owing to the opening of a War Memorial at Belstone, a holiday was given.' This must have been the War Memorial Institute Hut built of wood by the men of the village. It was later burnt down after a 'beating of the bounds' and replaced by a Church Hall, which subsequently became the Village Hall. On 2 December a social was held in the hall to raise funds for the school sports and for hot cocoa to be given to the children at dinner time.

During the early 1920s and beyond, with the First World War fresh in people's minds, long before it was considered wrong by some to express patriotism, the children regularly participated in local ceremonials. Empire Day was 24 May when 'the children were taken to the top of White Rock and there unfurled the Union Jack, singing patriotic songs at the same time.' Two days later the school was closed, and the children were celebrating with their friends in South Zeal the opening of that village's latest facility, the Victory Hall. We have already seen that fundraising was undertaken to provide hot drinks for the children and two other entries in the Log show that individual members of the community also added their personal assistance. On 11 November 'Mr

Pease sent another basket of apples to be distributed among the children. This is the third time we have received gifts of apples from Mr Pease.' There were many similar notes relating to the continuing generosity of both Mr and Mrs Pease. The entry for 5 June 1923 reads 'Mrs Pease still continues to send a large bucket of milk daily for the country children. This has continued ever since 14th May and the kindness is greatly appreciated by all.'

The school, in March 1924, and no doubt influenced by its popular headmaster, adopted as its motto the inspirational phrase 'Onward and Upward'. Respect for the past, and recognition of sacrifices made are indicated in the Log by entries such as that recorded in 1925 on 11 November when 'the children were marched to attend a service at the Village War Memorial.' The memories of war would never recede for those who lived through either of the major conflicts of the 20th century but in 1927 there was already concern about the health of children that resulted in a regular visit to school of one visitor whom pupils regarded with awe. On 6 May it was noted that 'the school dentist inspected the children's teeth and extracted bad ones in many cases. Only a few objections were received this time.' The popularity of Mr Richards is legendary, his guidance to young people is spoken of as inspirational and one very small entry made on 27 May perhaps provides an insight into why this should be so: 'the headmaster was absent from school this morning owing to the death of his wife which took place during the night. He resumed duties in the afternoon.'

As a communicator of education he was obviously a man aware of the values of communication and the progress being made by the British Broadcasting Company. Established in October 1922, it was a further four years before it could make simultaneous, or network, broadcasts to the nation, through its eight individual stations that previously had broadcast to their own limited area. The 'Company' became a 'Corporation' in 1927 and within months, on 20 February the following year, 'an aerial for use with the Master's wireless set [was] fixed in the Girls' Yard.' His was very unlikely to have been the first radio in the area, but when few could afford such a luxury, the knowledge and information the schoolmaster gained from his wireless he undoubtedly shared with his pupils, and thereby the community.

Top: *Sticklepath before the days of wireless.*

Above: *Early deliveries by cart, c.1908.*

Below and right: *The village scene c.1930 shows how little change took place during the early part of the 20th century.*

When those pupils became parents, and television came this way, they often told their own children of the days when the master had told of the news from London, on the day it happened.

Since the advent of motor vehicles in the district Mr Richards had witnessed a virtual proliferation of private cars and waggons and recognised the dangers. In March 1928 he 'had a talk with the whole school' in which he warned them 'against playing about on the road to and from school, to keep on the right side of the road, and to exercise great care when crossing the road.' Addressing children, as yet, more used to the horse and cart, it was probably not vehicles in great number that he was warning them of, it was the ability of a car to move at tremendous speed that mattered. A car could kill at less than 20 mph.

Another, problem, more relevant perhaps to the majority, was the bucket toilet sanitation system. It was discussed by the Managers in September, who noted: 'a doorway was opened between the Boys and Girls 'offices' so that the buckets from the former need not be carried through the school.' Taking up Mr Richards' fears they also 'requested a footpath to be made from the School to Lady Well on account of the danger to the children from the increasing motor traffic.' This was provided in 1930.

Mr Richards was not a man that suffered fools gladly, as an entry in his Log the previous year on 22 May confirms:

School visited by Board of Education Inspector this morning. He arrived during the playtime and at once accused the Head Teacher of placing scouts to watch for his approach. He bases his accusation on the fact that he saw a girl run into school and tell the teachers that the Inspector had arrived. The master replied to his insulting remarks in no uncertain manner and it appeared to him that afterwards the Inspector went out of his way to ask questions in Mental Arithmetic too involved for any to follow and questions in Geog. that were purposely meant to confuse. This entry is made merely to explain beforehand any vindictive remarks that may appear on the report.

On the afternoon of 10 September 'Ray Kelly fell into the water contained in the tank and got very wet. He was sent home to change his clothes.' Many years later Ray, a pupil at the school from 1926–33 remembered the incident and added that he 'and other boys had caught some minnows in the leat and had put them in the tank at school.' Kneeling on the top and peering into the water to see them, his hand slipped and in he went. Retribution did not end with his getting wet as he was also caned. Pupils, he recalled, were allowed off the school premises at lunchtime and often played chasing games through the undergrowth around White Rock. In winter, they would go up to the frozen pond on Brennamoor, often getting a lift back on the horse and cart delivering bread but, if they returned late, they were caned.

There were rewards as well as punishments however as, on 19 December Geraldine Wickett and Hubert Kelly were each 'awarded 10/- prizes for essays written during Health Week and sent to the Royal Sanitary Institute.'

Village water supplies being used by Violet Mallet and Margaret Rose.

🦉 A Happy 🦉 Place to Be, School Life, 1960s–70s

Top: *A classrooom in 1966.*

Above and below: *Sticklepath School's Save Our School Campaign, 1979.*

Top right: *Making the model of Wiley Farm was also remembered by past pupils.*

Right: *Swimming lessons, 1978.*

In October 1930, the Managers expressed 'grave alarm' regarding reorganisation; which would mean the senior children going to Okehampton for their secondary education. In April of the following year the Managers declined to recommend one of the teachers to be dispensed with because of the proposed re-organisation, and unanimously threw the responsibility back on to the County Authority. The effort was in vain. The school was renamed Sampford Courtenay Sticklepath Junior School, all children over 11 years were transferred to Okehampton Senior School, and in July the Managers were advised that the County Authority had decided that Miss Finch should leave and be put on the unattached staff.

The entry for 13 July 1933 reads: 'On her way to school today, Evelyn Crocker was knocked down by a motor-bike. Her leg was injured but no bones broken.' On 13 September 1935 'the tank in the boys yard [was] raised and the base cemented in to prevent any of the boys from climbing up and being in danger of falling in. A netting of wire [was also] placed over it to keep things from being thrown in.' The Silver Jubilee of King George V was celebrated by parishioners and children. During his reign, and that of Mr Richards, the SS Titanic had sunk, a World War changed society for ever, workers had seen the first Labour Government elected, and women over 21 had won the vote. The rural schoolroom world ruled by Mr Richards was part of the changing times; and the King was ill. The school Log for 21 January 1936 reads: 'The master talked to the children this morning about the death of the King and the meaning of the phrase 'The King is dead – Long live the King.'

The entry for 31 March confirms, after 38 years, the end of another popular reign: 'From this date, I, Frank Richards, resign charge of this school.' The following letter had been sent from the Managers to Mr Frank Richards after receiving his resignation in January:

The Managers received your notice with deep regret but they realise that years pass on and they only hope that when the time comes for your retirement that you will be able to spend many happy years, made happier by the knowledge of how well they know you have served Sticklepath School and your County.

In fact, Gertrude E. Squires had already commenced her duties as headteacher of the school on 3 February. Like her predecessor she was to become a highly respected and much loved member of the community, destined to serve the educational needs of her young pupils for more than 30 years.

One benefit she received that Mr Richards had never enjoyed was electric light. It was installed in the school in 1936. In 1937 the headmistress ensured that the past was not forgotten. On 11 November a wireless set was hired and the children joined in the Cenotaph Service. In January 1938 the Education Committee authorised the provision of fire buckets in the school, much to the amusement of the Managers and staff since there was no source of water on the premises from which to fill them. After inspecting the school later in the year, a Ministry of Health Inspector wrote: 'I find that there is no water supply on the premises of this school.' He added: 'The water has to be carried an unreasonable distance and I recommend that this matter be given urgent consideration.' The Headmistress, however, ensured that the latest means of education was made available to her pupils. On 30 September a wireless set was installed and BBC School broadcasts used.

In 1939 war loomed once again and in March the Managers were advised of Air Raid Precautions. It was instructed that in schools with over 30 pupils, 'Managers should consult with the District Air Raid Wardens regarding the selection of suitable sites for trenches on the Common in the vicinity of the school.' This the Managers did and selected a site for trenches on the Common about 40 yards from the school wall. (There was no further mention of this and no one apparently remembers any trenches being there.) On 10 October children were fitted for gas masks by A.R.P. Warden, Mrs Burd.

For 70 years after the school was built, all waste water was allowed to run into the gutter in the main road. It was not until 1949 that pipes were laid under the school path to connect with the main drain at Lady Well corner. The bucket lavatories that the older generations still speak of today had been of use to several generations before 1952 when, after years of complaints, correspondence, and Inspectors' reports, flush lavatories and handbasins were installed. Disappointment awaited one pupil who greeted their arrival in the earnest belief that her prayers had been finally heard and her regular plea for safekeeping from spiders and other terrors anticipated to attack in her times of dire need had been rewarded. She recalled that at her first attempt to use the modern facility, she was refused admission to the newly installed inner sanctum. The toilet was there, but no running water was connected to provide its major modern benefit to users. For a few weeks, the flushing of the lavatories had to be carried out with buckets of water from the rainwater tanks; the only source of water within the school. Then a rotary pump was used to take water from the tanks to a storage tank above the toilets. This, apparently, solved the problem except when there was insufficient rainwater or when the pump itself failed!

The name Gilbert Harding still reminds many people of the television programmes round about

Class 5 on a trip to London, 1969.

Sticklepath School, 1969.

Above: *Class 1 of
1979, with Mrs
P. Wedlake.*

Right: *Mrs D. Wedlake
and Class 2, 1979.*

Below: *The entire
school in 1979.*

1950 and the reputation this television personality gained for himself. To some local people, his name is forever coupled to the subject of Sticklepath School toilets. The story is rather vague but the fact that he wrote to the *People* newspaper about the school's sanitary arrangements is clearly remembered. The only mention in the school records is found in the minutes of the Managers Meeting of January 1952 when comments were made about 'the article in the paper'. Whether this publicity resulted in the ensuing improvements is uncertain. It may have been mere coincidence that the long-awaited flush toilets and water supply were installed later that same year.

From the day of its opening until 1952, all drinking water was carried from the spring at Lady Well. Often when the water in the tanks had frozen water for all uses had to be brought in by hand. When storage tank supplies ran out, or during droughts, the local fire brigade would be summoned. Even after tap water was available from December 1952 there were times when the old method had to be resorted to. For five days in 1960 there was no supply owing to workmen having broken the mains whilst digging up the road. That same winter, a North Devon Water Board tanker came to fill the tanks during a freeze-up. This must have brought back memories of the bad old days when Okehampton Fire Brigade came out to do the same thing.

An entry made in October 1958 reads: 'The name of the School was changed to 'Sticklepath, Okehampton', leaving out 'Sampford Courtenay'.' By 1966 Gertrude Squires had completed 30 years' service as headmistress at the school and the Managers were preparing for her departure at the end of the year. In June, four shortlisted applicants for the post were interviewed and Mr V.W. Hutchison of Grantham, Lincolnshire, was appointed 'after considerable deliberation'. On 1 January 1967 Mr Hutchinson brought his wealth of experience to Sticklepath as the village school's headmaster, experience that was soon to be called upon by the community. In March, his school Managers held a meeting with Mr Brotherton, the Assistant Education Officer, to discuss the Authority's long-term proposal to build a new Area School to replace the schools in Sticklepath and South Zeal. They learned that the Authority already had two sites to be considered, one at the lower end of Sticklepath by the bridge and the other on the road leading to South Zeal. The stability of schooling provision in the villages that had been enjoyed for almost a century (although some children might say endured) was considered to be under serious threat.

For the next seven years the proposal to build a new primary school, large enough to provide for the educational needs of children throughout the entire area, was a controversial issue. In the midst of it all, in 1970, and almost unnoticed, a small part of the school's history disappeared. The rainwater tanks, which had provided such a long and essential service to the school, were finally disposed of; but the school was still threatened with closure. From the outset the Managers of both schools, similarly threatened, could not agree on either of the sites proposed. The County Planning Department's recommendation that the Sticklepath site was more advantageous received the approval of the Education Committee and support from the County Council. The Managers of both schools came into conflict at joint meetings and could not agree on a choice of site. A public meeting was called in South Zeal but did not resolve matters.

Opposition to the scheme from all quarters continued and despite proposals put forward for alternative sites the two sets of managers could not find any of them mutually satisfactory. As the impasse continued the belief spread that the County's instigation of the matter had been premature. Time was passing and with the eventual sale of the proposed site in Sticklepath, for housing development, it seemed that the death knell for the two village schools would not sound their passing. Another omen of hope was the discovery by Mr Hutchinson, Sticklepath School's headmaster, of his school's big brass bell, originally installed in 1879, but found tarnished and forgotten in 1972 in a coalshed. Cleaned by the crafts department at Okehampton School, it rang out again at celebrations marking the Centenary of the school to which it had summoned the first pupils.

With the benefit of hindsight some now consider that opportunities were lost during these years of indecision and that a school situated at Ford Cross might have far better served the local population than the eventual outcome of the conflict. It was an outcome that was to satisfy no one. Sticklepath School was doomed to closure, South Zeal to remain with its 19th-century Victorian premises. Despite its 21st-century extensions, the school is still considered to be in need of an extra hall if it is to continue coping with around 200 pupils.

In the 1970s the opportunity to establish a school, suitable in size to provide education for children from many local villages, and adequate for such service well into the 21st century, was lost. The consequence was to bring parents and parishioners out on to the streets to protest against the closure of Sticklepath School. 'Please spare our local school – it's so good' was the heading of an article by Keith Whitford, published in the *Western Times* of 29 July 1983. Contained within the article were the words that parents of pupils had long feared, 'Devon County Council has published a notice of closure to take effect from July 1984.'

Chapter 6
Industry in the Area

The earliest evidence of the occupation of land by people comes from moorlands and downlands of the South, including the high moorland of Dartmoor. No one can tell when the cultivation of crops began but it is considered likely that wandering tribes or families would select a place where their simple tools would give them a return for their labour greater than the more fertile lowlands, with their dense covering of natural growth. The earliest settlers in this locality selected the slopes surrounding the highest point in the area on which to live. For thousands of years others followed suit, and those of us that live beneath the beacon have hardly distanced ourselves from it.

The cultivation of soil and the domestication of animals provided the foundation for community life; and it is a safe assumption that animal husbandry came first. Sooner or later, their attempts to rear the young offspring of animals they hunted led our ancestors to succeed in breeding animals in captivity; and they also found Cosdon. To our forefathers its height provided a place of safety, the high place on which to honour their beliefs, and land that was free from the dense scrub and trees that covered the land and valleys below – a perfect place.

Historian talk endlessly about the burgage strips of South Zeal but there is other land in use nearby that, despite its almost modern development and useage, provides clear visual reminders of the earliest field systems. The ancient small inclosures had well-defined boundaries, composed, some suggest, of stone cleared from the land. Next time you are travelling from Whiddon Down towards South Zeal, or walking

Above: The Nine Maidens, Belstone, attracts attention from young and old.
Below: Aerial photograph shows clearly signs of the old strip-farming methods.

from Zeal Head cross roads to Ford Cross, look toward the slopes of Cosdon hill, at the smallest enclosures in use today, let the mind's eye divide the larger ones, and allow the centuries to drift away.

Food production was originally for self-supply and a man's holding was rarely larger than that which he and his family could keep under cultivation. By the late-Saxon period they had the benefit of the plough, which became so firmly established that land measures, such as the furlong or the rod, were derived from its use; holdings were also measured by its work; bovate, hide, and the carucate (Latin caruca meaning plough). The Domesday survey's information on the 'Manor Tauetona', records that, 'thirty ploughs can plough it.' By the time that the earliest, disputed, records suggest that South Tawton had become a hundred (1243, 1269) the majority of the manor's inhabitants were engaged in tin mining in the area. As Stannators, they enjoyed the remission of some taxes and while also enjoying venville common rights; they were certainly not only relying upon agriculture. Between the 12th and 14th centuries, entrepreneurs became intent upon establishing new towns as centres for commerce or industry. By the middle of the 13th century the developers' eyes turned to the settlement that they intended to turn into the town of South Zeal. For whatever reason, their ideas fortunately foundered, but the town layout survives to this day.

In 1299 when lord of the manor, Robert De Tony, was granted the right to hold a market and two fairs in the newly created borough he must have had high hopes for its future development. Premises that could provide traders and merchants with commercial outlets were intended to line the central highway through the 'town,' with the cottages and houses having their burgage plot, or 'borough acre' as they're known locally, to provide for animals, fowl, and produce. All of this was intended to encourage newcomers to the 'town', but the villagers were not reliant upon his expansion for employment.

There had been fulling mills operating in Zeal as early as 1263 when it was recorded that 'Humfridus le Fulur' or Humfrid de la Sele was paying an annual rental of 2s.6d. for water from the Blackaton (Lovebrook) to Ralph Tauney. The fulling process was applied to woollen or worsted fabrics with the objective of turning a soft cloth, woven or knitted, into a firmer one. Originally treading the cloth underfoot in water did this. Later it was done by using waterpower driven hammers. Reference to the rental of water rights are found again in 1421-22 in a document regarding a dispute:

Willm umfray Burgoyne w'ch rent a water-course the pliff affirmeth to be the same that be conteyned in the saide anncient deed, and for that the said deft. did not disprove the same.

Details are unknown but clearly Willm won the day:

... it is therefor ordered and decreed by this court that the s'd Wm Burgoyne... shall enjoy the s'd water-course, conteyning in bredthe fower foote, to the said mill in Sele... without anie lett or interruption of the s'd Alexander Knapman.

Members of the Beacon Players celebrating with an Olde Englishe Fayre, 1952.

There are other records of disputes regarding water rights, and the diversion of water in the northeastern region of the moor, in 1275 regarding a mill at Wyke, and again in 1277 another in Suthtauton, or South Tawton as it was becoming known. It is these disputes that confirm the conflicts between tin miners who were claiming their ancient rights to water, and others who now needed it. Most of those in the village community who farmed the land were small, subsistence farmers, holding their land from a higher landlord, the lord of the manor, who was also a subsistence farmer growing food for his family and establishment. He looked to his tenants to carry out the commoner work, of ploughing, harrowing, weeding, haymaking, harvesting and carrying; their remaining time they could devote to their own land. His tenants might be Freemen, who could leave the manor at times, or villeins, who could not do so without their lord's permission.

Devon at the end of the 13th century, and well into the 14th, appears to have been a place where problems between the miners and farmers were commonplace and disputes regarding the ownership and the possession of water rights were even referred to Parliament. In 1300, in an ancient petition, Roger de Novaunt, John de Denhm, Will'me de fferers and John de Prouston, at a Parliament held at York, brought bills against the Stannators for 'many grievous oppressions, etc.,' and Mons. Hugh de Courtenay, Sire Will'me Martin, John de Stonore and Will'me de Burne were appointed to 'oyer & terminer les trepas', although it was noted that they had 'done nothing as yet.'

In 1300 the accounts of Thomas de Swenesey, clerk warden of the king's mines mention moneys received from the king's manors of Dertemore, Lydford and Wyke; as in Week in both Southteign and Chagford. No fewer than 80 part-time tinners worked claims in the Suthtauten manor area in 1337, not to overlook the mines at Throwley and towards Drewsteignton, and in 1377, almost eight decades after Roger de Novaunt, John de Denhm, Will'me de fferers and John de Prouston had taken their petition to York, the Stannators were still a cause of problems for the general population. The complaint was, predominantly, that the miners were abusing the privileges granted them in their Charters and confirmed by King Edward I, grandfather of the the newly-crowned Richard II. The people vociferously protested that while the Stannators ought to be digging for their tin only on wastes and moorland, they were claiming the whole of Devon for their Stannary. Pit-workings with their ugly residue were a blight on the landscape. Streams that kept the wheels turning as they ran past mills were also important to the common people for providing water to their houses and cottages. The Stannators, complained the people, were diverting these streams to serve their own purposes only, to the destruction and disruption of many communities.

By now though radical changes to farming were under way; Black Death, the pestilence that swept across the countryside in 1349, had decimated the population of South Zeal where an additional burial ground is thought to have been necessary in land bordering the northern edge of burgage plots at the bottom of the village. The heavy casualties among villein tenants sped up the enfranchisement of those villeins that survived.

Apart from food, the most important commodity derived from the land, was wool. Steps had been taken during the reign of Edward III (1327-77) to foster the weaving industry and the production of woollen cloth. Farming, of course, was continuing to expand as the corn mills confirm, and Geoffrey Colet and Mary his wife who had a tenement in Sticklepath in 1407 are considered to have perhaps been the first actual farmers to live in that village. Reddaways were also farming here in the 13th century, among them one old reprobate who gambled away some of his land at cards, also keeping a pack of hounds. Legend has it that long after his death, the old man and his pack of hounds were to be heard hunting around the neighbourhood fields and copses. Seven centuries later J.I. Reddaway bought back 'Reddaway Close', one of the fields gambled away by his ancestor. The name of Reddaway Farm is often said to have derived from an outcrop of red sandstone but there is no red soil on Reddaway; an alternative explanation is that this old sub-manor owes its name to the ancient Mariners' Way. The Anglo Saxon 'rad' meant 'path' and the sailors' route passes through its yard.

The sea, and the armed forces, offered young men a way out of the labour attached to farming and with heroes to follow from local families such employment would also have proved attractive to those who cared nothing for the soil, and less for the prospects attached to tin mining.

In 1450, one Nicholas Radford, solicitor, was 'indifferently chosen as arbitrator' between Henry Wyke and Willm of the one part, and Richard Wyke of the other part, to arbitrate concerning the title of a certain tin-work called Bobhill and Bobhill Coombe within the forest of Dartmoor. It appears that the arbiter carried out his duties 'by which the sd Rich. Wyke should release to the same Henry and Wm Wyke all his rights, title, and Claim which he then had to the s'd tinn works.'

The opportunities for work in the mining industry did not limit local men to digging for tin ore. In 1461 a John Wykes Armiger was Controller of all the king's gold and silver mines in the county of Devon. In June 1550 at Chagford Coinage, William Knapman Junior is recorded as presenting more than

⟞ Mining ⟝

Above: *The land held riches, the rich held the land – South Tawton Quarry and its miners.*

Right: *Ramsley Mine.*

Top right: *The wheel at Ramsley.*

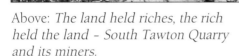

Ramsley miners posed outside the Dry, c.1905. Left to right, back row (standing): Will Gillard of South Tawton, Mr Wonnacott of South Zeal, James Wedlake of South Zeal, Dick Northcott, John Lee from South Zeal, Albert Hellier of Sticklepath, Will or Bobby Tucker of South Zeal, Partially hidden, Mr Gidley, far right end, Johnny Roberts; also standing to the right are: with white jacket, Samuel Earland, wearing a cowboy hat, Alfred (Alf) Parker, wearing check suit, Mr Pengelly; middle row (seated): Samuel Earland, son of Samuel in back row, ?, Jim Sleeman, Alfred Sleeman (Jim's brother), Ern Osborn, George Pyne of South Zeal, Will Osborn (brother of Ern), Sid Pengelly (son of Mr Pengelly standing to his right), Will Lentern of South Zeal, William Earland (brother of Samuel sitting on left, and son of Samuel standing, with white jacket), William Powlesland; front, sitting: Jim Weaver, Jim Langmead (with beard, from South Zeal), Bill Padden, Alf Treleaze, Dick Clarke, from Cornwall, Tom Crocker of South Zeal, holding a pipe, Tom Crocker of South Tawton, John Osborn (father of Ern and Will in the middle row).

5000lbs of tin, which indicates that he and/or his family had extensive mine workings. The tin at the time would have been worth 4d. to 5d. per lb. A conveyance of 1559 confirms that a John Knapman was the purchaser of a Drewsteignton mine, Bradford Tinworks, and since we know that the Knapman family had other mining interests already, it seems to show the local mines were quite productive, and the industry was expanding. Evidence of mining continuing to provide employment in the area, as well as being in conflict with rural industry, comes with the contention of water rights in a case between the Burgoynes and Knapmans in 1590 when Thomas Dunnynge stated that:

He hath oft times heard to contentions between the miller of Wyke mill which grendeth by the water descending from Lovebrook to the said mill, and so from thence to ffrog mill; and that when the miller of Wyke mill was accused fourteen years ago, he declared that he turned the water on behaulf of ffroggy mill... and was discharged.

'Ffroggy Mill' was the ancient manorial mill of Aysh, dating from Saxon times, in Throwleigh parish. In the early-17th century the Knapman family were involved in a dispute with John Newcombe, owner of a corn mill, regarding water rights to their tinworks and tinmills in the South Zeal and Drewsteignton area. Newcombe had diverted the tinners' leat to his mill, claiming that he was entitled to do so when the tinners were not using it. Judgement was going against him when the purpose of the leat was said to appertain to 'divers tinworks', not his corn mill, possibly Ffroggy Mill. However, after arbitration the Knapmans agreed to use the water between 1 November and 15 May each year and let it be diverted to Newcombe's corn mill for the remainder of the year.

Throughout the 17th century there were many disputes regarding water rights, including a court case heard at the Exeter Assizes in 1699, between Bartholomew Gidley, the then lord of the manor of Gidleigh, and the tinners of the Bradford Tinworks mine, sometimes called Bradford Pool. 'The Bradford Pool Case' by Lynette Costello, in *Transactions of the Devonshire Association*, Vol. 113 (1981) tells all. In 1565 John Dymocke and his wife 'of the Manor of Sticklepath' are said to have owned '10 water mills in Sampford Courtenay parish' but, how many of them were in Sticklepath is not known. During the eighteenth century, it is believed that at least seven mill wheels were turning along the 600-yard stretch of the village street. To drive these wheels water was diverted from the weir on Taw River, taken beneath Skaigh Lane, and directed by way of a lane-bridging leat to Cleave Mill; housing now occupies its position.

Situated within sight of Lady Well, the mill was referred to in 1795 as Wilmott's mill, but it burned down eight years later. The ruins remained for some seven years before two serge-makers from Horrabridge purchased the site and converted them into a woollen factory. The venture proved to be a success for George and William Pearse who remained in control of the mill for about 30 years.

During this time, packhorses were kept busy transporting bales of cloth and raw wool up and down the steep old high way that lay conveniently at the factory's door, and much of that cloth was being taken to Plymouth, for export. A century later, in 1910, a descendant of the mill owners, Colonel Cecil Pearse, then aide-de-camp to the Governor of Assam, was on a mission to the Nizam of Hyderbad. When Colonel Pearse was introduced, the Nizam said that the name 'Pearse' was known to him. Colonel Pearse admitted that he could offer no reason for this but the Nizam insisted that the Pearse name was one that he knew. He eventually found the explanation for this among some old papers and business documents when bills revealed that the Maharajah of Hyderabad had purchased scarlet cloth from the Pearse woollen mills in Sticklepath. The scarlet cloth had been made into uniforms for the Palace Guards and, over a century after being made, were still in use.

Home for the owners of Cleave Mill was a large thatched house in the main village street but this was later divided and can now be seen as two houses, 'The Retreat' and 'Staplers.'

The general decline of the woollen trade throughout Devon around the middle of the 19th century brought about the closure of the Cleave Mills which were purchased from the Pearse family by Harry Littlejohns in 1890 to be converted to flour and grist mills; still powered by water. For almost a century the mill remained with the Littlejohns family, brothers Harry and George following in their father's footsteps, and a third generation, Harry, and his wife Violet, seeing its final days as they introduced and developed farm machinery contracting in the area. Housing, incorporating old mill-buildings and original walls, now stands on the site of Cleave Mill.

On the site now occupied by the National Trust Finch Foundry Museum, the two manor mills two formerly provided employment in Sticklepath. Their wheels were powered by water from the leat after it left Cleave Mill to run behind the houses and through Hayes and Mill meadows to the next places of production. Operated by John Bowring and John Stanbury respectively, the manor mills were already well established in the early-19th century, one as a corn mill, the other a cloth mill. It was the latter that William Finch took over 1814, as Stanbury's tenant, in order to convert it into an iron smithy, or foundry; but there seems to be no record of casting being done

❧ Cleave Mill ❧

Below: *Cleave Mill once powered serge production but ended up grinding pig-corn.*

Below: *Cleave Mill was fed by an over-head leat (top left in picture).*

Above: *Water rights in use at Cleave Mill; Sluice operator, worker and villager collecting water*

Right: *Harry Littlejohns, owner of Cleave Mill.*

Above right: *George Littlejohns at Cleave Mill drying house.*

there. The present-day appearance of the premises defies the reality that a full three storeys of the old cloth mill were needed to house the forge. The title 'Finch Foundry' continues to be used today but as business first began to grow, the need to expand grew with it, and in 1835 the corn mill, previously in Mr Bowring's hands, was swiftly converted to the needs of the Finch family.

Even as the conversion continued, a mile or so away from the foundry other industrialists might already have been taking an interest in the local landscape; or what lay below. At the north foot of Ramsley Hill between 1851 and 1856 Fursdon Mine, listed as Manor Mine in 1854, was established and more work was becoming available. Until the end of the First World War the Finch family operated the foundry and then Albany, James and Thomas Finch formed a partnership and purchased the properties to enable further expansion which was to have seven of the Finch family men working there at one time. In the multi-fire-heated foundry workshops, craftsmen using skills and methods that had served their ancestors since the time of Waterloo produced all manner of agricultural equipment.

One water wheel was needed to work the paddle type fan forcing air through underground ducting to five hearths and two furnaces beside which the sweating blacksmiths worked, another provided power to the tilt or trip-hammers that forged the

tools, while yet a third wheel was needed to provide power to the almost never ceasing needs of a massive grindstone constantly circling as it sharpened a never ending stream of tools. Even assisting wooden ship construction was not beyond the firm's capabilities; it supplied ready-cut boat knees to the boatyards.

The reputation of the handmade agricultural edge tools made by Finch Bros., the billhooks, scythes, hayknives, shovels, hoes and special ladle-shaped scoops for the china-clay industry, spread not only throughout the kingdom but also to wherever there might be a demand for quality products. As the firm's reputation grew it became the sole importer and agent of American farm tools: 'Lake City' axes and 'Batchelor' hay forks. They traded in seed lips, mole traps, binder twine and grindstones, and acted as wheelwrights making carts and wheelbarrows; as gate and hurdle makers; as builders and builders' merchants, and as coal merchants and sawyers.

Only about 20 men are thought to have been employed at the foundry just prior to the Second World War, but an old employee claimed that 400 swan-neck hoses were being made in one day by five men from the cutting of the steel bar to the polished and varnished end product; and that other tools were being produced in similar quantities.

New industries were already emerging in 1939. The future potential for road transport for business and pleasure had been recognised by motor car

Foundrymen at work, but not a wet child in sight – summer perhaps?, c.1950.

❧ The Finch ❧ Foundry

Mr K. Mallet working at the grindstone.

Top left: *Albany Finch outside the family foundry.*

Above: *Roger Bowden's early interest, assisting the foundrymen working on the shaft.*

Above: *Locally made tools on display at the Dartmoor Folk Festival.*

Left: *Foundry workers, c.1900. Left to right, back: W. Westaway, Jack Powlesland, Christy Osborne, Centre: John Mallett, A.G. Finch, Joe Hellier, Aubrey Tucker. Front: Alf Hooper, Lawrence Taylor, Mr Gee ('Whoaup Gee').*

proprietor and haulage contractor Charles Bowden, working nearby wheelwrights, James Cook & Sons. In the village Frederick Wonnacott was repairing boots and shoes for villagers, probably including Albert Bowden the dairyman, John Mallet carpenter, George Hussey the tailor, and Mrs Edith Arscott the local hairdresser, not forgetting Mrs Lucy Gater the district nurse.

After the death of Albany Finch in 1945 the family business became a limited company with Ralph Finch, Charles Bowden and Richard Barron as its directors who ensured its survival until 1960 when the south wall of the foundry collapsed. It is thanks to Richard Barron, helped and encouraged by a few friends that much of the flavour of the original foundry can still be enjoyed by visitors today. It was he that set out to create a museum of rural industry. At his untimely death in 1964 that project was continued by the Trustees of the Finch Foundry whose dedication was rewarded when they could open their museum to the public. Today, the National Trust has assumed responsibility for the foundry's future and with considerable investment and the goodwill of many volunteers it is likely to be a long one.

In the area of the bridge, old deeds mention a bone mill being here in 1848 and the sites of other mills are close by. Formerly there seem to have been two grist mills here, known as the Sticklepath Grist Mills, or as the Western and the Carnall Mills. During the latter half of the 19th century they were owned by William Fewins, but were later being taken over by the Finch brothers. After one wheel was removed the second continued working a threshing machine until 1939 and was only broken up ten years later when the last of the mill buildings and sheds were converted into flats.

A seventh mill in the village is mentioned in 1800 as 'Scaw Mill' probably situated at Bridge Cottage on the South Tawton side of the Bridge; if this wasn't the aforementioned but as yet unidentified 'bone mill,' it would be the eighth mill mentioned. Two of Sticklepath's historic mill wheels survive; one at the Foundry Museum and the other at the home of Maurice and Sue Pritchard, close by the bridge.

In the days when the foundry, farming, builders and stonemasons, serge factory and grist mills all created employment, local people had little need to seek work elsewhere. Local industries working to capacity could absorb available labour and until the beginning of the 20th century there were also the two copper mines. Greenhill, Ramsley (at either end of Sticklepath), Ford Arsenic and the Copper works (operating for the first decade, and briefly revived in 1920), ensured that competition for labour was keen.

Inviting further investigation are two items briefly mentioned in *The Story of Sticklepath*, first published by the WI in 1955 referring to a tannery in the village, and of candles being made in the village also:

a curious small candle making industry connected with the bone mills in an old building, the remains of which is now a shed in the Devonshire Inn car park. Tallow from the bones was made into candles or rush dips, the pith for the wicks being supplied from rushes gathered in Hayes Meadow, next to the Chapel.

Mr Gerald Bastable, of South Zeal, whose interesting articles on Ramsley Mine we would refer you to in past issues of *The Beacon* provided us with the following information regarding the mine that has left indelible marks upon the landscape;

1851-56	Fursdon Mine, listed as Manor Mine 1854. At North foot of Ramsley Hill.
1852-53	Lease sold to a London Co. who started another adit in another part of the sett.
1854	Series of Chancery suits.
1856	Devon Copper and Silver Lead Mine advertised.
1857-59	Ramsley Hill Mining Company Ltd. formed to take over Manor Mine, liquidated in 1858.
1859	Fursdon Mining Co. Ltd. formed for the working of Ramsley Hill Mine.
1868	Fursdon Copper Mine. Lawsuits and company wound up in Stannary courts.
1870	Property acquired by Fursdon Great Consolidated Mining Co Ltd.. Languished.
1876	Title changed to Wheal Emily. Dissolved June 1883.
1881	Sett taken over by Emily Copper Mines (a.k.a Wheal Emily.)
1888	Emily Copper Mines becomes South Tawton Copper Mines Ltd..
1900	Property acquired by Ramsley Exploration Company.
1910	Finally wound.

The ownership of the various setts lay with the Fursdons and still does. The setts would normally be leased for a 21-year period at a Royalty of 1/15th. At the end of the lease any 'good' created by the lease holders would revert to the landowner.

In 1922 local labour found yet another potential employer opening up for business when the Hayes Tor road-metal quarry was opened close to the main road just above Sticklepath School, and it is in the school records that notes can be found of near misses when quarry material landed unexpectedly in the

👉 Sticklepath 👉
and South Tawton
Quarries

Left: *Sticklepath Quarry below White Rock 1937.*

Below: *Visitors at South Tawton Quarries.*

Bottom: *South Tawton Quarries.*

playground, and similar hazards caused teachers to make note of incidents, and their concern. Quarrying, however, was terminated in 1947 but, two years later, a tarmac plant was installed there instead. It continued providing local employment until 1950, after which its machinery was eventually dismantled four years later; but not before it left a mark in the memory of some people who were young at the time:

Courtin? Well, it wasn't like it is nowadays you know. We didn't do anything really wrong but there were some tomboys among us. If it was a nice evening we might walk up Skaigh, or get up behind White Rock, or down in the old tar works, but it was mucky round there and years after it closed down you'd be scared of your father or mother finding the stuff on your clothes. It was all good fun though, but mind you...
(HVW - Sticklepath 1999)

Shown on geological maps of the area as totally isolated in the region, providing an almost freak deposit of lime, are the quarries at South Tawton that also provided employment. No other similar deposits are shown anywhere near to them; which would have made their value to the area considerable indeed. John Darch, whose family has long been associated with the area, remembers his father being the last man to take lime from the quarry; and also recalls another business that benefited from the sales made at the quarry. There is little if any sign now of the inn that stood near the corner of the lane that led to the quarry entrance, but when drivers and carriers queued to wait their turn to have their carts and waggons filled it was the pub that satisfied the men first.

Another industry that provided employment, by day and by night, but which is often overlooked was one that satisfied the need for horses; usually but not always associated with the inns. From the earliest of coaching days, 'Oakhampton' is shown on travel and carrier records as the local centre of the trade; through its mid-Devon position on the North/South and East/West highways. At regular distances, generally ten miles, the drivers changed their team of horses which, one instantly realises, should exclude Sticklepath or South Zeal from having derived any benefit from such business; had they not been so conveniently placed. Their hills were alive with the sound of the hooves of extra horses, desperately needed at times by coach drivers and carriers whose vehicles could not be driven uphill without extra helpmates being attached to the regular team, or held back in safety as they came down into the valleys by an additional horse pulling back at the rear of the coach, waggon, or cart.

With the wet and winter seasons accounting for two thirds of the year, at least, there was a continual need for extra horses whichever way the travellers were coming or going. In the worst of the winter weather a coach, its driver, its guard and their passengers could easily be stuck in one or the other villages; those travelling west in South Zeal, those heading east in Sticklepath. At a cost of course the inns could provide accommodation, with innkeepers purchasing extra provisions from the local population, and also employing some to provide laundry services or, eventually, to help clear the roads.

In the mid-19th century there was plenty of opportunity with a great deal more coach traffic on the roads than might be expected including The Regulator, from Falmouth to Exeter every evening, except Sunday, at six thirty; The Times, from Truro to Exeter on Monday, Wednesday, and Friday evenings at seven; The Royal Mail from London to Falmouth every night at nine; The Royal Mail, from Falmouth to London every morning at four thirty; The Times westbound on Tuesday, Thursday and Saturday mornings around nine, and The Regulator from Exeter to Falmouth every morning, Sunday excepted, at nine thirty.

In addition to the local carriers there were the regular area carriers also providing services to Exeter from 'Oakhampton' where William Davis despatched his waggons from the Exeter Inn every Monday and Wednesday, those owned by Russell & Co. left almost daily from their warehouse, while those belonging to William Alway and Alexander Northan, left from their respective houses, every Monday and Thursday. Then there were the return journeys. Local carriers serving the surrounding districts including Throwleigh and Gidleigh, and carriers from Moretonhampstead, Drewsteignton and Crockernwell also came through South Zeal and Sticklepath on their way to 'Oakhampton' to connect with John Baker's Vans, leaving from the Golden Lion, every other Tuesday for Plymouth, and for South Molton every other Friday, or William Always' waggon with Tavistock its destination every Wednesday.

The arrival of the steam train, seen here on nearby Fatherford Viaduct, bought many benefits for trade and industry.

Other than farming, and that today as a minimal employer compared with the past, none of the industries mentioned survived - but without a knowledge and appreciation of them, our own inheritance would be the poorer.

Our list could certainly be expanded since we have barely looked, here and elsewhere, at the industry that continued behind the closed doors of dairies and kitchens where butter and cream was produced; in the yards of company's such as that of the Counter family in which many tradesmen, stonemason, carpenters, and builders first learned their crafts; in the workshops of the boot and shoemakers where skills were passed on; or in the bakeries where bread was baked overnight to be ready for the early rising parishioners and people yet abed many miles away.

There is still a great range of occupations being followed by people living beneath the beacon, but a century ago our predecessors would not have believed it possible that Tim Argles would one day advise Radio Devon listeners about their gardening problems by sitting in a room and talking into a metal object, or that Laurie MacMillan could similarly speak to the nation from a BBC studio in London, passing on news of same-day events occurring on the other side of the world. They all would have appreciated the work of carpenter Ray Souness and blacksmith Dave Denford and understood that accountants like David Youle and David Capon were providing a service, even if not to them. Only the educated few, however, would have been able to pick up Michael Jecks' medieval mysteries and enjoy a tale well told. As far as Mike Hall's televisions, Jon Padfield's washing machines and Norman Butlin's community computers were concerned, such machines might have been considered devil-made or life threatening and, have sent panic stricken parishioners in search of their equivalent of Revd Barry Wood and Dr Andrew Stainer Smith.

Top: *Mid Devon thatcher with his son who is learning the craft under his father's tuition - examples of their work can be seen on various village houses.*

Above: *The Dairy School was run in Church House.*

Left: *Farming survived the Industrial Revolution, until now at least, but will future generations only know of sheep safely home from photos such as this one from Addiscott?*

Chapter 7
The Parish and the Church

For many who come upon St Andrew's in South Tawton for the first time, it is perhaps the embattled, double-buttressed, three-stage tower of the church that impresses them. This granite-cloaked Mother church with its tower of 75 feet, was built in the third or 'florid' style of English Gothic pointed architecture, which prevailed from the middle of the 14th century for 200 years. Within its walls can be found signposts to 700 years of the history of the area and its people, each one inviting detailed consideration.

As early as 1327, with the presence of Willus de Batteshull, the connection of the Battishill family with South Tawton church is recorded. In Baring Gould's book, *John Herring*, the Battishill family is included in the form of a portrait by an old man living in his ancestral home, a 16th-century house, West Wyke, in the parish of South Tawton, who declared: 'My family is gentle, and of ancient degree. We appeared in the *Herald's Visitation* of 1620 in four descents, but I have title deeds that show that we were lords of the manor of West Wyke from the time of Edward III.' An owl to be found on a side boss in the north aisle is considered by many to be intended as a charge in the Arms of the Battishills of West Week. On the wall near the south entrance two memorials can be found, to the memory of Thomas Battishill, and his wife Aphrah of Drewsteignton.

The Northmore family is recorded as first residing in the parish in 1332 but in the 18th century became more associated with Okehampton, providing the town with an MP and continuing the connection with the parish through a charitable bequest. A few yards from the stopped north door, and the war memorial above it, a stone commemorates Joane, daughter of John and Joan Northmore, who died at the age of 28, and without having married, in 1699. The leger stone for her mother who

St Andrew's Church, South Tawton, c.1904.

died in 1686 is to be found in the north aisle, as is a stone to her brother's wife, Grace, who died in 1721 but of her father's memorial there is no trace. It was probably lost during the restoration work undertaken in 1881.

The treasure trove that is the inheritance of the present and future generation are the accounts of the South Tawton churchwardens, commencing before the Reformation and which, from 1524, provide a vivid portrait of local personalities down the years, their work for the church, and also a clear indication of events, visits and political changes that had some impact on the mid-Devon community. Latin, somewhat rurally contracted, was the language used in the earliest records, interspersed with neo-English words or phrases. The compiler of these records in 1524 is referred to as the 'Custos' (warden), responsible for the goods and chattels of the store 'instaur' of the church. Henry Smith was receiving two shillings (10p) a year in 1526 as keeper of the cemetery, with a few pence added some years later for also looking after the hedges. Four horsemen of South Tawton are among those most constantly claiming expenses in the early accounts, for often riding to Exeter to the Episcopal and Archidiaconal Visitations; one of the riders was, of course, most likely to have been the vicar. Other entries relate to expenses incurred, generally, by four men journeying to Exeter, in charge of moneys that had been levied on the parish, including the king's subsidies or Peter's Pence. 'Four men,' are referred to yet again, riding to Chagford or to Dunsford, to military musters or on business connected with them, and of their going before justices or commissioners on divers matters. Whether these 'four men' were always the same, or whether a vicar, sidesman, tithing-man or holder of similar offices on official

South Tawton churchyard.

St Andrew's chancel, South Tawton, before 1910.

Cottages and church, South Tawton.

South Tawton church gate, steps and stile, c.1903.

🖚 North Wyke 🖛

WYKE (WEST)

Above: *Building a hayrick at North Wyke.*

Right: *North Wyke – the west front of the house.*

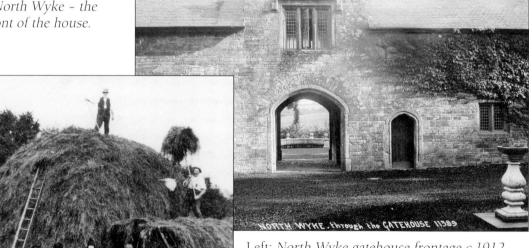

NORTH WYKE through the GATEHOUSE 11389

Left: *North Wyke gatehouse frontage c.1912.*

duties might have been accompanied by guards while travelling is not known but it is likely anyone carrying taxes or parish monies would be accompanied by a constable. John Battishill, Henry Gidley, Thos. Yeoland and Richard Waleys were recorded as being parish constables in 1533. There is no reference in early records to a parish clerk. The word 'clerk' does appear but is thought to relate to a person in holy orders as opposed to a layman. In 1552 the church accounts show Simon Downe and John Ascot as 'gardiani Instaur Sci Andrei' but four years later John Dunning is the 'Hed Warden' and his receipts include an item relating to St Andrew's 'warden', a seemingly lesser person.

An accountancy hierarchy had obviously been established in the village church but was there a power struggle going on between those responsible for church goods and chattels? In 1562 a 'Chief warden' is recorded as being in control, of necessity it seems. While wardens Richard Stronge and Bernarde ffrende 'made of there ale clere wt other thynges geven & gatheryd iiij li... ', they also 'aske alowans of xvii d. spend, & dyd losse by iiij pysterlyns & Span'ys mony wyche they had of the olde wardens iij s.' Income from 'alle & gatheryng', two years later had rocketed to 'xl viij s. viij d.' for some reason, but in this year, 1564, there was the need for 'Reparyng of the churge howsse' at a cost of 'xxij s. ij d.' and a payment made for 'ye mayking of Bottes xiij d.'

There are occasions when attempts to interpret old, hand-written documents excite the researcher and one such occurred when looking at accounts for 1568. It suddenly seemed likely that the churchwardens had paid for the erection of a scaffold in South Tawton. The excitement died when further reference to payment made for the transporting of 'shynnell' from 'Wynckley' and consultation with a local builder confirmed the suspicion that roof repairs had required scaffolding. Control of accounts and finances, c.1571, was back in the hands of a 'Warden,' supported by someone called the 'Collector.'

The sum of £18.13s. 4d. was the annual value placed upon the rectory and parsonage of South Tawton, together with all tithes, fruits, emoluments etc, when it passed, by Grant in 1563, to John Wyke, of North Wyke; who promptly charged his son, Roger, £24 annually for the rectory and glebe land alone. Church staff expanded between 1586 and 1591 during which time, in addition to the warden's accounts, there are also accounts rendered by the receiver(s) and collector(s), for goods and repairs to the church.

One of the jobs was that of 'dog-whipper,' a distant relative perhaps of our recent but obviously not innovative post, the dog-warden. In the 16th century the parish was satisfied to pay its dog-whipper around 16d. per annum, to effectively keep dogs out of the church and yard, but his present day counterpart, according to comments in the local magazine, has yet to attain such high regard.

The early South Tawton Register of Baptisms includes these entries:

1543 Eliz: dau of George Burgyn 24 May
1551 Margt dau of George Burgyn 5 Janry
1551 John the sonne of no bodye 17th Febry
1554 John son of George Burgin 13 Mar
1556 William son of George Burgyn 22 Feb
1558 Robert son of George Burgin 12 Aug
1588 Johan the supposed daughter of William Hayforde as it appeared by the confession of the mother of the saide childe unto the Justice and to the mid wife... in her travaile.

Births in the Burgoyne family thereafter continue and ensure the family connection with the parish continues also. The family marriages are similarly recorded; with marriage there was celebration, and the church could now celebrate with bells.

A 'Keper of ye bels' appears in the records in 1529 when John Wells (or Veale) is named as such. The inheritance of today's bellringers of a tower full of appealing bells can be attributed to many bellfounders. John Noxworthy used a team of four oxen to help remove and return a bell he re-cast in 1525-26. Thomas Geffray (or Geffries), bellfounder, Sheriff of Bristol in 1525, received £6 for his work on the bells in 1533, and £4 the following year.

An inventory of church goods, taken by command of Edward VI in 1553, showed South Tawton in possession of five bells admitted to the custody of John Webb, Richard Friend, William Sloman, Thomas Keland and others; most parish churches had only three or four. The 1569/70 records confirm that the 'great bell' and 'lytell bell' were recast by Thomas Byrdall of Exeter and his assistant John Bursedon. After borrowing a 'cable rope' from Inwardleigh to lower and hoist the bells, they carted them to Honeychurch where they also had recasting work to complete. The South Tawton great bell weighed 1944lbs before recasting and 2491lbs afterwards, the little bell 624lbs before and 805lbs afterwards. The parish gave the Byrdall 102lb of broken metal and made three payments of £4, £4 and £7 to him for the work.

The records relating to the old rood screen and loft reveal some 16th-century conflict after Queen Elizabeth's Injunctions of 1559-60. The rood loft had probably never been used for liturgical purposes, because of access problems, but, nevertheless, an order was given for its removal. This was obviously ignored in the parish because in 1563 the 'Hedwarden' and others at South Tawton were excommunicated after the 'Rode Lofte was not taken

⊰≈ The Bells ≈⊱

Top left: *South Tawton Bellringers Deanery Competition 1991 - shield winners Nicky Wonnacott, Sid Cooper, Cecil Allen, Nora Bertram, Edgar Bertram and John Cooper.*

Above left:
Gooding's bell being held, balanced upright by experience ringer Nicky Wonnacott - ready to strike when the photographer gets out of the way.

Far left: *Recast by Ambrose Gooding in 1744*

Left: *Rehung in 1931. The present striking point is indicated by the helpful hand of Nicky Wonnacott - the chisel marks made during previous tunings show clearly around the rim.*

Bottom: *Former South Tawton ringers.*

down' and it had to be dismantled at 'a cost of xiijd'. Two years later Richard Hole was paid 'iiijd' for 'cottyng the byme yn the rode loft.' The rood screen remained in place until 1826 when the greater part was removed. The bottom panels finally disappeared during the restoration work of 1881 but 21 years later the church's beautiful rood screen was erected, the chancel portion given by Mrs Helen Kingsbridge and her children in memory of Mr William Lethbridge of Wood, while those portions to the north and south were the gifts of the Revd W. Wykes-Fynch MA and Mr William Lethbridge Junr.

For the visitor the church contains many interesting items, some of which may not be readily apparent. The oldest decipherable leger stone in the church can be found at the west end of the north aisle commemorating 'John Hole, the son of Thomas Hole, buried the xii of April, A. dom. 1607.' Between the steps at the south entrance and the font can be found the primitively lettered gravestone of 'Elizabeth Hole and her sonne, buried Jan. xiii, 1653,' with the arms of Hole of Blackhall, impaling the arms of the Weekes.

In the period before or soon after the burial of Thomas Hole the role of the parish clerk had been determined. The Register of Burials for 15 January 1622 records the final resting of 'James Beard, formerly Parish clerk of this church.' The parish was obliged to support the Parish Clerk, whose duties were multifarious. He had to sing with priest, read the epistle and lesson, and join the clergy in ringing the church bell since, in pre-Reformation times, this was not a job for a layman and was an act undertaken while wearing a surplice. The clerk had need to be a scholar in order to fulfil his duty as a schoolmaster. He was called upon to attend the priest both in the church, and out, and in funeral or other processions was given the responsibility of carrying the vessel of holy water, which he sprinkled far and wide with the aid of a long brush. This distinctive office (aquae bajalatus), the benefice of holy water, did bestow upon the clerk some benefits of his own. It entitled him to go about the parish with his, often mentioned, holy water bucket at certain times and claim from each house 'a stretch of corn,' or, at Lammas time (1 August) when men had shorn the sheep, to collect 'some woole to mayke him cotts to goo yn the parsch livery.' It was the parish clerk that would have assisted with, if not supervised, the installation of the stone-framed slate monument, dated 1651, commemorating Robert Burgoyne and his wife Margaret, the daughter of Olive Whiddon, of Gidleigh, and their family. On this the adults kneel before open bibles, whilst behind them kneel their sons and daughters, 'sized' to show their descending ages. The baptismal records show three of these to be:

1635 Philip son of Robert Burgonie & Margt 18 May

1637 Margt dau of Rober Burgonie & Margt 24 Aug

1641 Francis son of Robert Burgonie & Margt 27 Dec

Burgoyne mural monument.

❧ Church Features ❧

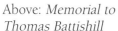

Above: *Memorial to Thomas Battishill*

Right: *An unusual resident in St Andrew's, Sheila-na-gig.*

Below: *Heraldic carvings in the church.*

Below centre: *The Norman font on its way back to church.*

Above: *The present clock mechanism.*

Left: *Eagle Lectern in memory of members of the Mackay family – a gift to the church in 1897,*

Below: *Church organ.*

Bottom left: *Monument to 'Warrior' John Weekes of North Wyke, Constable of the Parish in 1553.*

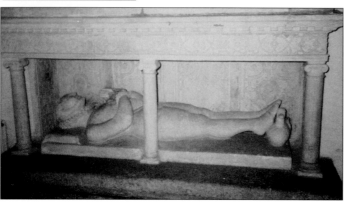

Those who died before the erection of the monument are identified by the addition of the symbol of a skull and include a baby in a cradle and an infant in a shroud. For several generations the Burgoynes owned the manorial 'great house' in South Zeal before it was purchased by the Oxenhams in 1700 and later became an inn under the sign of the Oxenham Arms. The manorial chapel that served the manor provides the origin of the present-day church in which can be found the north and south chapels, with a priest door in the latter; the chapels being associated particularly with the historic Wyke and Burgoyne families, respectively. Granite is used predominantly throughout the church, which has north and south aisles, and the several stages of work in its building can be observed in the masonry. Alterations, which lengthened the south aisle, appear to be confirmed by the presence of two piscinae and by changes in the exterior stonework. Beer stone was used in the arcades, which consist of five arches on each side, with a mixture of the two in the chancel.

In the late 16th century a new pulpit was required and John M. Batrome was commissioned to provide it. When he visited the church 'to view the place for the pulpett' he was entertained with a drink at the cost of 'ijd'. 'John ffrynd's boy' who fetched 'Mr Ware at North Wike when the pulpit should be sett up' received a penny for his long walk, and to John Gaidon and John Oxenham were also paid for fetching the 'stoope' (pedestal) for the pulpit from Seale. The payment made to John Batrome for the pulpit is recorded as being 'xvis' and when he and his men arrived to install it in 1586 they were provided with a breakfast costing 'iiijd' by Mr William Bourne. Andrew Casligh who looked after the church bells and acted as carpenter and odd-job man about the church and churchyard was paid 'iijd' 'for brads and nailes', and a 'matte', purchased for the pulpit, is recorded as having cost 'ijd'. The pulpit costs did not end there; in 1612 John Rogers received a penny for 'myndynge the pulpitt,' in 1672 a whole sixpence was expended on a 'stock to goe up into the polpit,' but when this interesting item eventually disappeared is unknown. The present pulpit, of early 18th century origin, made of oak inlaid with lighter wood and showing the four evangelists and the arms of the see, stood on the south side of the nave until 1881 when it was moved to the north side, lowered, and provided with stone steps.

In 1903 the stonework was removed, and E.T. Rogers of Exeter completed the existing woodwork on the base, stair and balusters. The records of expenditure for this, or any other church, often illustrate incidents, or conjure mind-pictures of characters that illuminate the past, inspire understanding, and induces admiration. South Tawton disbursements for 1681 were 'as followeth':

	£.	s.	d.
To Rich: Weekes Esqr. who was the former Churchwarden	5.	0.	6.
to Tom Knowline for 2 yeeres aenuall rent		16.	8.
to Rich; Arnoll for washing of the Church	1.	13.	6.
to Nath: Wood masson for glassing the Church windows & for mending of ye tiles of the tower Church & porach and sawder	2.	12.	8.
to Rich: markes & his sone 4 dayes to tend the plumer		6.	0.
for 4 sembs- of wood for ye plumers use		5.	0.
to the visatation Coort & for the booke of Artickles		10.	6.
In Charges toward Mr Bowers appeeransce before my Lord Bishop & for a greate many peoples being theare to testifie ye treweth against him.	5.	0.	0.
to Kath: Drew for keeping the Clock		6.	6.
for 2 new bell Roapes & for Carage		12.	6.
to Roger Battisshill for work done about the bells		4.	0.
to Rich: Cousen for his labor About the bells		3.	0.
for Ringin the 29th.of May		5.	0.
In charges towards Mr Beeseis, his man & Mr Penniton & for a dinner for them and for as many of ye pishoners as woold eate	1.	10.	0.
for washing of the Sirpleses 6 taimes		9.	0.
for washin the Communion table Cloth 3 taimes		1.	6.
& for makin Cleane the plate 4 taimes		2.	0.
for bred & waine for 9 Communions	6.	0.	0.
for Charges In & towards the Coort for recoverin the pulpit Cloth & the Covering of the Cushin wch was Imbe...	1.	10.	0.
for Ringine the 5th of November, & for Candle light		12.	6.
for Charges in & towards the Coort to prosecute those wch doe refewes to pay theare Church rates	2.	0.	0.
to Mrs Pearson & to Mrs Parsson & theare 7 Children whoe weeare bound for new England to theare husbands but weare taken by pyrates & sate a shore att ye lands End thy having a sertivicate to travill to lincolne wch was theare whome thy being in extrem need		5.	0.
To Mrs Katherin Medland & her Familie being 5 in number coming			

	£.	s.	d.
from Ireland weare cast away wth the lose of all theare goods, havin a passe to travell for redding in Barkshire.		2.	0.
to Sara Browen & her sick child		1.	0.
to Thomas Edwards A sick man of the same company			6.
to 4 men wch served his Majestie in f landers having a passe to goe to bosscastle thy being in need & dessairing releese		2.	6.
To Francis King & his waife & 3 Children havin a passe for hartland being in want & dessairing releese		1.	0.
to 2 protastant ministers wch came from Fransce dessairing releese		5.	0.
to Jo: Eaane his waife & 2 Children havin a.passe for pensansce thy being miserable poore		2.	0.
to Rich: Baker a verie Impotent & miserable spectackle to be hould		1.	0.

The bell-ringers today no longer ring in 5 November and have yet to discover when this celebration, of the man some say was the only man of honest intent to get to Parliament, actually ended. The bells of St Andrew's regularly ring out across the countryside thanks to the team of ringers led by Nora Bertram, their captain. Like those who heaved upon the bell-ropes before them John Cooper, David King, Jane Youle, Brian Jeffrey, Ruth Rockey, Sid Cooper, Andrew Sampson Bryan Wooland, Nick Wonnacott, Linda Sampson and John Coulthurst, regularly record the passing of the years, and strike the right note at services, weddings, funerals and festive occasions alike. With time honoured tradition to guide him Nick Wonnacott is also 'Tower Keeper' responsible for 'greasing clangers, painting the bell frames, checking the jute bellropes that cost £700 to recently replace, and keeping out the birds.' Traditional payments appear in the church records from 1733 onwards which show that for over a century £1.13s.4d. was paid annually to the ringers and in that year of 1733 was accounted for as:

Pd for ale for the Ringers the 29th May   5s.0d.
Pd for ale for them the 11th June   6s.8d.
Pd for ale for them the 11th October   6s.8d.
Pd for Ringing the 4th and 5th November 15s.0d.
                          £1.13s.4d.

It is perhaps fair to note that 6s.8d. would purchase quite a few gallons of local ale and that Fawkes' failure now commands a higher fee; for ringing through the midnight hour perhaps. The ringers were also responsible for sounding the curfew and when

Richard Drew observed this in 1665 he was paid, for ringing the curfew bell at '8 of the clock' at night and at 4.00 in the morning each day for one quarter of the year, the princely sum of five shillings (25 pence).

The bellringers of 1745 received 15 shillings if they tolled a tribute whenever the Bishop came by; and by then the church had six bells. In 1744 the bells were recast by Ambrose Gooding of Plymouth but the inscription of bell four stating that 'A Gooding cast us all six' has, until recently, been challenged by the church because the churchwardens' accounts show that Ambrose Gooding was paid for casting five bells only despite the instruction, 'When I begin then all strike in I II III IV V VI. AG 1744', which Gooding also inscribed on the bell when he recast it that year. A 1995 report by expert John G.M. Scott concludes:

Gooding was almost certainly casting the old five into six, as the weight of the old Tenor was given as over 22 cwt and the Treble as over 7. If the other bells were on much the usual scale, the old 5 would have weighed about 62 cwt, and the new six about 55, so Gooding would have had some metal in hand, which was probably allowed for in the deal. 18 shillings was spent on timber for the house to cast the bells in, and 9s.4d. for 52 niches of reed to thatch it. They bought 40 seams (packhorse loads) of hardwood for melting the metal, bricks, charcoal, &c. Ambrose Gooding was paid £57.5s.0d. in two instalments, and Oliver Langmaid was paid £2.6d.0d. for carriage of Mr Gooding's tools, for wood, and for Ale when the Bells were cast, and Ale for the men that helped.

On bell three Gooding left a goodwill message to sound down through the centuries 'Prosperity to this parish,' while on bell five he noted his paymasters of the day: 'Jno Noswrthy, Vicar. Francis Moore, Richard Lethbridge, Wardens, AG 1744.' The sixth bell provides a timely reminder '1744. I to church the living call, and to the grave do summon all.' Bell two was recast by Mears in 1857, all bells were rehung by William Aggett of Chagford in 1904 and the treble recast by Talors of Loughborough in 1913. Gillett and Johnston, of Croydon, recast the second and fourth bells in 1931, tuned all them except the fifth, and rehung all six in a new cast-iron frame.

The ringing of bells on New Year's Eve is not such an ancient tradition but owes its origin to the introduction of change ringing around about the middle of the 17th century and an account entry in 1794 confirms that the parish 'Laid out to ringers as usual Ringing out the Old and in the New Year – 2s.' They also received two shillings for ringing in Easter Monday and for some years in the first quarter of the 19th century the ringers received a similar amount for 'ringing in the New wardens.' In 1821 a west gallery was installed, replacing an earlier one used singers and instrumentalists, and a combined barrel and finger organ made by H.P. Dicker of Exeter in 1854, installed 'to restore psalmody in an approved and fit and decent manner' was later housed within it. The gallery installation never met with everyone's approval, was considered neither fit nor decent, and was regarded as unsightly. Messrs Hayward & Sons of Exeter removed it in 1881 during extensive renovations when the tower was opened up and the north aisle extended eastward to provide an organ chamber. Old box pews were replaced with new seating, and the present oak prayer desk and choir stalls were installed. Some roof timbers were known to be suffering from damp and decay, so their renewal, together with that of the porch roof, was included in this major undertaking which concluded with renovations made to window chacery and the installation of a new heating system.

In the same year the north doorway, traditionally regarded as the devil's doorway, was closed up and the doorway of the rood stair opened. Six years later, in 1887, the organ was completely rebuilt by Henry Jones & Sons, South Kensington, with this work funded, as a Jubilee gift to the church, by Mr William Lethbridge JP, of Wood. A further six years elapsed and the new century was three years old before the old vestry was converted into an organ chamber, and a new vestry added. During the 1881 restoration work, unexpected and serious problems had been revealed in the church's waggon roof. The plaster was condemned as unsafe and was hastily removed.

An inscription to be found on a stone-faced sundial near the top of the turret at the south-west corner of the south aisle reads 'O brepit non intellecta senectus,' or otherwise, 'age, as it creeps on, is unperceived' but the ravages of time, reflected in church maintenance requirements, were rarely less than very expensive when perceived by the congregation – of any period. Those expenses were met down the centuries variously by tithe payers, hardpressed congregations that willingly contributed every penny, or portion of a penny, they could afford, and individual benefactors able to contribute in pounds; their efforts provided succeeding generations with a valued inheritance. Look now upon St Andrew's' magnificent waggon roof and, while it remains an architectural gem, the achievements and intentions of the original builders can only be imagined. They used laths and plaster to fill in the square panels formed by the intersecting carved timbers and this whitewashed filling, reflecting and enhancing natural light, helped considerably to illuminate and show up the beauty of the timber carving. Prior to the Reformation, many such in-filled panels were decorated with religious painting or designs and the churchwardens' accounts of 1557-58 suggest that South Tawton church may have been embellished in this manner since there is record in the accounts of the payment of 8d. 'for taking downe of the pycters on the Rowffe of the Church.' Consider today that 'rowffe' and attention will undoubtedly be drawn to carved angels attached to the wall plates at the springing of the braces, and to the variety of devices carved on the bosses of the nave, chancel, and both aisle roofs. High overhead, the works of unknown artists bear witness to the passing of ages by providing us with pictures of Royalty, reminders of famed local families, and a glimpse of fashions from past

Choir outing in a charabanc, thought to be heading for Plymouth, c.1928.

centuries. To look upon the long-dead Henry, the fourth of that name among these chiselled-stone or carved-wood characters, seek out the crowned head and bearded face, then find the fashions of the Yorkist-Lancastrian period, disclosed in reticulated head-dresses; reminders of troubled times. Another boss carries the device of a double-headed eagle, associated with the Hoare family of Oxenham but the boss with two heads upon it remains a puzzle.

A long-established resident in this mid-Devon church is a figure with a seemingly foreshortened head, when observed from below. It was identified by an expert on church and cathedral bosses, Mr C.J.P. Cave, MA, as none other than, Sheila-na-gig, a curious pagan character whose history is definitely pre-Christian, and whose seductive role in life is associated with fertility. This imported personality has a friend however, since another boss provides a splendid example of the pagan 'green man'. The presence and the identity of this ancient one is recorded by Mr William Wordsworth in his excellent book of that name but he fails to mention that more than just one green man can be found on bosses in St Andrew's. Above every aisle their faces can be easily recognised. All but one have leaves coming from their mouth or ears. One, most carefully concealed, and perhaps the most ancient of all, can be found only by close observation, near the pulpit, peering through leaves that to the casual glance will certainly keep him hidden.

Carved by craftsmen, these colourful characters from our pagan past indicate the area's connection with tree-worship, opposed by St Boniface, but also evidenced around 1989 by the discovery at Bow of the remains of a Bronze-Age wood-henge or tree temple close by his birthplace – and this parish

Furthermore, it is possible that not only green men are present in St Andrew's. Close by the south chapel, observe another face; with feminine features. Partly concealed by foliage, carved carefully, could this be their most rare counterpart, the green woman? Many, having seen one in France and another in Germany, believe so. Another connection with the ancient past is clearly revealed on the boss in the nave depicting a maze, its circular route suggesting connections to both pagan and Christian Glastonbury to the east, to the tribes once residing throughout the South West, across the waters at New Grange, and to many places of Celtic and religious significance adorned by similar work.

Among the church's many other possessions of interest to visitors is a bowl-shaped granite font, a reminder of the Norman church, and one probably ejected from the church by Puritans during the 1640-16 Commonwealth period. Its original pedestal was lost or destroyed, possibly during the same era. Baptisms continued throughout the two decades with the old granite font replaced by a pewter bowl or basin; a trend of the times. With the Restoration many fonts were returned to churches, but not so in South Tawton. A font of Renaissance type made of wood and clay, which was painted, was certainly used in the church and its details were recorded in the *Rough Notes of Churches* published by the Exeter Architectural Society in 1849. What became of this font is not known but the bowl of the Norman font ejected by the Puritans was found in the old Vicarage gardens. In 1908 it was taken back to the church and erected near the south porch where it remained in an ornamental fashion until it was re-installed in the church on 1 March 1934. The present font in use was a gift from by Henry Arthur Hoare in 1851 and was moved from the north side of the nave to its present position when the north (devil's) door was stopped up in 1881.

Tithe payers of previous generations earned their pennies from the land and gave what they could to the church.

Chapter 8
The Helping Hand

Charity, it is said, begins at home. For our predecessors there was no other way of dealing with life's cruel impositions other than helping each other; charity in the area of home. When virtual slavery kept the peasant tied to the land, there was only the community to turn to in times of trouble. It is true that parishes, later, had responsibilities thrust upon them, but it is people that make parishes. Neither parish nor government does more than re-distribute money provided by people in various ways. Residents who experienced the years prior to the First World War refer to the caring community then as something real, reliable, and very different from today. Much earlier, the helping hand often came from the parish, with funds for those in need (when 240 pence = £1) or offering of a modest home. Now we have the State, and various Housing Associations - so, has the helping hand survived, and did the past help shape the present?

Almost century ago the poor people of Sticklepath shared the benefit of charitable gifts made to the parish of Sampford Courtenay, one of which was John Tickell's charity. There is an entry (some of it illegible) in the churchwarden's accounts which reads:

By the Will of the late William Tickell Esq. of Bath the interest of 100 (£) stock amounting to 3. 5s. 0d. is to be distributed at Christmas by the Rector and Churchwardens, this 100(£) stock was bought in the three per cent. Annuities 31st October 1817 in the names of the Rev. William Beauchamp, Rector, John Brook and Robert Woolridge, Churchwardens.
        signed by J. Heathman, vestry clerk.

The record showed there was a sum of £90. 0s. 4d. in the Devon and Exeter Savings Bank, No.G. 100 No. 89237, entitled:

John Brook surviving executor of John Brook who was the survivor of the Rev. William Beauchamp, John Brook and Robert Woolridge, some time Rector and Churchwardens of Sampford Courtenay, &c.

There appears to be no record how this came to be substituted for the sum of consols but the income was 2. 5s. 0d. The income was drawn every year and distributed with income raised from a charity established by one, John Sloman of Throwleigh. To found his charity he had given 'Beacon Garden' to the parish, and its lease to Mr Sidney Boult at the time, was providing 2s.6d. annually for distribution, on Easter Monday. In 1911 a total of 2.7s.6d. was distributed. The sum of 1.10s.0d. went to Sampford Courtenay and 17s.6d. to Sticklepath. Some 18 needy parishioners received amounts varying from 6d. to 2s.6d. each.

Those who founded such charities laid down some very strict guidelines as shown in the transcription made by C.A.T. Fursdon in 1934 of a legal document drawn up in 1583 - we recommend its reading in full. The following provides a good sample:

BE IT KNOWINGE to all men by this psent Indentures that I William Smythe, in the pishe of Southtawton in the countye of devon, Tann, to have geven and granuted and by this psentt wret-tinge doth cleyrly geve and granntt & confirme unto the Empetentte poure people and to thyr successors wythin the pishe of Southtawton in the countie of devon, three steures and ffower Ewes. TO HAVE & TO HOLD All & singler the three steures & ffoure Ewes, expssed & specified & evy partt & pcell therof unto the said poure and to theyr successors ffor ev, to such use as in this deed indented shalbe wretten, to the use of the said empetentt poure & to theyr successers for ever. AND ALL so I, the sayd William Smyth, have before the seelinge of this deed deleivered ov the three steures & ffoure Ewes in to the handes of my welbeloved in christ Richerd Smythe, Alexandr Wells, William Wells, William Smythe, jun, Richard Wells, the sonnes of the sayd Richard Smyth & Alexander Wells, in the pishe & countye aforsayde duringe theyr lyfves. TO HAVE & TO HOLDE the three steurs & ffoure Ewes, or the just valew therof, ffore the saide Enpetent poure & to theyr successors to grannte, sett & lett & inploye the same goods & chattels to suche Reasonable

British Legion Carnival, 1934.

Women's Section British Legion, 1940.

gainne & prophete for the said empetent poure as they saide Richarde Smythe, Alexander Wells, William Smythe, Richard Wells, Allways at theyr discrycion shall thynke best to be done for them. AND ALL so, wee the saide Richard Smythe, Alexandr Wells, William Wells, William Smythe, Richarde Wells, doth covenanntt promys and grannt to & wyth the said empetentt poure & wt there successors to inploye & bringe the three steures unto ffouer kyne in such order that allways maye contenyew, remeayne, stande insteed unto us Empetent pours & unto oure successers – that is to saye, the genne, the incres, the good godly profyt shall comon & above the stocke of the foure kyne &.ffoure Ewes all wayes to be delyved unto us the Empetent poure wydow & fatherlysse children wthin the pishe of Southtawton aforside, by the handes of us Richard Smythe, Alexander Wells, William Wells, William Smythe, Richard Wells, or one of them, allwayes wyth the consennte of the minister, vicker, or curett of Southtawton, upon good fryday (after) morninge prayer in the same day, yerlye so to be done & pfermed for ev unto such as be comfortlyce unto gods saynts and not unto Idellotter.... dye dames, catterpeller, euseurpers off gods benifyttes. AND ALL so, wee the said Richard Smyth, Alexandr Wells, William Wells, William Smythe, Richard Wells doth covenannt & promys that one off us inmydyatly aft the date heare of, ones evy yere yerelye duringe the lyfves, to wrette & rejest & sett it down upon the heed wardens books of Southtawton the wholl some of these forsayd goods & chattells that ..th ptendeth & belongeth unto the empetent poure & in whos handes the goods doth remayne & then shalbe, & also to awnswer ther the disatr... tinge unto the poure, the gaynne & incres wherby the Inhabytannce maye know yff they doe contrarye to the trew meaninge heere in, that then, the heed warden to call them forth by law & to causse them.to eld theyr acompt of the sayd goods & chattels, unto the sayd heed warden. AND ALL so, wee the sayde Richarde Smythe, Alexandr Wels, William Wels, William Smyth, Richard Wels, doth covenannt promys and grannt for us & for oure heyres, executors, administrators, to & wyth the saide empetent poure people, and to & wyth theyr successers by this psents that after the death and decesse of us Richard Smythe, Alexander Wels, William Wels, William Smythe, Richard Wels, that then oure heyres, executors & administrators or assignes, or one of them, shall then paye or caus to be well truly payd and delyved over ffour Kyle & four Ewes, or the just value off them, that is to SAYE, Sex pound Sexton shillings lawful moony of England, unto the heed warden of South Tawton aforesaid, off

Clockwise from top: *Zale Fayre. OAP Dinner in South Zeal, c.1950. Sticklepath WI staging a knit-in, 1976. David and Diana England share their garden in South Zeal with visitors Terry and Brenda Kempster during 'Open Gardens Day' 18 June 2000.*

❧ Charity ❧ and Fund-Raising Today Comes in All Shapes and Forms...

Top left: *Revealing evidence - Jon Padfield and others at a Sticklepath Fashion Show.*

Left: *Gardening expert and broadcaster Tim Argles at his 'potting shed' with Martyn, a visitor from Hampshire*

Top right: *George and Faith.*

Above left: *STOC – Cobbled path restoration at Sampford Courtenay.*

Left and below: *Richard Hart just manages to get the door closed after collecting another load of donations from generous people in the district; South Zeal and district Eurolief contributions are sorted at Dawlish, packed, and then driven by volunteers direct to those in need.*

Above: *Sticklepath Fireshow 1999 and the set nearing completion.*

them, or any of the be three unto required by the heed warden, & then the sad heed warden & his successors to inploye, grannt, sett & latte these ffouer kyne & ffouer Ewes to the use off the empetentt poure and to ther successors wythin the pishe aforsayd ffor ever, so to be inployed, done, & parformed in evy thinge according to the true meanings in this deed above wretten WHER by the sayde empetentte poure maye be the better releivede, and not to los the yoke and borden of others.

THEREFORE, I doe putt intriste under god to see this gyfte delyvered, pformed from tyme to tym, & so from yere to yere, and not to be troden under fote, the mynister, vicker, or curet of Southtawton ffore ever. AND ALL so, this deed intentede to lye in the box for the poure, or by the rejester booke in the coffer, or chist, for the poore, wythin the church of Southtawton.there to remayne for ever. BE caus that svannt which received one talent of his lorde, & gained nothing therwyth but went his wayse & hid it in the grounds, was cast into utter darknes, wher wepinge & gnashinge off teeth shalbe. the five folishe virgens, because they had no oyle in theyr lampes, were not suffred to enter into the marige. Moreon in gene 4 god asked caine where is abel they brother, what sayth hee, am I my brothers keeper. So these carelys mynisters & riche ffrannclynges, these covetous felloues saye, have wee the keepeinge off the poure. in Exod 3 and 22, Eccle 21, the prayer of the poore, the cry off the own pssed. I have harde theyr crye ffrom the face of theyr task masters for I knowe their sorowes & am come downe to delyv them, and againe, in the 2 booke of macha 3 god sent onias the prest that had such monye layd up for the upholding of wydowes & fatherlysse children, the sprate of almighty god shewed himselfe openly, and delyved them from the men of warre, daniel 4 wherfor o kinge be content wt my counsell yt thou mayest redem thy sinnes wt almesse. Eccle 19, and thyne offences wt moye to poore people. math 19. marke 10. luk 12, yf thou wilt be perfect go & sell all yt thou hast & gyve to ye poore & yu shalt have treasure in heaven & co & folow me, when hee hard yt sayenge he turnd his backe to christ & beed him fare well & some ther be when they se nothing but psent death then lash out & liberally geve unto ye poore, but wherfore is it, because they can kepe it no longer, ffor I thought it bett to send my workes before me while I live in this world and wholl, than to have the sent aft me, I know not by whom whan I am gone. 2 corem 9. Exo 25 and 35, Eccle 25 ffor god loveth a chearfull gever & Saint James sayeth, 2 ch, yff ye fulfyll ye royal law thou shalt love god above all thinge & thyne neyghbour as thy self and at ye resurreccion

aft this lyfe at wch tym evy man shall geve accompt ffor his workes, for ther shalbe judgment mcilesse to him yt sheweth no mcie, and mcie rejoyseth agaynst judgementt.

DATED the xvii° day of June in the xxv° yere off the raigne of ours sovaigne ladye Elizabeth, by the grace of god off England Frannce, and Ireland, quene, defender off the ffayeth etc anno Dni 1583. By me Willm Smythe, senn.

Backed/Selled delyved unto Richard Smyth, Alexandr Wels, and to John Connybye, one of the empetet poore of Southtawton & to his successers wythin wretten. In the psence of Thomas Ware, senn, William Borne. grom, Elynor Ware wt others.

If you skipped through to this line, we still recommend you to return to William Smythe's Indenture. Join him in 1583 as he decides how his 'three steures & ffoure Ewes' can best help others. Let the centuries disappear as his beliefs, trust and mistrust, reveal a personality worth meeting. With that suggested, we'll continue.

To ensure that local charities complied with the provisions of the Charitable Trusts Acts 1853 to 1894, an inquiry was held on 19 February 1912 in the parish of South Tawton as part of county-wide inquiry considering 'Endowed Charities.' The inquiry had access to an 1824 'Report' which, with inquiry notes, provides extensive information regarding individual charities, and reveals some local disputes relating to them; space permits us only to include extracts:

Burgoyne's Almshouse It appears from an entry in the register of this parish, supposed to be in the handwriting of the Revd Thomas White, vicar of the parish about the year 1750, that Robert Burgoyne, by his will, gave in 1656:

... to 11 esquires and gentlemen of the county of Devon, and the parish of South Tawton, as trustees, three almshouses and a field, called the Jamphay, with the gardens and appurtenances, for ever, to the use of three poor widow women to live in, each of them to receive 6s.8d. yearly, to be paid quarterly out of the rents and profits of the said field; and the residue and overplus of the rents and profits of the same, to remain as a stock for the keeping and maintaining of the same house in continued repair, or building new houses for other poor women, and giving them like allowance, or for enlarging, the allowance to the poor widow women who should reside in the said houses.

A lease was drawn up on the 28th September 1728, whereby William Oxenham, jun. esq., Thomas Hore,

'Sticklepath Jazz Band.' c. 1920.

Sticklepath WI - presented an 'Austrian Evening' in 1958.

George Hunt, Francis Moore, sen., Francis Moore, jun., James Battishill, John Oxenham, John Dunning, sen., John Orchard, sen., Oliver Long, jun., Philip Burgoyne, William Steere, Thomas Hole, and John Battishill, of South Tawton, accepted responsibility, as feoffees, for 'the better preserving and keeping,' of the land called Jamphay and three almshouses on it, 'lying within the borough of South Zeal, in the parish of South Tawton.' They, in turn, intended to let the land to James Lethbridge on a 99-year lease and maintain the almshouses, and the three poor widow women residents, from the rent received.

Unfortunately, it appears that the almshouses burned down before this arrangement was completed and William Oxenham paid £29 to have them rebuilt. He was reimbursed by James Lethbridge who did eventually take up the lease on the land and also agreed that he or his successors were to pay:

... yearly to the said feoffees, or their successors, or to the three poor women, from time to time inhabiting the said almshouses, the rent of 20s.; and also yearly paying to the said feoffees, the further yearly rent of 6s.8d. towards repairing the said almshouses.

The lease doesn't re-appear until 1815, when Thomas Lethbridge, the survivor of the persons on whose lives it was granted, died in his hundredth year. The field called Jamphay, adjoining the almshouses, had been let for some years by Thomas Lethbridge at about £4 per annum but in 1814 he let it to George Drew at a £8 per annum. Unfortunately, both of them died before a year's rent became due.

After their deaths, Thomas Lethbridge, the younger son of the above-mentioned deceased Thomas Lethbridge, agreed, with George Drew, the younger nephew of the above-mentioned deceased George Drew, to let the field to him. The amount of the rent to be paid for it, however, does not appear to have been finally settled between them. The widow of George Drew, the elder, paid £4 to Thomas Lethbridge the younger, for one half year's rent, due at Lady-day 1815. At Michaelmas that year, George Drew the younger paid him half the same sum for half a year's rent due. George was also a butcher and between 1816 and 1818, in addition to the part payment, also provided meat to Thomas, valued at £14.12s.0d.; before discovering that Thomas had no right to the field. Not surprisingly, George refused to pay Thomas any more rent but found the parish officers of South Tawton, on behalf of the charity, asking for it instead. At first he offered to pay them the rent for Jamphay, but later withdrew the offer relying it seems on the difficulty of anyone ascertaining in whom the legal estate was vested in trust for the charity. This was a successful ploy since he continued to occupy the field without paying rent to anybody until c.1823 when he returned possession of the field to

A Mothers' Union sale – included in the photograph are Nelly Kelly, Maud Jeffrey, and Rosie Coombes.

Traditional pancake races were either revived or introduced in South Zeal during 2000.

Teams entering the Fancy Dress Football Competition at Zale Fayre, July 1986.

the churchwardens of South Tawton. Also at that time Thomas Lethbridge showed the churchwardens that since his father's death he had laid out between £4 and £5 in the repairs to the almshouses and paid £13 to them. They had agreed to accept the £13 from Thomas in satisfaction of the rent received by him from George Drew, who then agreed to pay the churchwardens £5 in satisfaction of the residue of the rent which ought to have been paid by him for his occupation of Jamphay. With the matter clarified and concluded the vicar and ten respectable persons of the parish were appointed as trustees for the almshouses. As the field was estimated to be worth from four to five guineas per annum the charity still suffered a loss of rent but at the time it was considered highly advantageous that settlement was achieved without recourse to legal proceedings.

For the use of the poor, Oliver Lang by his will of 19 August 1654 gave the churchwardens and overseers of the poor of South Tawton, and their successors, thereof, a yearly rent-charge of 30 shillings. during the term of 300 years, issuing out of a close of land, called Brushcombe, in South Tawton. John Northmore's will, in 1718, shows that from Coombe, an estate in Drewsteignton parish, he gave one moiety of the rents thereof to be applied to the poor of South Tawton parish, and the other moiety to the poor of the parish of Okehampton, whom might otherwise be 'reduced to poverty by sickness, suretyship, or fire,' or who were 'overburthened with children.' and 'should not be relieved by poor rates, together with the particulars of the property and of the rent thereof.'

Out of the estate called Higher Cullaford, by his will in 1727, William Oxenham gave £5 to be paid yearly to the South Tawton poor, by the minister, churchwardens and overseers, by quarterly payments. William Battishill, by his will, gave £20 to South Tawton parish, to remain as a stock for ever, to be disposed of by the churchwardens and overseers, and the profit thereof to be distributed to the poor, at Christmas every year. He also gave £20:

... to be lent to poor tradesmen without interest, for one year, and no longer, by the consent of the said officers, with the approbation of the parson, vicar or curate, and so to remain as stock for ever.

According to the register, the £20 was lost in lending it out. Returns made to Parliament in 1786, state that with 'two sums of £20 each, given by William Battishill and Edward Northmore, together with a collection, land was purchased, then let for £4.4s.0d. per annum.' Income derived from rent was given for the use of the poor people. By indentures of lease and release, bearing the dates 22 and 23 December 1730, Johanna Neale:

... in consideration of £80 conveyed to William Oxenham and another churchwarden and Thomas Hore and three others, overseers of the poor of South Tawton, a field, called Derracombe meadow, in that parish, in trust, to permit the churchwardens and overseers of the said parish, for the time being, to receive the rents thereof, and pay the same to such poor persons of the said parish, as should be at the monthly meetings of the parish officers and inhabitants, thought to stand in need of relief, so as such poor persons should not receive any monthly relief.

John Dunning bequeathed, in 1781, an annuity of five shillings payable out of an estate in South Tawton, called Scurhills, to poor labourers in husbandry of this parish, not receiving relief.

By declaration of trust dated 22 November 1887 William Henry Kelland provided the sum of £8.7s.6d. for investment. Dividends were to be used to supply of clothes, medical or other aid in sickness, food or other articles in kind for the benefit of deserving and necessitous persons resident in the said parish. As with other benefactors he insisted that the funds of his charity:

... should in no case be applied directly or indirectly in relief of the poor rates of the said parish or so that any individual should be entitled to a permanent or recurrent benefit therefrom.

The inquiry in 1912 was held in Church House, South Tawton, attended by the vicar, Revd T.F. Boultbee, Messrs J. Tucker and G. Grendon, churchwardens, Messrs G.D. Cann, William Endacott, D.S. Warne, Robert Holman, and the clerk to the Charities, Mr J. Sampson. The charities, by the time of the inquiry, were being administered as one, as United Charities regulated by the Scheme of 17 February 1906 but there were more. Mary Ann Buse, a widow, who died 13 April 1902, by her will gave to the vicar and churchwardens of the parish of South Tawton, £20, to be invested by them in Consols. The whole of the income in 1912 was paid to one poor labourer who was unable to do any work and had a large family. Jane Harriet Bliss, by her will, 5 September 1901, bequeathed £150. Investment interest was to benefit the poor inmates of the Church House of South Tawton, or failing such for the sick poor of South Tawton parish.

In his will, dated 10 March 1906, John Sampson gave £200 to be invested, and interest used to provide gifts to the deserving poor of South Tawton on Lady Day in every year; and a further sum of £200 to be invested, with its annual income devoted entirely towards any fund which might be established for providing a parish nurse for the parish.

On 12 June 1939 the Board of Charity Commissioners for England and Wales approved a revision of the charities, which became 'The South Tawton Charities,' with seven trustees; the Vicar for South Tawton, ex-officio trustee, four Rrpresentative trustees, appointed by the South Tawton Parish Council, each appointment being for a term of four years; two co-optative trustees, being persons residing or carrying on business in or near South Tawton, each appointed for a term of seven years. Irene Madders is the present Secretary to the charity and its trustees. Charity income was then, and still is, applied to benefit poor parishioners who did not receive Poor-Law relief, other than medical relief, for any of the following:

Contributions towards medical and surgical appliances; travelling expenses, e.g. towards attending hospital, dispensary, and infirmary; the assistance of persons, under the age of 21, who are preparing for, entering upon, or engaged in, any trade, occupation, or service for their advancement in life, or to enable them to earn their own living as the trustees think fit; to supply clothes, boots, linen, bedding, fuel, tools, food and any other articles in kind not exceeding £20 in any one year; temporary assistance by way of a loan, or otherwise in case of sickness, special distress or unexpected loss to an amount not exceeding £10 in any one year; temporary assistance by way of loan or otherwise not exceeding £20 in any one year, to mothers qualified as aforesaid, who have three children or more under the age of 16 years.

Throughout much of the 20th century many among the rural population were very poor indeed, with no National Health Service to help the sick, or a range of Social Services payments and grants to call upon for assistance. Within the living memory of many people times were very hard and difficult for country families. They recall the parish charities being highly valued, and often needed, by their parents and older people when it cost 6d. to see a doctor, and a doctor's home-visit had to be paid for.

Despite the NHS and DSS availability these small charities inherited from bygone days continue to serve the community, administered by trustees with discretion both in regard to applications and modest payments made from interest received from investments. In 1997 the Charity Commission approved a request made by the trustees for the amalgamation of all the charities into one. The 'South Tawton Charities' were then legally formed, retaining objectives established in past centuries, and the body will continue, 'For the general benefit of the poor of the Parish of South Tawton.' The trustees have chosen to wind up the Robert Burgoyne Charity as they

are no longer obliged to provide almshouses for 'three poor widow women to live in,' or to ensure that 'each of them to receive 6s.8d. yearly.'

Help for the community coming from within has, if anything, increased considerably over the years and while our guide to present-day 'helping hands' cannot include every generous individual, it is intended as a tribute to all that uphold the principle.

For many years Bert Stead has assisted with charitable activities, members of Sticklepath Sports and Social Club have been organising events, including the highly successful annual Pram Race; donating the proceeds to local groups, organisations and charities. Sticklepath Fireshow organisers are similarly motivated, and with an able team, Pauline Fletcher assists the continuity of the village Annual Flower Show. Cogs and Wheels, the Finch Foundry based ladies' morris dance team has not only been freely adding their individual style of entertainment to local events, as well as making county-wide appearances, but have also been able to donate over £600 for charities and organisations in a short time.

Generosity knows no bounds, as those who work tirelessly for British Legion, Cancer Research, the Lifeboat Association, Mencap, Hospiscare and many other organisations would testify. Primary School children donate their toys to those with none, support appeals from Blue Peter, and enjoy participating in fund-raising for their own school; which also finds local supporters and local support invaluable. 'Members of the Friends of South Tawton County Primary School' were delighted with the success of the 'silent auction' recently held in Victory Hall, South Zeal, in support of the school that had raised, at the time of a report in the *Okehampton Times*, December 1999, the magnificent sum of £1196. People in the entire area, and beyond, continually respond to Devon-based 'Eurolief' as a report in the *Express & Echo*, also of December 1999, shows:

... the last load of goods collected in South Zeal, Sticklepath, and the area around Okehampton that was destined for the children's orphanages and the hospital units being assisted by Eurolief has been received in time for Christmas. Clothes and blankets, typewriters, sewing machines, bicycles, and toys... donated during recent months... The jumpers knitted by so many generous people for the small children have brought comfort to many and the toys so generously shared by our own young people have been particularly appreciated.

Members of the Cosdon Group of Friends of St Loye's identify a specific need, work hard and gain support, as evidenced in another newspaper report– this time in the *Okehampton Times*, during June 2000:

The group of 'Friends' from around and beyond the South Zeal, Sticklepath area is renowned for its fund-raising based upon its members toy-making talents and nimble needlework. During the past year those talents ensured that £1900 was recently handed over to St Loye's in Exeter to assist its work in helping those with handicaps...

There are those who work for the community without whose efforts some of our most useful facilities or services would certainly suffer. The committee members that sustain our village halls and playing fields, the organisers of the Youth Club, the Jack & Jill Club and the Playgroup. They tackle fund-raising not for themselves, but for the community which that benefits from so many events, among them Christmas Bingo fun, Zale Fair, the annual opening of private gardens, coffee mornings, sales and bazaars.

In November 1999, *Express & Echo* reporters noted that:

It is now certain that Father Christmas has confirmed that he will be in South Zeal on Saturday 4th December in plenty of time to find the Victory Hall in which South Zeal Pre-school Playgroup organisers will be holding their Christmas Bazaar from 10.00am - noon.

Individuals respond readily to needs that matter to them and regularly find support for their efforts. Lesley Wright from Ramsley has walked hundreds of miles accompanied by her dog, Meg, to raise funds for the Canine Defence League and other animal charities while others open their homes to assist a cause close to their hearts, as noted in the *Okehampton Times*:

When Bill and Joyce Worthington declared their historic home to be an 'open house' for visitors to a fundraising 'coffee morning' organised by them to assist fundraising for St Mary's Church in South Zeal they could hardly have wished for a better response from the public... The combined generosity of all those people has resulted in over £900 being raised.

Ann and Roger Bowden and Jacquie and Roger Yeates regularly open the gardens at their Sticklepath and South Tawton homes to visitors to raise money for charity.

In recent years the volunteers that comprise the Sticklepath and Okehampton Conservation group, STOC, have extended their help to the local community, and others around the region, through countryside care and conservation work. Members of the community often help them and they certainly rallied around when the revival of pancake races on Shrove Tuesday 2000 proved popular. Inside the tiny church of St Mary's, Revd Barry Woods and Mrs Wendy Kitchen from South Tawton were busy cooking pancakes for the refreshment of parishioners and visitors, thanks to Vera and Clifford White for donating eggs and Barry and Joyce Woods from Dartmoor Dairy for providing milk and eggs. Prizes were provided by Pauline Baker of the Kings Arms, Linda Trussler, Andrew White of Maid Marion Stores, George Henry of the Oxenham Arms, Jacquie Jordan and Jan Berry of the Cosdon Group. Assisting as race marshals were Pauline Baker, Dawn Watkins and Peter Kilgannon, and the raffle was run by Sherri Henry. After eliminating around 16 competitors in the heats, Emma Jeffries and Pat Brocklesby, with frying pans refilled, raced over the near half-furlong course again, from Parish Church to Post Office, in a final pancake-pitching duel that made Pat the pancake-race champion of South Zeal. Finishing the day's racing was an event for toddlers with Harriet Graham (3), Emily Boother (4), Bethany Webber (3) and Phoebe Jordan (2) ensuring that the revival was for everyone. Judges declared them all joint winners, to the approval of the crowd. Within little more than an hour a successful event raised almost £70 for the church, because the community cared.

Scouts, Cubs, Beavers and Brownies would not exist in the area but for the helping hands of people such as Michael and Caroline Boother, Jill Watson, and those that help them help the young ones in the community.

Members of the Women's Institutes are ever ready to serve their communities and while they, those we've mentioned, and many more beside, continue to inspire the next generation, the 'helping hand' principles will continue to flourish beneath the beacon.

Top: *Carnival Princess 2000, Jennifer Howard.*
Above: *Campfire and sing-song, firm favourites each year with Guides and Brownies visiting the annual camp at Taw Bottom.*

The Bundle of Sticks *production in 1931 led the way for future players.*

In 1960 the Merry-Go Rounders brought Dick Whittington *to the village stage with Diana Endacott (England) in principal role, Raymond Souness portraying King Rat, Susan Roberts as Fairy Gossamer and Marcella Wedlake as the Pearl Sprite, all more than ably assisted by E.L. Roberts, Jaqueline Hooper, John Brockman, Victor Sloper, Charles Jasper, Edward Hammett, George Hocking, Nina Roberts, Heather Roberts, Philip Gwynne, Brian Knox-Little, Joyce Brockman, and many others.*

Chapter 9
Entertaining Others...
and Ourselves

During the 1930s the stage productions in the area were generally based on entertainment presented in the style of a revue, invariably featuring a cast with a wide span of ages rising from very young children to older adults. Songs and sketches, music, verse and dance were all included in productions such as *Bundle of Sticks*, remembered by at least one performer for the dress she wore; much to her disapproval because her petticoat was shorter. Mrs Clark-Gray from South Zeal is remembered by many for having devoted considerable time and talent to producing shows that were always welcomed by parishioners and that involved people from throughout the area. Many of those who worked with her were well grounded in stagecraft by the time war broke out and made good use of their talent and training during the darkest years by entertaining others in the forces.

Towards the end of hostilities, in March 1945 'The South Zeal Drama Society' was formed with Miss Eileen de Burgh Daly as Chairman, Mrs W. A. Ebbutt as Secretary, Mr A. Fry as treasurer, and Committee Members, Mrs Box, Mrs Tippins, Miss Mary Crocker, Mrs Fawden, Mr Hicks, Miss Pam Hucker, Mr Scaife, Mr Underhill and Mrs W. Wonnacott. Their first production, *Legend*, a one-act play by Philip Johnson, was staged on 12 May at the Exeter Drama Festival and then as part of a 'Social' held on 24 May at the Victory Hall. The ambitious group also produced *Redundant, White Blackmail* and *The Bear* in the same year.

The Haxtons and *They Never walk Alone* were produced by the group in 1946, followed by the *Farm of Three Echoes*, a year later. In 1948 the 'Society' became 'The Beacon Players', staging three one-act plays, *The Proposal, The Anniversary* and

This early 'four-season' float confirms Carnival's long history of popularity, extended in more recent years since revival. However, the event is likely to need help if it is to continue for long in the new millennium.

The Bishop's Candlestick, with performances described by the *Western Times* as 'well unto the high talent one expects from this talented company, the members of which show an encouraging stimulus to break new ground rather than tread the stereotyped old.' Anton Tchekov was noted as, 'the Russian dramatist who is coming increasingly into favour over here.' The cast of *The Anniversary*:

... entered wholeheartedly into the spirit of the occasion, and we had some uproarious office scenes with Albert Stead as the harassed overworked clerk; Richard Barron, the underworked chairman of directors; Joyce Tippens as Tatyana, his sleight-of-tongue wife; Joyce Dennison, the victim of financial circumstances, and Reginald Styles, also responsible for production, the deputation's delegate.

The annual Hunt Ball, and the Art Ball introduced in 1950, are remembered as great occasions for dressing up. There were regular barn dances, the weekly 'hop' socials, visiting circuses, and, best remembered, the Carnival.

Newspaper reports in 1952 confirm just how popular the event had been on 8 November:

ELIZABETHAN TABLEAU WAS THE CHAMPION AT SOUTH ZEAL HEADED by a mounted marshal in uniform (Mr. John Holman), South Zeal carnival procession on Saturday night was a spectacular and colourful cavalcade. Included were coaches bearing the "Queen" (Miss Rosemary Wannacott) with her attendants (Misses Iris Sewell and Gracie Fildew) and the Okehampton Carnival "King and Queen" (Master Brian Vanstone and Miss June Lee). South Zeal's "Princess" (Miss Valerie Jeffery) rode in a car with her attendant (Miss Valerie Stevens). South Zeal Air Scouts, Okehampton Borough Band, Tavistock Cadet Force Bands, and Chagford Jazz Band provided music. Scenes from early English history and colourful outdoor settings of fact and fantasy imparted beauty and imagination to the carnival. Nearly 20 tableaux wound out of the narrow village street and threaded their way along the Dartmoor heights and back to the starting point.

The champion tableau was "Queen Elizabeth and Sir Walter Raleigh," entered by South Zeal Guides. Other efforts of considerable merit included "A Japanese Tea-garden," "The Snow Queen," "Mary Quite Contrary," "Jingle Bells," and the runner-up in the original class, "Robin Hood and his Merry Men." One which did not figure in the prize list, but which struck a topical note, was a miniature reproduction The Cenotaph surrounded by a scarlet Field of Remembrance. The carnival was well supported from Okehampton, the visitors' class being won by "Destination Moon," fresh from its triumph at Okehampton carnival.

The Beacon Players were responsible for an amusing turnout, "Dairy Show Supreme Champion," showing a "dairy cow" whose milking qualities were suspect. Any resemblance to the chase was purely nominal In "A-Hunting We Will Go."

In a football match South Zeal beat Devon County Police by 8-4. A dance was held in the Victory Hall, refreshments being supervised by Mrs F. Delbridge and helpers. Proceeds were in aid of the parish church, South Zeal Football Club, the Victory Hall, and South Zeal Guides, Brownies, Scouts and Cubs. Officials were; President. Mr. T Bakewell-Green: Chairman of committee. Mr. G. Perry; hon. Secretary Mrs. K. J. Jackson: hon. treasurer, Mr. A. Nash. Awards:-

Artistic – Japanese Tea-garden (Mr. L. Lentern and company). Mary, Mary, Quite Contrary (1st South Zeal Brownies). Comic – Dairy Show Supreme Champion (The Beacon Players), A Hunting We Will Go (Mr. J. Cooper), Original – Queen Elizabeth and Sir Walter Raleigh (1st South Zeal Guides), Robin Hood and his Merry Men (South Zeal Wolf Cubs). Visitors' class- Destination Moon (Okehampton Rugby Club Colts), Present – From Okehampton (nurses, and District Hospital), Santa in Toyland (Messrs. T. C.

Guides and Brownies on parade at Church House in South Zeal.

Westcott and company). Children five to 12: Artistic - Christine Tippins, Jeremy Fford, Gay Bisett. Original- Jane Hakewell, Joan Wonnacott, Mary Reddaway. Comic - Barry Redstone, Leonora Styles. Cynthia Chowings. Under five: Artistic - Marilyn Tucker. Joan Tucker, P. Buxton *Original - Naomi Barron, Mary Reddaway, Ron Gillard. Comic - P. Sealing, David Emery.*

The champion float the following year, Old Stage Coach, was entered by the South Zeal Social Club but the float that took to the prize-winning trail in 1953 was the Beacon Players' entry 'Pot Luck,' taking 1st Prizes at South Zeal and Exbourne and 2nd Prizes at the Okehampton and Hatherleigh carnivals. The weather on Saturday, October 24th was not kind to South Zeal carnival in which fourteen tableaux, mounted characters, and children in fancy dress, accompanied Carnival Queen Miss Susan Ffoorde, her attendants Lorna Elsworthy and Gracie Phildew, and the prince and princess, Harold Sleeman and Ann Redstone around the route. Confirming the memories of some, whose comments to us can best be translated as probably meaning, 'it was a long walk in the wet,' the press reported:

Even the stoutest hearts may well have quailed at the prospect of facing a two-mile jaunt (the processional route was extended this year by taking in Sticklepath) under such conditions, and it says much for the toughness of the villagers that they stuck it out to the 'bitter end'. Among the many who did just that were the following award-winners;

Riding Class - 1, Brenda Jones; 2, Barbara Murrin; 3. Geraldine Easterbrook.

Artistic - l. Snow White and the Seven Dwarfs (South Zeal United Football Club); equal 2. Won't You Buy My Pretty Flowers? (the Parish Church); and Cinderella-Ballroom Scene (South Zeal Brownies).

Comic - 1, Pot Luck (the Beacon Players); 2. The Poachers (the Victory Hall).

Original - 1, Old Stage Coach (South Zeal Social Club); equal 2. Autumn Days (Old Age Pensioners) and Venetian Gondola (Sticklepath Social Club).

Children, 8 and under, fancy - 1, Mary Needham; 2, Sandra Osborne; 3, Nicholas Norman; 4, Naomi Barron.

Comic -1, Philip Selling.

Original -1. Mary Gillard; 2, Gay Bissett; 3, Leslie Howard; 4, Frank Wonnacott.

8-12. Fancy - 1, Margaret Reddaway; 2, Carol Hicks; 3, Graham McPherson; 4, Robert McPherson. Comic -1, Keith Redstone; 2, Barry Hicks; 3, Peter Bissett.

Original - 1, Terence Hooper and David Hunt; 2. Leonora Styles; 3, Marlynn Souness.

Over 12, comic - 1, Terence Leyland.

Original - 1, Stanley Souness.

Pairs - Marilyn Tucker and John Hicks

With another dozen productions to their credit by 1956 the Beacon Players, led by Chairman, Peter Jackson, Col. Erskine-Lindop their President, Elizabeth Macmillan Scott, hon. Sec., and Ian Abell, Treasurer, continued to receive praise in the December papers:

GOOD ACTING AT S. ZEAL DRAMA, farce, and the warmth of Devon's native humour, were neatly blended by the Beacon Players in the three one-act plays they presented on their home ground at South Zeal on Thursday, Friday, and Saturday, last. One of the trilogy was a first performance of Widecombe Fair, *written by Mr C.E. Robinson, who lives in retirement at Belstone. It deals with a decision by Uncle Tom Cobley's grand niece to round up a number of her sex, bearing the same names as the illustrious septet and visit Widecombe to celebrate the jubilee of the famous journey, but old sores were opened, and what started with the best of intentions ended in bad blood.*

...the mounting resentments, were brought out well by a cast consisting of Kathleen Hocking, Shirley White, Jenny Sewell, Gwendoline Legg, Dorothy Drew, Winnie Roberts, Emma Yeo, Gertie Harvey and Geraldine Abell.

The portrayal by Joe Quick of the tramp, in J.M. Synge's, *The Shadow of the Glen* was noted as 'an acting highlight.' Local chemist, Albert Fry, was appreciated by the reviewer for his performance as 'an unexpectedly animated corpse' and the 'slapstick comedy in the best Mack Sennet vein (was) liberally dispensed by the entire cast... '. G. B. Shaw's *Passion, Poison, and Petrifaction* was much to the reviewer's liking. It was another of his plays that the company selected for its June 1951 Festival of Britain Presentation in which, as the press reported: 'The atmosphere of London four decades ago was cleverly recaptured... when the company... gave [an] accomplished performance of Pygmalion.' The group's hon. Secretary, Joyce Barron, was reported to hav 'handled her dual personality with resourcefulness, bringing to bear large reserves of emotion,' and as Alfred Doolittle, the Cockney dustman, 'Christopher Lovell came close to stealing the show.' W. H. Vipan was credited with being scene builder and decorator.

Was it he, we wonder, who also led the group in creating and building carnival floats used by members? The Beacon Players were regular participants,

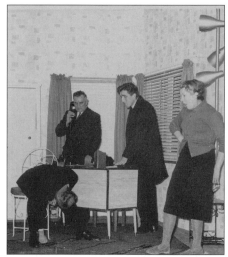

Above: Arsenic and Old Lace, *1952.*
Cast included: Dorothy V. Gardiner,
Victor Walker, John C. Jevons, John
A. Norman, John Oliver Jane Sewell,
Sylvia Lambert, Albert Stead, Peter
Jackson, Ronald Styles, Albert Fry,
Chris Lovell, George Hocking and
Victor Walker.

Top right: Busybody, *1967, included*
Maggy Thomas, Tony Taylor,
Maurice Roberts and Ken Chapman,
Sheila Holman, Cherry Hindmarch,
Colin Trump and Jean Chapman.

Above:
Widecombe Fair,
1954. The cast
adding
to the Cobley
myth were
Kathleen
Hocking, Shirley
White, Jenny
Sewell,
Gwendoline
Legg,
Dorothy Drew,
Winnie Roberts,
Emma Yeo, Gertie
Harvey and
Geraldine Abell.

Left: *The annual*
Arts Ball became
a popular event
for the Beacon
Players and
parishioners.

The Beacon Players

Left: *In 1953 the Beacon Players produced* Blithe Spirit *with Marion Walker, Ivy Hallowell-Carew, John Norman, Albert Stead, and Jane Sewell, with Joyce Barron, as Madame Arcati, and Margaret Fforde as Elvira.*

Right: *The cast of* They Walk Alone, *the 1946 Beacon Player production; Albert Fry, Ivy Carew, Rosemary Wonnacott, Richard Barron, Alexis Yates, Ronald Styles and Joyce Tippen.*

Below: *A reminder of the Beacon Players' production of* Babes *in 1951.*

The producer seemingly found a village equal for Peggy Mount *in Joyce Barron who waspishly played the roost-ruling Emma Hornett, central character in the Merry-Go-Rounders' 1959 production of* Sailor Beware! *Philip Gwynn (her downtrodden husband), Nina Roberts, Jacqueline Hooper (the betrayed bride), John Brockman, Maurice Roberts and Sheila Holmanall helped the team sail on to success as they 'toured 'the play around the area.*

and prizewinners, not only in this event but also in other canrivals around the county. In her 1954/55 report Joyce Barron noted that 'Our comic tableau, 'Boadicea Rides Again' won second prize at South Zeal and District Carnival in October.' She also added that:

Our greatest misfortune this year was the death of Mr Jevons who was our good friend as well as a keen and tireless worker on our behalf. We are happy to know that the proscenium in the Victory Hall which he designed has been completed. This will be of inestimable benefit to us in future productions, as well as improving the appearance of the hall and stage from the audience's point of view.

She was absolutely right and a great many people have gained benefit from Mr Jevons' work.

Programme adverts from the period provide useful information. By 1958, when the group produced The Ghost Train, adverts confirm that Mr Fry, the chemist, had handed the reins to others. A.C. Lovell at Moorside Drug Store, South Zeal, now offered, '[everything] for your toilet requirements, cigarettes, confectionery, library, etc.' It was possible to 'Meet 'Teddie Deakin' in person in the bar of the TAW RIVER INN, Sticklepath (built in 1660)' for 'CITY ALES & STOUTS; J.E.B. Price is proclaimed as being the 'Tobacconist: Newsagent: Book Seller,' also providing 'Fancy Goods; and Haberdashery,' while

trading as a 'General Dealer' in Sticklepath; J. & R. Redstone are listed as grocers and greengrocers in South Zeal while both the Rising Sun and Seven Stars are 'free' houses . The Express Typewriting Service , for typewriting and duplication, is located in South Tawton, Established 1946, with Regd. Office; 108 Friern Park London N12. For their 'Guns - rifles - ammunition - fishing tackle - golf, tennis, and sundry sports - hunting crops and knives,' playgoing programme readers were advised to visit 'C.H. SPORTS (EXETER) LTD. 94 Queen Street.'

Anyone planning to do that on Monday 3 February may well have assisted the Players by returning 'weapons' supplied by C. & H. Sports for use in the production. If it was a lorry they were going in, they might also have volunteered to return the 'properties' on loan from British Railways, and Devon County Constabulary. Well, someone was going to have to do it.

On 3 May 1958, a new theatre group emerged, led by Margaret Hocking, to present their 'Merry go Round' of songs and sketches, with handbell ringers on the bill. What really rang the bell was the show title. As 'The Merry-go-Rounders', the versatile company produced straight plays, comedies and pantomime - with *Cinderella* in 1959. That year they also 'toured' the comedy *Sailor Beware!* to Gidleigh, Chagford and North Tawton. *Dick Whittington* was produced in 1960, *Little Women* in 1961 and *Miranda* in 1962, by which time the company had already contributed £383.10s..0d. to the Cancer Campaign Fund. In 1996 the press reported that:

CONTINUING their efforts for deserving causes the South Zeal Merry-go-Rounders delighted large audiences last week with a freely-adapted version of "Little Red Riding Hood." During the past eight years the company has raised £600 for cancer research. The proceeds of their latest production will go to the N.S.P.C.C.

The pantomime in six acts, filled with talented comedy turns, spirited dancing, and music to the toe-tapping melodies of yesteryear got a rousing performance from a cast of 30 who did wonders to perform at all within the congested limits of the Victory Hall stage.

In the title role Marcella Wedlake was coy and winsome, and mimed well to the loud speaker, while Ken Chapman was professional and as polished as could be as Mother Hubbard. The husband and wife team of David and Diana England as Polly and Simple Simon provided much tuneful singing, and a dramatic climax in which Simon, a curious blend of Britannia and St. George, despatched King Wolf after a stirring sword fight. In wolf's clothing, Ray Souness convincingly menaced the forest glades and died nobly. Susan Roberts as Prince Charm-ing lived up to her character, and the contrasts between good and evil were nicely demonstrated by Wyn Roberts (the Witch) and Linda Hooper (Fairy Queen).

Comedy, largely uninhibited, flowed easily from Johnny Norman, Tony Mortimore, Laurie Ainsley, and John Soper, and other parts were suitably played by Sheila Holman (Grannie), Timothy Hocking (Tommy Tucker), Maggy Thomas, and Madge Kelly. Tiny tots and teenagers rejoicing in the names of The Smarties and The Spangles, joined forces for chorus work and dancing. They were Susan Dymont, Jane Holman, Yvonne Howard, Hazel and Dulcie Cooper, Diana Holman, Rita Granger, Susan Maguire, Angela Woods, Susan Dominy, Shirley Madders, Shirley Mortimore, and Ann and Jacqueline Pillivant. The pantomime was devised and produced by Margaret Hocking. The painted backgrounds were all home-made, as were the dresses, made by parents and friends.

Behind the scenes were Steve Sillifant (piano), Maurice Roberts (stage manager), Doug Howard and Derick May, (electricians). Laurie Ainsley (drums), Sally Smithson (prompt), Mary Hooper, Oliver Hooper, Joan Norman, and Cynthia Souness (dresses and make-up).

There then followed a 20-year hiatus in panto production until February 1987:

WORTH WAITING FOR

THE people of South Zeal have had to wait for just over twenty years since they last had their own pantomime. They certainly welcomed 'Red Riding Hood' when she came back to the Victory Hall at the end of the week. Packed audiences watched a fast-moving, colourful and lively pantomime. The players worked to a complicated script which somehow brought in Mother Hupboard (so spelt), a Prince Charming in all but title, fairies and a witch to complicate even more than usual the life of Red Riding Hood, the Wolf and Granny.

The cast was an entertaining mixture of children and adults and - most important of all - the entertainment kept on the move.

Beryl Crump as fairy Hopeless grabbed the stage. when she was on, young Stuart Birch and Richard Sampson compelled attention and applause as Grabbitt and Floggit. John Candler played a major continuing role and John Birch, as Mother Hupboard had a strong stage presence which helped to keep things going with a swing. But all the principals, Ursula Radford, Sandra Darkin, Nicola Peacock, Andrew Sampson, Sarah Birch, Roger Wools, Rachel Fanconi, Karen

Darkin, Anna Curnow and Winifred, Glyn, kept up a high level of entertainment.

They were more than adequately backed up by the children and junior dancers, Lisa Holman, Jenny Mort, Emma Reeves, Joanna Mort, Andrew Darkin, Sarah Woods, Joanne Nunn, Laura Norrish, Rosalind Stainer-Smith, Rachel Pollard, Debbie Mills, Chris Owen and Ross Clarke. The pantomime was written and directed by Roy Radford and Howard Baker was musical director.

"D.D.S." (Okehampton Times)

We were privileged to lead a very enthusiastic team that responded to the suggestion that a village 'drama group' could be re-established to introduce young people to live theatre and raise funds for village projects and community groups. At a meeting in Buttercup Cottage in the autumn of 1986 the 'South Zeal Players' decided to 'do a panto.' A much-loved teacher, Elinor Warnock, volunteered, with Debbie Retallick, to get the schoolchildren involved. Sharon Pollard Dorothy Flower and Edna Gay started to create what has developed into a valued costume wardrobe, while Winnie Roberts and Ray Souness, members of the 1966 production, added their expertise and encouragement to an increasingly confident and able company. Even the youngest children were soon talking 'upstage' without turning their backs on their audience and kneeling comfortably through musical numbers with a clean, downstage, profile. Enthusiasm was shared by everyone; talent provided sparkling performances; audiences generously showed their appreciation.

The success of Red Riding Hood, returning over £500 profit, permitted the South Zeal Players to immediately revive the tradition established by its predecessors of devoting funds to local causes. But it was not until after their second production, in February 1988, that funds raised by The Last Fairy Tale also ensured that the they could pay for the regilding and restoration of the two clock faces on St Mary's Chapel; a project that those in the company remain proud of to this day, and one which parishioners and visitors will long continue to enjoy.

During that panto-less period, other very entertaining projects were launched in Sticklepath and Wood; both of which continue to entertain, and excite. The Dartmoor Folk Festival and the Sticklepath Fireshow each have a committee, people dedicated to the continuity of successful annual events. Talk to the Festival committee members and within a few phrases the conversation turns to one man, Bob Cann, to whom we record our tribute. Bobs inheritance was folk music. His grandfather played a concertina and created step-dancing competitions for country dancers in the days when performers that could rightly be considered

Carnival

Above: Good Golly – there was always good fun at carnival – pre pc humbug – and long may the fun continue.

Top left: *Beacon Players' float took first prize in South Zeal Carnival on Saturday 24 October 1957.*

Below: *Will carnival memories of Patricia and June with Maurice Wonnacott captured here help carnival continue? We can only hope so.*

Above: *'From Beyond' - the Easterbrook family carnival float in 1966 with Jo, Aaron, and Aidan Easterbrook and Clare and Katherine Foulger.*

Above: The Last Fairy Tale *was the South Zeal Players' panto for 1988 that also put a smile back on both faces of the village clock thanks to the efforts of Elspeth Brint, Roger Wools, Melanie Mills, Stuart, Sarah, Eileen and John Birch, Sandra and Karen Darken, John Candler, Lisa Holman, Richard Andrew Sampson, Philip Radford, Jenny Morton, Emma Reeves, Cara Clarke, Jonathan Wools, Keren Wools, Clive Madders, Sonia Cann, Ross Clarke, Andrew Darken, Julian Pillar, and many many more in a marvellous company.*

Top right: *A principal boy in panto's truest tradition, Susan Roberts.*

Below: Red Riding Hood *returned to revive panto in 1987 with Sarah Birch, in title role, Ursula Radford, John Candler, John Birch, Roger Wools, Beryl Crump, Sandra Darkin, and Nicola Peacock, in a strong company.*

Bottom: *An earlier* Red Riding Hood *was the six-act panto produced in 1966, with Marcella Wedlake in the title role, Ken Chapman as Mother Hubbard, the husband and wife team of David and Diana England as Simple Simon and Polly, Ray Souness convincingly menacing as King Wolf, and Susan Roberts as Prince Charming. Wyn Roberts made a convincing Witch, Linda Hooper sparkled as Fairy Queen and comedy, largely uninhibited, flowed easily from Johnny Norman, Tony Mortimore, Laurie Ainsley and John Soper, all backed by an excellent supporting players, singers and dancers of all ages.*

Above: *Fireshow – more magic with the puppets.*
Left: *Bob Cann.*

spectacular used farm wagons as a stage. His three uncles taught him to play concertina at the tender age of three and a half; Uncle Bob played mouth organ, Uncle George played concertina and Uncle Jim favoured the melodeon.

By the time he was 11, young Bob had taken up the melodeon himself, and mastered it so well that was in demand at barn dances; cycling to them with the instrument strapped on his back. Early on, Bob played in a melodeon, piano and drums trio, with a Mrs Eccles and her son, Raymond. As his teenage years passed by he cycled further afield, playing at ever more dances and picking up a great many new tunes from other players and bands. Next came The Kestor Rocky Band, new players, new horizons, on one of which he foresaw future happiness. Bob met Joyce at a 'sixpenny Hop;' they married in 1947.

Folk music found a new following in the 1950s. As a member of The English Folk Dance and Song Society Bob was instrumental in forming many new folk clubs. Like many Dartmoor musicians, he combined his music with his cattle and sheep farming, first at Batworthy and later at Ford, but when the

EFDSS held their first competition in London for solo instrumentalist in 1957 it was Bob that won the top award.

Wherever there was folk music to be played, dancers to be encouraged, or festivals to be assisted to flourish, Bob Cann could be found at the forefront. Bob was one of the original helpers of the Sidmouth International Folklore Festival; and later received a Festival Award. His own Pixie Band may generally only have comprised six marvellous musicians but over the years many hundred more music makers climbed on stage to join them. Having often worked with Charlie Bate, the 'Gentleman of Folk,' Bob was particularly proud of receiving the first award given in his name, The Charlie Bate Award, at Cornwall's Folk Festival in Wadebridge.

When Bob and Joyce had retired to South Tawton they only swapped one full-time job for another. Bob began the Dartmoor Folk Festival, first at Wood before it settled in South Zeal, in which he revived competitions created by his grandfather. Necessary finance was raised by Bob and his team of willing helpers and he travelled miles to seek out suitable bands, dancers and entertaining acts. Since then, hundreds of original acts, dancers and bands have visited South Zeal. Thanks to Bob's perseverance, the dances his grandfather created and the traditions they both fostered are being carried forward by the young people.

Bob's services to folk music were appreciated by every audience he played for, and still are whenever the Kestor Rocky Waltz, Briarfield Jig, Ford Farm Reel, Pixie Jubilee Jig , Ripple of the Teign, or any of his music is heard. His services were recognised by the English Folk Dance and Song Society when awarding him its Gold Medal. The appreciation of the nation was expressed in 1989 when he was awarded the British Empire Medal.

Sticklepath Sports Club had been organising a traditional bonfire in the village for the enjoyment of parishioners and visitors on 5 November for some years when, in 1984, the Wren Trust, the Okehampton-based Arts Group ,were working with South Zeal Youth Club, and, according to legend, one Taffy Thomas suggested that the club should organise a story-telling fireshow.

Well versed in arts grants and community funding, Paul Wilson and Marilyn Tucker of Wren Trust also recognised the potential for the project to be combined with Sticklepath's annual bonfire. Their efforts, combined with those of creative artists, musicians, bonfire builders, lighting technicians and pyrotechnic personnel, established a new event in the area entertainment calendar when Guy Fawkes encountered Uncle Tom Cobley and his companions in a fantasy adventure, 'Widecombe Fair.' The show's reception ensured continuity, celebrated with a Birthday Cake storyline the following year. Since then the show has become an annual one, organised by its own committee; apart from the Sports and Social Club.

The Fireshow quickly developed its own traditions by including giant puppets, pageantry, groups, a torchlight procession, and music and songs woven into a spellbinding stage show performed on a gigantic bonfire; before it erupts in flame and fireworks illuminate the night sky. The area behind Finch Foundry continues to house the event, thanks to the support of the National Trust and the great many adults and children from the surrounding area who work voluntarily throughout the year to ensure its continuation.

Little is leaked about the storyline prior to bonfire night, and afterwards most people seemingly recall the spectacle rather than content but Lady Howard's Dog and the Chinese Pagoda of 1986 and '87 were less well remembered than Guy Fox, the 'ducky' Drake and the sinking in flames of a galleon during the Armada; but watched on this occasion in 1988 by over 1500 people.

This was also the year for another revival; and co-incidence? On 25 August 1988, the *Okehampton Times* proclaimed:

SOUTH ZEAL CARNIVAL BACK
Twenty years after it last rode through the streets of the village the South Zeal Carnival has been revived this year. Mrs Wendy Redstone, a moving spirit in the revival, said, "The first procession of which the present committee has detail of is the one of 1918. It is known that there was, as with other carnivals, a break in the period 1939-1945. It was re-started in 1948, lasted for about 20 years, and then the 20 year gap began until this year."

Kit Cornthwaite, a very much appreciated former landlord of the Kings Arms, encouraged a team of like minded people to help Wendy and the committee; Oxenham Arms regulars joined forces with local companies, farmers, traders, and individuals; ensuring Carnival Day, Saturday 3rd September, became a success and the event become re-instated in the area's entertainment calendar.

By that time the Players were beginning to think about their next panto and early the next year the dozen or so adult South Zeal Players found themselves among a cast of about 50 rehearsing for another production that included primary school pupils and youth club members. Thanks to the unstinting efforts of everyone, *The Crock of Gold* in March 1989, and also *Mean King Mouldybones* in 1990, ensured that, with public support meaning even standing room was taken, the company could continue to provide funds, equipment, and professional work skills too at times, to local organisations until the curtains came down on the brief panto era.

The Sticklepath Fireshow however had continued to annually illustrate Guy Fawkes' adventures... among the Planets in 1989, the Aztecs in 1990, and in the following years in Camelot, and in pantomime. During the next four years the shows drew increasingly large crowds, which required ever more vigilance with safety precautions, public parking and crowd control. Having joined the South Zeal Players for both the 1989 and the 1990 production, Jillyann Healey was used to crowd control, at least on stage, where she helped the entire company with her expertise as choreographer and encouraged and inspired the young ones to excel. She was later to lead the adult performers to new heights as their Director after the Players began to widen their repertoire to satisfy their need to include productions with a more adult appeal.

An 'Old Time Variety Show' in October 1990 set the Players off in new directions and group members again confirmed their abilities the following April with *Anything Goes*, a 1920s–30s revue directed by Jillyann Healey and Produced by Eileen Birch. The Players continued with an impressive list of productions:

Dec. 1991	Dickensian Christmas (inc. excerpts from Dickens)
Feb. 1992	Candlelight Cabaret (supper, songs & sketches)
Feb. 1993	*Peter Pan*
Oct. 1993	*Those Were The Days* (celebration of the '60s in Community Festival)
June 1994	*What About A little Drop 'o' Cider?* (for Parish Council centenary)
May 1995	*There'll Be Bluebirds* (celebrating the 50th anniversary of VE Day)
Sept. 1995	*Tom Pearse's Legacy* (for National Trust Centenary – Finch Foundry)

Two months later the grounds of Finch Foundry played host to the Sticklepath Fireshow with its story of 'Treasures of The Deep,' not only another scorching tale but also undoubtedly the tallest so far; the fire-set built by Barry Drewing and his crew was the biggest by far since the Fireshows began.

Over 30 local primary-school pupils gave up much of their half-term holiday for rehearsals and puppet-making workshops to ensure that the enormous puppets created by artistic director Hilary Gillespie could help unravel the mystery of Guy's involvement with an underwater world.

A cast and company exceeding 100 revealed the final secrets of the tale and the crowd witnessed Guy, clutching a king's ransom in jewels in his hands, engulfed in the volcanic destruction of Atlantis, and firework fuse-lighter, matchless Dave Denford, set off one of the finest firework displays ever seen in the village. A new and marshalled system for accommodating cars and parking, with support from the police, was required to cope with the growing number of visitors. When a similar crowd of around 3000 returned the following year, Guy was still up to his spectacular tricks in a Games Show and Lottery-based extravaganza filled with all-singing, all-dancing, large-than-life puppets, designed, constructed and choreographed by Hilary 'Tuppence a Yard' Gillespie.

The fireworks, from the Firework Company of Uffculme, were still under the control of Dave 'Safer than Houses' Denford, and Dave 'The Relay' Blencoe returned with even more lighting and sound equipment. Walter Shortage and the Hosepipe Banned, supplemented by Sam's Amazin' Keyboard and Strings added live music for the wide-eyed crowd admiring the giant set constructed once again by Barry 'A-pence a Foot' Dewing. Many people contributed to the 'family night out' but some in the area were concerned that the event was becoming a victim of its own success.

Earlier in 1996, in February, the South Zeal Players had confirmed their continuing success with a production by Eileen Birch, directed by Jillyann

Healey of *The Snow Queen*. In January 1998, with Jillyann as director, the group achieved new heights in Alan Ayckbourn's masterpiece *A Chorus of Disapproval*. Eileen Birch directed their 'Cabaret Evening' contribution to the WI buffet evening in May and John Candler more than capably directed the Players in Peter Gordon's *Out of Focus*.

In November 1999 the death of Jillyann Healey was a tragedy deeply felt not only by the Players, but by many other theatrical companies, both amateur and professional, and a great many members of the public, all of whom appreciated her work, her talent, and her dedication.

In their next production, *Snapshots*, in February 2000, the Players presented cinematic memories of the 20th century after which, in June, Eileen Birch produced and directed local school and village children in a short play presented during the Millennium Street Party.

During the mid-summer of 2000, with cottage fires still alight, the next Dartmoor Folk Festival consumed many hours of the organising committee's time. The success of the most recent Fireshow will hopefully secure its survival beyond the millennium year. It takes a month or more to construct the bonfire, honeycombed with passages and providing artist walkways, so, local people will soon be encouraged again to bring out their bulky rubbish, and local builders invited to add demolition material and anything that will burn; all behind a super 'stage' set that hides everything.

It is behind the scenes that the real work of entertaining the community takes place, and we recognise the values of the coffee mornings, bingo, pub quizzes, concerts, choral nights, jazz evenings, fayres and festivals, football, cricket, safari suppers, snooker, tennis, bowls, barn dances, exhibitions, talks, silent auctions, group meetings and many other activities. Rural communities have managed to entertain themselves for centuries so, when asked, 'what do you find to do in the country?' you have to smile, don't you?

The past inspires the present while securing the future. Broom-dancing tuition in Victory Hall during the Folk Festival weekend ensures the continuation of traditional dance.

Chapter 10
The Way it Was

The lives and times of people that knew much of the 20th century from personal experience, by working in the area, being born here, or arriving as evacuees fearful of their future, we are fortunate enough to be able to draw from recorded interviews, letters, notes, and our records of conversations held during the compilation of this book.

In the 1920s, on the day before her 15th birthday, Olive Hooper was taken on as a tweenie maid by Mrs Cooper, a wealthy lady, who lived at Great Tree, Sandypark, and whom Olive came to regard with respect, affection and enormous appreciation. A 'tweenie' worked between the ladies' quarters, and the kitchen quarters; she cleaned and might also learn to cook. As a tweenie maid Olive first earned five shillings per week (25p), and lived in; when she left eight years later she was earning £36 per year.

She had a nice big bedroom, and food and working clothes were provided. The housemaid's bedroom was next to hers, then came the parlour maid's, and then a door, between the workers' and the ladies' part of the house. Olive recalls:

I had to get up 6.30 and have a kettle of boiling water ready for the Lady. The housemaid had to take up the water and she often had to wake me up... it nearly always was half past six... There was a great big black stove - oven and everything for cooking - I had to black-lead that, then I lit the fire and got it all going. From 7 o'clock I went up into the ladies' quarters - I had the hall to do - a great big hall - all polished wood - always polished - with great big carpet in the middle. There was a door between quarters - linoleum where we were - and past the door there was all carpet... in the middle of the corridor... and wood strips down the sides that had to be polished.
I used Mansion polish... in a flat, red tin... and I used to use Zebo to clean the stove and Brasso to clean brass; they used Meppo in the north.

I used to come down and have breakfast at 8 o'clock, and helped the cook at 12, no earlier than that because I was working in the ladies' quarters - there was so much cleaning and polishing to do, the bathroom, a vestibule...The chauffeur there -

Frank Rogers - he could turn his hand to anything - the things he did - marvellous - brilliant man His was an easy job with only the lady - she went out in the car - 30 miles an hour - went to Paignton once a week in a Sunbeam, always a green Sunbeam...

Once a week I had a day off, but didn't get out before 3 o'clock... when I was first there I had to be back by 6.30. I walked to Chagford - the cook knew somebody there - I went in for a cup of tea, and then walked back again. When I got between 16 or 17 of course, I began to like the boys, and one time I promised to see so many I had to go home on me own because I didn't know who to go home with. They were lovely days.
We didn't have chaperones except when we went to dances - Jack worked in the garden and if we wanted to go to a dance - only if Jack went and took us - used to be the parlourmaid the housemaid and me - Jack had to take us - have a taxi - take us and bring us home again - he lived in the gardener's cottage - supposed to look after us. I was a bit wild, always up to some nonsense - just larking about. I had a good place and I stayed there for eight years and got married to Jack from there. [My lady said] "Olive, if you buy a white dress I won't have to pay for it, but if you buy a dress that you can wear afterwards I'll buy for it for you." My Lady was a lovely lady... I went and chose it for myself - it was beautiful dress, it was blue, right down to my ankles it was... and it had sleeves like lace, material and lace... and a little white collar inside and a little collar outside. She wasn't very happy that we got married - she wanted us to stay there and work see. All my family was up north... but not one of them could come down... in the days when life was very hard... the train journey... and we were a family of eight... I came from a family of eight... expensive... when they got on... and they were married.. they came down to see me a lot.

Olive and Jack went to live in South Zeal after their marriage.

Top: Frank Richards lived opposite the chapel.
Above: The flagpole destined for White Rock.

Mr Bill Adams, now living in Launceston, was kind enough to write to us. Born in 1924, he went to Sticklepath School from 1929 to 1936. He recalled:

We lived at Cross Cottage which was 1½ miles from Tongue End and my father worked for John Reddaway at Reddaway Farm. I walked approx fourmiles to school and if I got wet I was sent down to Finch's Foundry to dry out... it was of course much larger than it is now and a man named Tim Mallet used to lie on his stomach over a grinding wheel all day and every day just grinding hooks. My best friend at school was Colin Bowden... on various high profile days (i.e. St George's Day) we marched to the flagpole overlooking the village and hoisted the appropriate flag. I can remember at school being let out to watch the fair engines passing as that was very colourful and of course very slow. There was a chap who drove a steam lorry and when he passed me on the road he always threw out a cigarette packet containing cigarette cards. The lorries always filled up with water nearly up the top of the hill, past the quarry and Pixie Nook.

My headmaster was Frank Richards who lived in a cottage opposite the chapel. Things are flashing back and forth in my mind but I believe another teacher was called Miss Elston. Just before I left

Sticklepath School I was due to sit my scholarship at Okehampton Grammar School and were very poor and a bit tattered. On the Friday night before I sat Frank Richards took me to a shop in Okehampton and bought me a suit of clothes and I ended up looking like Lord Fauntleroy !

However that was the sort of person Frank Richards was, the kindest person ever but at the same time very strict.

Amy Bertram worked for the Kingsford-Lethbridge family. She recalls:

There were estate carpenters and masons then... but there was no electricity in the 20s... no hoovers - it was all brush and broom - rub an scrub. I remember the oak floors I had to polish. I started at 7.00am, with general housework, then there was the polishing, dusting, cleaning stair rods... and grinding coffee beans; I used to like that and I finished about 5 or 6p.m. There wasn't much time for recreation. but we went walking. We had dancing classes in Wood... Lovely... Mrs Edwards came from South Zeal and played concertina - beautiful music got the girls out to join the boys. Wood was lovely in those days... lovely lawns. We were not allowed to sit on the lawns every day - only at special times - we had to be careful. There was a little lake - and a rowing boat to row across the lake. I paid 6d. to go across once. My grandmother was a dressmaker, she could do anything... strip a dress to pieces and make another - put a collar and cuffs on. Did it for a lot of people - made men's shirts - half lining - long tails - [lots of] people came to her; there was a chapel down there at Taw Green... she used to play organ there.

Mr Avery was headmaster at our school. I walked in to school from Wood... often got wet... was dried off in front of fire. I got awful colds. Mr Avery very strict - always had stick under his arm - waiting for his chance. Some boys stood up to him... were rude to him... but he always got the better of them. There were four rooms. Miss Tucker, a relative of Mr Avery's, took sewing and knitting and things like that and Miss Read took the little ones... the babies they used to call them. She liked singing best - all kind of songs - war songs... 'Land of Hope and Glory' and that sort of thing. In the 1914 war...her brother joined up....came back after six or seven months - wounded on the Somme... a bullet in the wrist. He gave it to mother, and she kept it for years.

Dorothy Vanstone recalls living at Taw Green and walking to school although others walked 'from a good mile further on'. Some of her memories follow:

There was a range and the oven at school - we cooked pasties. Mr Heard was headmaster... he had a stick. I was given it once... for no reason at all! He changed the desks for tables and chairs - we did not like them. I was good at sewing. I worked at Crows Nest for six months then down at Wood for six months as parlourmaid in both places... went down to Elderton's in Sticklepath and stayed there three years -learned to cook with them. Winnie Roberts' mother was cook. I went across the road to get the water for the house - six days a week.

Met my husband when going to chapel at Taw Green - had a bike and rode there - Mother lived there... he worked on the farm with horses - horse-smith - with shire horses - ploughed the land, reaped the corn [and] sowed the land again.

Many people have been kind enough to spare their time to enable us begin to record their comments on various aspects of everyday life. Several parishioners passed comment on the topics of illness and childbirth:

I was ill once but no doctor came - Miss Stewart was very good to me and got me well.

... by the time the doctor came my son had been born - Nurse Holman [an] Irish lady brought my baby into the world, and others... She had several on the go. Nurse Holman was alright, she lived in South Zeal [and was] related to the Holmans, Bill Holman perhaps. not the one that later kept the shop.

My babies I had at home [and they were] delivered by Nurse Holman - I was a long time in labour with one... from Saturday to Thursday.

And on the politics of the area:

When I was young my father and my grandfather used to tell me how all the old men got drunk in South Zeal on voting day... they'd be wearing their rosettes - one was one thing... one was another.... Then they got drunk and set to fighting...

Shops in the villages:

Tailors?... my uncle was tailor in Sticklepath, next up from Taw River.

The Throwleigh road oil-man was George Garish [who had a] shop at the Old Store... lovely little shop... sold all sorts.... lovely shop... Pete and George Garish...

Of Zale Fair and other happy days:

There always used to be an Aunt Sally... pipe in his mouth... you had to try knock it out. And there were the girls... the Stanley girls... gypsy girls, who used to do the dancing - lovely they were - ever so interesting. They sold all sorts of things at Zale fair, rattling things.

I saw the Victory Hall foundation stone laid [see bottom of page] - Mr Stanbury from North Wyke laid the foundation stone [and} I saw it with another girl [names] Palmer... they were nice people - ever so nice...

The British Legion - I belonged to it once - I loved it - Mrs Jackson lived up behind Owlsfoot Garage... right up over... she was President... lovely meetings... lovely times. Once a year she had us all up there during the summer - made lovely junkets - I was always interested in eating!

... we went dancing in Victory Hall when the black soldiers were there. I danced with a black soldier - they were billeted here - some at Owlsfoot, some in South Tawton.

Then there were those who came as strangers, and found friends. When evacuees arrived, villagers, including Muriel Endacott and her stepmother, were asked to go to Victory Hall:

[it was] just like a market, all these children and several grown ups. We had a bigger house than most... with a bath - children there, mother and I didn't make any quick moves [and then] saw [a] bigger girl - asked if she had anywhere to go - 'No, but I would like to go with you, but I have my Mum as well' [she said]. [Her] mother was a teacher, but not like a teacher at all [and her] father was also a teacher. Mrs Styles with Peggy came to us [and] Mr Styles went to Broadclyst. Mrs Styles

The Foundation Stone being laid in preparation for Victory Hall in 1922.

Top right: *Charlie Curtis ready for war.*

Top left: *War time 'somewhere in England' and local people in the services and away from home keep their spirits up.*

Centre left: *Stagecraft learned from Mrs Clarke Gray was put to good use by Joyce Knapman (Worthington) entertaining forces friends in* Cinderella.

Above right: *For Maurice and Winnie Roberts it was a wartime wedding - the first in South Tawton.*

Above: *Charlie Curtis recalled that wartime friends, seen here outside their billet, were people you could trust with your life.*

☜ Memories of Wartime ☞

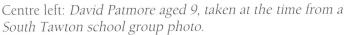

Top left: *Evacuee, David Patmore (10), with younger brother and cousin on Ramsley Common.*

Top right: *Evacuees in 1942 - years later many recall with gratitude the welcome they received; and the hard work on the farms.*

Centre left: *David Patmore aged 9, taken at the time from a South Tawton school group photo.*

Centre right: *St John's School, Walworth, photographed two days before they were evacuated to South Zeal on 22 September 1939.*

Above: *The Suez crisis brought tanks yet again to the old A30*

Right: *Territorials, including George Hooper and Albie Osborne.*

and Peggy stayed with us for a long time, until they took a vacant cottage. There were a lot of Polish people in the village, they were liked, and a handful of girls married polish men.

Letters added further memories, these from Mike Hawkins of Luton:

I write to set down as far as I can remember, my memories of my evacuated years to Devon. We lived in Battersea, my father working for the Gas Light and Coke Co., prior to joining the Army in 1940. My brother... and I were evacuated to Clannaborough Farm near Throwleigh at the end of 1939. I was under five years old but one of my clearest early memories is of the Endacott family and one of the farm workers, sitting around a large table with an oil lamp in the middle... I remember little of the first year or so probably due to my age, but we were treated very well as members of the family and on reflection our standard of living improved.

Clannaborough Farm was a large tenant farm, growing wheat and potatoes. It had cattle for milking, a large number of chickens, pigs, two working Shire horses and a tractor. There was a large orchard with many varied fruits and as such the farm was almost self-sufficient and we enjoyed a good and varied diet. Once a year we all picked wurtleberries (blueberries) which grew wild on the moors in the summer. [We] also used to picnic at the place I think called Shelley Pool.

Initially my brother and I attended a school at Providence and later, when he was older, my brother went to school at Chagford. The school at Providence was one large room with a partition in the middle and was attended by both the local children and the evacuees... the head teacher was a Mrs Amy Harvey... the school had about 20 pupils from age five upwards.

We are regularly had a lift to school from Throwleigh village in a converted biscuit delivery van but later had to walk there and back. From about 1943, I used to bring in the cows on the way home from school, for milking. We used to attend church on a regular basis, alternating between Throwleigh, Gidley and South Tawton. I used to attend Throwleigh church on some Sunday afternoons for Sunday school lessons... the Endacott family had family pews near the front. At one of the churches, I used to hand pump the organ bellows for use during the service.

Some time in 1940/41, my mother and youngest brother were evacuated to Higher Poltimore... the owner, Mrs Elliott, was Mr Endacott's sister (Mr Elliott was an Army captain). We used to walk and visit my mother on most

weekends. My sister was born in Okehampton in August 1942. During my time at Clannaborough I remember various things but not necessarily in the correct chronological order.

I used to deliver milk once a week on Saturdays to a Miss Walker, who lived near West Week. I also used to attend a big house near Spains Bridge (I think that's the name, it's a first Bridge from Clannaborough towards South Zeal) and got 6d for grinding coffee beans. A Mr Osborne who lived on the outskirts of Throwleigh, used to cut our hair and he was also the local shoe repairer, both being carried out in his garden shed. He had three daughters and lived next door to the Hill family who had a son called Norman (nicknamed 'Rabbit').

We had many walks across the moor during the summer and vaguely remember a reservoir created by flooding and a few buildings [which] could be seen below the surface.

A farmer at Throwleigh (I think named Polson) used to makes scrumpy and sell it from his farmhouse as there was no inn or public house there. At Clannaborough then, there was no electricity or running hot water and any hot water for washing or bathing had to be heated over the open kitchen fire and carried in buckets upstairs.

There was a lull in the bombing of London and we went back home for a few months but returned to Clannaborough, and my mother to Higher Poltimore, when the flying bombs (doodlebugs) started. Some time late in '43 or early ''44, the Americans camped on the moors adjacent to Clannaborough and we supplied them with hot water, eggs and other items. I remember they gave me chocolate, gum and I was allowed to watch films on their mobile cinema. They obviously moved on after a while, no doubt on transit in preparation for D-Day.

This reminds me about when we all visited the cinema in Okehampton to see the new film 'Lassie Come Home.' On the way back, the car had a puncture on top of the hill leading down to Sticklepath and I remember being given a mug of cocoa by Land Army girls from the nearby farm.

Once a year all evacuees were entertained in a large house near Throwleigh, with extensive gardens by Mr and Mrs Rashley and I think this is now known as Throwleigh Manor. As a Londoner I had never seen large lawns and statues of birds before... I seem to recall we had a regular gymkhana in the village, with the usual stalls containing home-baked items and marching and gunnery display by the Home Guards.

Ploughing competitions were held and one near South Tawton was for both tractors and horses. Once a year we all went on to the moors to round up wild sheep for shearing and dipping. The shears were all driven from one engine, which also ran the threshing machine, mill and other machinery in the farm outhouse.

One of the occasional farm workers who lived nearby at Clannaborough cottage was found asleep in the hedge early one morning near his home; evidently he had walked to the Rising Sun had some scrumpy and didn't quite make it home.

We celebrated VE night in Throwleigh in May 1945 but had left Clannaborough and were back home for VJ night in August. To summarize my memories, they are... of being well looked after, attending church, school, farm smells, harvesting wheat, collecting eggs and generally having a happy time.

I was personally looked after by Mr Endacott's sister, who was known by me as Auntie Marion, and I suppose she became my substitute mother whilst living there.

One evening, a visitor returning to the village gave his time to telling us of his memories of the area. Like Mr Hawkins, other evacuees have written to us, or to others and local people have also added their reminiscences from all of which we take the following extracts:

When war was declared we shot out of London expecting bombing to start, and went back when it didn't, then there was another scare and we got sent to Horsham, and then got sent back again; and then the bombing started and we got packed off to Waterloo to catch a train. It was all bewildering at times. I remember the train from Waterloo... it was smo... dusty... then we arrived at Okehampton and came out to South Zeal, to Mrs Osborne's. I was intrigued by her door, it was cut in half and I'd never seen a stable door.

At home the trams were going up and down a hill all the time... when the air-raid warning started up they used to stop on the hill... there was a terrible grinding noise... it was frightening. the town was noisy... then we were in a village that was so quiet... didn't roam far from the house... the bakery [was] most the impressive thing... The bakery smell... beautiful... pasties... Devonshire buns.

An evacuee at Woodball recalled:

Americans often called, landing their flying jeep, a two-seater aeroplane, in field opposite Mrs and Mrs Lashbrooks. Woodball was lonely, the wind was very noisy... we went to Okehampton School in a brown utility bus... a new bus... but you really felt it, there was nothing soft about it... it brought

us to the top of the lane. We didn't go out at night.... frightening.... they had no lights in London but it was darker here... and we were not country people. I wondered what was lurking in hedges.

In South Tawton, one unlucky evacuee was caught red handed:

... pinching Mrs Brimblecombe's gooseberries... Mrs Moore saw us and split on us... Mrs Violet Moore... she had a dinky little shop... the doorbell clanged. I used to rush in to buy Spam, corned beef, and a packet of cigarettes 'for mother' but it wasn't. We got our sweet ration there... there were two glass display cases... home made ones.... It was a lovely shop.

The same shop also impressed Diana England:

As soon as you opened the door it was the most wonderful smell, [an] Aladdin's cave - I can't describe the smell but it was just lovely. Even as a child I noticed it... not the smell of sweets, not of leather goods, it just had its own smell. She sold pots and pans - dishcloths, didn't give up till the 60s. I should think [she] sang in the choir - dear old lady, a spinster all her life [with] glasses, grey hair... the shop was absolutely full, just enough room to stand there and be served - she just had enough room to stand behind the counter and serve you - and she had just enough room for a little passageway to go through to her living quarters - a real Auntie Wainwright's - yes a good description.

But, to return to the reminiscences of our evacuee with a ponchant for gooseberries:

There was a transit camp in South Tawton... Canadians... in field before the new house where vicar lives. They used to have Whist drives in the hall - dances there too - and the troops came down.

On hobbies, one memory was of model making and egg collecting:

I made aircraft models - balsa wood kits from Okehampton. They were quite big... supposed to fly but never did. You'd wind up the elastic and they shot along the ground. but they were precious. [we also] went bird nesting with local lads - egg collecting [and] collected lot - only taking one - it was not illegal then.

It was not unusual for evacuees to return home, often

Top: *Sharing food in wartime came naturally to some, and everyone shared work in the field.*
Above: *Some recall that after the war the local blacksmith soon became mobile, taking his trade on the road to visit clients by appointment.*

only for brief visits though, and what they found there stayed in their memories. When David Patmore was in the village he told us that he:

... went back to London, but the V1s started so back I came to Ramsley... to Pinecroft... but, now I see it and I'm sure the door has been moved. Our flat in London was in a block... the doors and windows blown in... the windows got blown in countless times. Incendiary bombs came in through the roof and went right down through the flats, but there was more damage to the roof caused by the ack ack guns... on the cricket field opposite.

One of the first main casualties of David's war was the shelter he was supposed to stay in. It suffered a direct hit and everybody in it was killed. Depite the horrors in the city, however, he was not immune to homesickness:

I still got homesick and once started walking to London from Ramsley; I was picked up by a man in a car who brought me back. This was a sanctuary - in London in the air-raid shelters you weren't really sheltered it was a psychological thing - we

were safe here. Tommy Hall and his brother Bobby were at Zeal Head. In South Tawton there was Lennie Lewis, and Willie his younger brother. Freddie Tomlinson was another friend... he worked at Viger Farm. worked hard there... but there was no cruelty - none of the evacuees were unhappy. The quarry was a lovely place - hundreds and [there were] hundreds of jackdaws there - open undulating ground [and] no trees... mossy. I went rabbiting there, with George Hooper, the postman setting up tra [and] we sold the rabbits.

There was a plane that came down... but several people can't remember the Wellington plane landing opposite Minnimores [on] the other side of the road and other side of bridge - the field, past the one with bit of a slope, the one further in. it looks like a landing field. All the children went... they let us into it - had a go at the guns, didn't fire them of course [as they were] empty. The plane had damaged undergear... it belly flopped. I think there was an injured airman on it... shot at [but] not injured through landing. The plane was taken away within 48 hours... wings off... on to the back of a lorry - back to be repaired I suppose.

When added together, some of the briefest of memories can not only clearly conjure up pictures of past times but also provide valuable information. One person recalled how 'A German plane came low over South Tawton, engines roaring, being chased by British plane. A boy slung half a brick up at the German.' Another remembered 'children making their own amusements, rolling bike wheels, noisily, around the lanes.' 'Propaganda films' were put on 'warning that 'careless talk costs lives,' and that, 'coughs and sneezes spread diseases;' at least one of which should be revived!'

One memory of childhood was of 'a raft on the Quarry Lake supported by four tin drums - one leaking' and of being 'unaware, pushing it out to the middle, nearly getting drowned frantically peddling back.'

'The best thing about the villages' claimed one of our contributors, 'was that there was nothing bad about them!' 'Sunday school in 1945' provided poignant memories for some. 'Nearing the end of war [there were] hundreds and hundreds of bombers coming over - so noisy - pulling gliders. People jump[ed] up and down with glee, waving them on.'

There are also wartime memories of "Gas masks, being checked in Victory Hall and babies cocooned inside a box-like mask. Helping to make cider in the cider house (now Stable Cottage) in South Tawton' was another recollection, 'with a horse turning the press. I was sad to see the orchards go.' 'Shire horses were used on the farm... Freddie used to plough up the mangle wurzels [and I rode the horse back [to

South Zeal in 1904.

the field], fed and cleaned it.' There are memories of very cold winters, and 'one bad wartime winter when we couldn't see over the hedges.' The house next to the Seven Stars was apparently taken over by Army officers and sergeants. and people woke at night 'as tanks went through the village – troops in transit camps moved out quickly.' On one occasion, 'Back lane, the road from Zeal Head to Sticklepath, was lined with vehicles - bren-gun carriers, tanks and lorries sheltered by tall trees. Walking down there in the dark took some courage.'

'Carbon tape ribbons - dropped by the Germans - were draped over telephone lines and masses of it strewn across the field past school. From the top of the church tower one could see Exeter burning with the glow of the fires lighting up the sky.'

Memories of farm life include:

... keeping out of the way of the couple of people using hand scythes to cut corn around the outside of the field to allow the tractor and threshing machine in. Halfway through the threshing, the rabbits ran out and were chased, bashed, and caught by us kids.

Finally – as tributes to writers and researchers of the past that influenced and inspired us we have the recollections of one Ethel Legge-Weeks. In 1902, Ethel recalled having, some six years previously, visitedTaw Green with 'old Mr Mark Cann' who remembered that a 'John Weekes' used to live at Mullins Mill. She noted being shown, on the left-hand side of the road approaching Taw Green from the north, on a corner opposite Taw Green farmhouse, the foundations of 'a cottage once occupied by a John Weekes.' Tradition has it that Weekes was reputed to be a 'witch' and that even 'Old Andrew Arnold' never passed his door without repeating the Lord's Prayer, backwards.

They seem to have been enemies anyway, due mainly to the ownership of North Wyke by Andrew Arnold, a property to which John Weekes continually claimed to have better right. An indenture of 1819 confirms that a certain 'John Weekes' was the tenant of a property known as Moleys, or Mullins Mill. An indenture of 1840 indicates that a John Hooper was by then the tenant of Mullins Mill (Ethel concluded that the cottage could never have been a mill).

We feel privileged to be given access to private letters, that may or may not have been answered. These include the following:

Dear Mr. St Leger Gordon,
I have just read your book Under Dartmoor Hills *and enjoyed it very much. South Zeal was the one I was most immediately connected with, the first time was 1912. My father motored us down there to spend a holiday at Mr and Mrs Madders farm on the South Tawton road. He stopped at the Cawsand Beacon Hotel and found that it was run by a second cousin called Jim Trace. In conversation with him it transpired that my great-grandfather had owned the Tin mine on South Tawton road. Could you shed any further light on this subject? I would be most grateful if you could.*

My next visit was about 1924 when I was in practice as Dental Surgeon at Kingsbridge where I spent three most enjoyable years. I next visited it in 1948 when I hoped to show three friends an ideal village but was I disappointed. The golden thatch and pink distempered walls had all gone. They were replaced with tin roofs and grey walls. Even the Cawsand Beacon was taken by Lloyds ank. Bye the way did you ever know Chris Sharp the Dr who had a practice in the bar parlour of the pub at Sticklepath ?
Lawrence A. Trace, Boxmoor, Herts.

We wonder... did anyone?

Local area moorland has so much that attracts young visitors, said Mark and Debbie Lewis visitors with their family from Massachusetts.

Throwleigh: those with long memories say little has changed over the years, photo c.1906.

The area's most 'remembered' shop. Miss Hill, c.1905, is standing in the doorway of the South Tawton Shop that was to become regarded as real wonderland by later generations

Sticklepath Post Office.

A workshop photo found among local papers but, as yet, it is unidentified – can anyone remember this forge?

Harvesting taking place at the 'Golden Row' field at North Wyke on 22 August 1902.

An area of Sticklepath village, c.1913.

We Will Remember Them

24th Field Ambulance 8th Division

I am still getting on all right, and am proud to think that I am doing my bit for my King and Country. I cannot understand how the young men at home do not come forward and do their bit with us. The experience I have had during the time I have been out here is small compared with hundreds of other men, but I have seen enough to convince me that the nation we are fighting is a mad lot. For instance, the church in this village where we are billeted is smashed to pieces, there is not a sound window in the whole building, and the roof is completely smashed in, leaving only the bare walls, even the clock is smashed to pieces; and nearly every town and village that we have been to has been the 'bull's-eye' for them.

There are hundreds of innocent people's houses around here smashed to pieces, some with all their furniture still in them, but very seldom we find anything that will be of any use again. Of course you have read about the great battle that took place in this district some few weeks ago (Neuve Chapelle), that was the most exciting experience of my life, and I don't want to go through such a time again. For days and nights we were carrying wounded, catching a few hours' sleep and a bit of rest when we... got the chance. We got relieved at the end of four days, and we were jolly glad when the time came, because we were all dead beat; we came back to our billets and had a rest, then we went back to the trenches again, but it was much quieter then.

I am glad to say I have enjoyed good health during the time I have been out here; we have to look after ourselves very carefully, because we never know where we have to sleep. We have slept in a barn, stables, and all kinds of places, but all the men of our unit have been pretty free from sickness.

A LETTER RECEIVED IN 1915 BY VERA WESTLAKE IN RESPONSE TO THE GIFT OF SOCKS
WHICH THE LITTLE GIRLS, UNDER MISS COUNTER'S DIRECTION,
SENT TO MEMBERS OF THE DEVON REGIMENT.

No 5 Infantry Base, France.

My Dear little Vera,

It is with the greatest of pleasure that I write you these few lines thanking you so much for the splendid pair of socks that it was my good luck to receive to-day. It was so very good of you young girls to deny yourselves sweets, etc., and saving your half-pennies to buy wool, thereby enabling you, with teacher's help, to do something that you must have liked doing very much. I must congratulate you on the way that the socks were knitted, and for such a young girl I think it is magnificent. Referring to mistakes, I can find none; and the cigarettes, which I soon found after reading your letter, were splendid. There is nothing so good to a soldier as a few cigarettes, and once again I must beg to offer my most sincere thanks. Regarding your wishes, we hope that they will come true, and we shall come out victorious again. So now little girl I thank you again and send best wishes for your health, and may your work bring prosperity.

Your soldier friend Sergt.————— 1st Devon Regt.

P.S. No doubt you will be pleased to hear that I am a Devonshireman man, my present and past home being Barnstaple, N. Devon.

MR GEORGE VIGERS RECEIVED THE FOLLOWING LETTER FROM THE KING:

31st March, 1915
Privy Purse Office,
Buckingham Palace.

Sir,

I have the honour to inform you that the King has heard with much interest that you have at the present moment six sons serving in the Army and Navy. I am commanded to express to you the King's congratulations, and to assure you that His Majesty much appreciates the spirit of patriotism which prompted this example, in one family, of loyalty and devotion to their Sovereign and Empire.

I have the honour to be sir,
Your obedient servant,

F.W. PONSONBY
Keeper of the Privy Purse

The King also sent a letter to Mr Kennett, expressing his sympathy with him at the sad loss of his son.

THOSE FROM OUR VILLAGES WHO FELL SERVING THEIR GOD AND COUNTRY GAVE
THEIR LIVES THAT WE MIGHT LIVE IN FREEDOM.

THE GREAT WAR 1914–1919

John Henry Barkwell	William Henry Bowden
James Box	John Brimblecombe
Samuel Cann	William Endacott
Alfred Hellier	Ernest Hellier
Archibald Roger Huggins	Percy William Bishop Kennet
Thomas Lethbridge	Benjamin Albert Mallett
William Henry May	Samuel Pearse
Thomas Powlesland	Cecil Rowell
Richard Allan Stansbury	Samuel Vigers
Thomas Vigers	Samuel Westaway
Albert Norman White	Frederick William Woolland

THE SECOND WORLD WAR 1939–1945

Phillip George Chapple	James Cottle
Reginald John Evely	Geoffrey Ford
William Ernest Keslake	Richard Lethbridge
Donald Edward Pitcher	Alfred John Taylor
Albert James Wright	

We Will Remember Them

Chapter 11
Gleanings from a Rich History

As any collector will confirm, it is difficult to dispose of items of interest and, for us, this applies to pieces of information that we have come across or others which have been drawn to our attention. Our book contains only a very small proportion of the material we have collected regarding the area in which we live; and that material continues to grow. Never have we given a talk on folklore or local history to a group without coming away with some interesting piece of information to add to our collection. Our conversations with the inimitable Douglas Mounce on Radio Devon have brought forth questions from listeners and prompted others to send us information. For all of this we are indeed extremely grateful but our collection of information started with notes and newspaper cuttings that caught our attention. It is our hope that this chapter will encourage others to gather more gleanings from history and create their own scrapbooks of the past. Even recent facts, still reasonably accessible, may not be known to many and an old report might correct, clarify, or add to our picture of the past; just a snippet can open up old pathways that cry out for investigation.

A relatively recent short report about a local conservation group that quickly earned the respect of the community as well as its appreciation will inform historians in the future... if the report is not lost:

Sticklepath and Okehampton Conservation Group (STOC) was established in 1991 as a result of a community project at Finch Foundry, Sticklepath. It was necessary to rebuild a double dry-stone wall taking a footpath through from the back of the foundry to Billy Green. Tuition was arranged and volunteers from the local residents. Okehampton College, Kelly College and The Leaze Centre for students with learning difficulties all helped to complete the project.

As a follow up to this venture, and the enthusiasm and satisfaction it gave all concerned, the STOC group was formed.

The aim of the group is to help improve the environment in and around Okehampton and surrounding districts by identifying and developing conservation work required by the community.

We wish to achieve this by encouraging the commitment of local people who want to learn about, care for, and work at improving the local environment in practical ways. The group is open to people regardless of age or experience, sex, background, or disability. It offers constructive and valuable opportunities to those who may be disadvantaged or unemployed and it gives the satisfaction of being able to do something positive to improve the local environment in carrying out necessary tasks that in most cases would not otherwise be done.

STOC is based at Finch Foundry, which is now run by the National Trust and is affiliated to the British Trust for Conservation Volunteers and where appropriate we can use their expertise for tuition purposes. Other experts, e.g. from the Forestry Commission, are also consulted to teach specific skills or co-ordinate particular projects.

We would only add that new members are always welcome.

Below: *Ian Bowker and STOC members appreciatmg that ancient walls, restored by the group of conservationists, very efficiently continue to provide shelter.*

Above: *STOC, the Sticklepath-based conservation group, tackle all kinds of work*

Beyond the headlines, local 'reports' to be found in old newspapers can often contain gems of information:

WATER WARNING BY CHURCH BELL
SOUTH ZEAL OBJECTION
T0 NOVEL METHOD
Criticism of the method adopted to acquaint South Zeal residents with the times when the water supply is turned off was forthcoming at the annual meeting on Saturday of Okehampton Rural District Council. In a letter Miss A. Lee complained that the pressure of the 'supply' was irregular, and referred to the fact that the church bell was rung when the supply was to be turned off. The letter continued: 'The only use for the church bell that I have known is to call to prayer. How is one to distinguish between the bell's normal use and its use for preventing cleanliness, which is supposed to be next to Godliness?' It was stated that it would be impossible to go to every individual with information 'as to when the supply would be interrupted and so the church bell was rung. A now plentiful supply existed and inconvenience to residents had lessened.' It was decided to reply to the letter, pointing out that the supply was now quite satisfactory and that the Council were taking steps to increase the supply in the event of a drought.
Western Morning News, *24 April 1932.*

In 1463 a murder was committed at Tawton Fords, attributed to one John of Ireland. While the existence of such a person in the county is disputed the question that remains is whether or not mistaken identity caused this denial since records show that one Ric. Irishe and his wife Isot held a tenement and 32 acres of land nearby.

In 1827 a case of fraud connected with Ford Farm came to a terrible conclusion:

EXECUTION OF JOHN ORCHARD
John Orchard, jnr, convicted at the Devon Assizes, of uttering a forged and counterfiet deed with intent to defraud, was executed at the drop in front of the County Prison, on Monday last. From the time of his condemnation he had devoted his time to prayer, and in preparation for leaving this world, admitting he had down a very wrong, but to the last, speaking of this offence as a matter not deserving such severe punishment; – in other quarters, however, it was thought differently of and strenuous exertions of his friends to save his life failed of effect. He took leave of his father a few days after the trial, and on Friday last, of his three eldest children by his present wife, the eldest
under 7 years of age. On Sunday he attended divine worship with his fellow prisoners, and with ten others received the Sacrament; on this occasion he desired the following verses, which he had selected as suitable to his situation and frame of mind, might be permitted to be sung; – his request was readily at acceded to, and the whole of the prisoners assisting him in going through it. –

> *When guilt distracts my labouring breast,*
> *Justice enraged and wrath I see,*
> *Thy Cross alone I seek for rest,*
> *And fix my hope, O Lord On thee*
> *Secured in Christ, th' eternal rock,*
> *No angry storms, no angry sea*
> *Can e'er my expectations shock,*
> *My hope is fix'd, O Lord, on thee*
> *Oft when death's awful gloomy veil*
> *affrighted nature dreads to see,*
> *What thought would then my heart assail*
> *Did I not hope, O Lord in thee*
> *But I can never, never sink,*
> *My faith a wreck can never be,*
> *Boldly I stand on Jordan's brink,*
> *And sing, 'My hope, O Lord, is in thee.'*

In the afternoon and this day he took his final leave of his wife; (who had went ahead and infant, the youngest of her four children), his daughter by his first wife, about 21 years of age, and an elderly female, understood to be in near relative of his wife. The prisoner conducted himself with becoming fortitude through this trying scene, and gave such directions as he considered necessary for the future disposal of his family.

When visited on Monday morning he was found in prayer, and appearances bespoke his having spent the principal part of the night in this way; he was early attended by the Revd Mr Chave, Chaplain of the prison, who had been constant in his attendance on him from the time of condemnation. The Revd Mr Burgess, a Wesleyan minister, who had constantly visited the prisoner, and his brother Mr Paul Orchard, understood to be a minister in the Wesleyan connexion, were also early at the prison, where they remained till within a few minutes of the fatal hour of twelve, the prisoner exhibiting up to this time equal firmness with that he had previously displayed, but as a moment drew near for ascending the platform his fortitude foresook him, and a considerable time elapsed ere with the assistance of two sheriff's officers he walked down the path-way from the governor's house; his eyes were closed and his ejaculations were incessant; his dress was that of a man on his farm – fustain jacket and trowsers.

While being ironed and pinioned in the press

room, he appeared scarcely conscious of what was passing, continuing his ejaculations without the smallest intermissions; the support of the officers was again necessary in ascending the steps, and been placed on the machine; the Chaplain in vain waited several minutes for the usual signification of the prisoner's being ready to join in the last service, when seeing his state, the Chaplain mercifully commenced the service, and all being ready, as he had nearly closed the service for the dead the bolt was drawn, the platform fell, and in a few moments life appeared to be extinct. The body after hanging the usual time was cut down, and on Tuesday morning at five o'clock placed in a hearse, to be removed to South Zeal for interment. —

Orchard was about 50 years of age, is said to be a native of South Zeal, but had lived many years as a farmer in the adjoining parish of South Tawton, and a few weeks previous to his apprehension had moved into St. Thomas, adjoining this city; — he is understood to have been held in estimation by many who knew him as a pious man, and it is said occasionally officiated as a Minister among the Methodists.

A vast concourse of spectators among whom were a considerable number of persons from the country, witnessed the execution.

Newspaper report, 18 April, 1827.

Documents relating to a specific property often provide an insight into the past. Jenny and Peter Brotherton own what once was the London Inn, South Zeal. Sharing with us a translation of the following document they take us back almost 250 years:

Devon)   *Be it remembered that on the 5th Day of Sept 1764 -*
To wit)   *James Lethebridge of the Parish of South Tawton in the sd (said) County, victualler (lnn keeper crossed out) and William Underhill of the same Inn Keeper (Miller crossed out) personally came before us two of his Majesty's Justices of the Peace for the sd (said) County and Acknowledge themselves to offer the sum of ten Pounds each to be made and levied on their goods and Chattles, Lands, and tenements respectively to the life of our Sovereign Lord the King - his heirs and successors - if the said James Lethebridge or the sd (said) William Underhill shall make default in the Condition Underwritten. The condition of this recognizance is such that whereas the above bounden James Lethebridge and William Underhill are licenced to keep two Common Inns and Ale-houses (each separate) for one Year from the 5th day of September present in the house where James Lethebridge now dwelleth*

- and William Underhill in the house known by the name of the London Inn - in the Parish of South Tawton - If they the said James Lethebridge and William Underhill shall keep and maintain good order and rules, and shall suffer no disorder nor unlawful games to be used in their said houses nor in any outhouse, yard, garden or backside thereunto belonging during the sd (said) term then this recognizance shall be void - Taken and Acknowledged the day and year above written before us - two of his Majesty's Justices of the Peace for the sd (said) County

(signed) Geo. Hunt J. Baring

We recognise and regret that little detail has been included by us about local families of historical note. The Battishulls, the Oxenhams, the Weekes, Finch, et al, they really deserve a publication devoted entirely to their exploits. A 'Coram Rege Roll' of the King's

Right: *The London Inn, South Zeal, once served travellers of the coaching era; photograph, 1904.*

Below: *Re-erection of the Oxenham Cross, South Tawton.*

Bench, dated '22-23 Charles II', bears record that Richard Weekes, of North Weeke, in the County of Devon, was held in goal, for being in debt. In return for a loan of £40, Richard had given a bond to a Mr William Jolly, gentleman, but not honoured the agreement. Only the local people probably knew the London gaol in which Richard Weekes resided, with normal fees paid. In 1811 it became the Marshalsea Prison that Dickens brought to the attention of his international readership in *Little Dorrit.* Alongside Marshalsea prison lay the burial ground of St George's in the Borough; and in the 1670-71 registers of that church, beneath the heading 'Burials' the name recorded on 5 February is 'Richard Week's, K.B.' There is further evidence that Richard died 'not worth a groat', as one note indicates, while another confirms that it was necessary to take up a 'gathering' for the deceased, a collection, made to defray the debtor's funeral expenses.

Old recipes have a fascination, or perhaps it's just that special treats remain as fascinating today as when they were enjoyed by our ancestors if we follow their guidance. In mediaeval days Easter biscuits and Destiny cakes were enjoyed locally but it seems that brandy in the biscuits was a Napoleonic variation. The following is a recipe for Easter Biscuits:

4 oz. Butter.	*4 oz. Sugar.*
2 Egg yolks.	*1 Egg white.*
2 oz. Currants.	*10 oz. Flour.*
1 teaspoon Brandy.	*Castor Sugar.*

1. Cream fat and sugar.
2. Beat in egg yolks.
3. Add brandy and fruit.
4. Work in flour, with a very little milk (only if needed) to make a soft paste.
5. Roll out and cut into big rounds (bigger than the usual biscuit size).
6. Bake in a moderately hot oven 15-20 minutes.
7. After 10 minutes, brush the biscuits with a little egg white.
8. Sprinkle with caster sugar.
Serve when cool, if you can wait.
The earliest Easter biscuits were 'quartered,' marked with a cross in a similar manner to hot cross buns that came later.

On birthdays, St Valentine's day and All Hallows Eve, the favourite treats were Destiny Cakes. The hot oil that is used is dangerous, so the following recipe is definitely not one for children to try; let an experienced cook do the work, and enjoy the results:

These elderberry funnel cakes are made with batter that is passed through a funnel or tube, to form letters, or 'divination' shapes.

3 eggs, beaten well   2 cups milk
1/2 teaspoon salt   4 cups flour
2 teaspoons, or slightly less, baking powder
A funnel or pastry tube with nozzle measuring 1/2" in diameter
1/2 cup elderberry preserves, or plum jam
6 tablespoons honey
2 cups vegetable oil for 'deep frying' in a fryer

1. Beat the eggs well, then add the salt. Stir the eggs briskly into the milk.
2. Stir the baking powder into the flour.
3. Mix most of the milk and the eggs with the flour. Keep a little milk/egg mixture aside.
4. Add the elderberry preserves, or plum jam, to the mixture. (The consistency ought to resemble a thick pancake batter.) If the batter produced is too thick to easily run through the funnel or pastry tube, carefully add more of the milk and egg mixture. If the batter is too thin to hold its shape... add a small extra amount of flour.
5. Heat the oil in a deep, wide, frying pan.
6. Pipe into the oil the fruit batter making initials, designs, or imaginative shapes.
7. Fry until golden.
8. Remove carefully from oil. Drain, drizzle lightly with honey.
Destiny Cakes are best served warm.

DID THE PUNISHMENT FIT THE CRIME?

In Sticklepath School, corporal punishment expired in 1962 but for half a century or more two strokes of the cane, usually on the hand, had been deemed necessary at times to deal with the top ten crime categories; and more. The cane came out first and foremost for 'Inattention,' then for 'Playing about and bad behaviour,' somewhat surprisingly ahead of 'Hitting or Bullying' while 'Fighting' was closely followed by 'Disobedience' at number five in the crime charts. Closely bunched came 'Neglecting work,' 'Talking' and 'Bad work,' with 'Throwing ink, stones, or books' remaining well ahead of that most antisocial crime 'Laughing aloud,' causing more than a little misery at number ten in the corporal categories. Those predecessors of some of today's local adults that did not achieve the heights of top ten crime were still not exactly rank outsiders in the punishment stakes when it was possible to be caned for committing the next most popular offences; 'making a loud noise, blowing a whistle, whistling, or blowing a trumpet,' or 'coming late owing to playing about,' 'interfering with next boy' or 'going into the Girls' Yard.'

Then there were cane-earning crimes that appear to be inexplicable; 'washing without permission' being one of them. Surely any child having committed the act voluntarily was more worthy of a reward than a caning; but there were also the crimes of 'tickling each other,' 'interfering with new boy,' and 'eating nuts' that also warranted the maximum penalty. Prompt punishment was applied with the aid of a cane for 'riding a pony over a girl and injuring her' yet 'sitting on top of desk' hardly seems to have warranted the cane, unless there was another pupil shut inside perhaps, but 'pushing threader into boy's nose' was probably inviting trouble. Corporal punishment in schools has been consigned to history but would the teacher who could see no wrong in caning two culprits for 'bad language,' understand the 'progress' made in modern literature, so called, and today's obscenity-ridden casual conversations?

Adult conflicts down the ages can often be placed in the 'pay up - or else' category where claims are made before a court; it is the outcome that often remains elusive where the records are concerned:

In 1287, Edward I was still counting the cost of having defeated Llywelyn ap Gruffud and annexing the Principality of Wales a few years earlier. He had already instituted the wool subsidy as a source of useful revenue, which hit West Country farmers and exporters heavily, and was not inclined to let a penny what was his by law pass by his coffers. Edmund, Earl of Cornwall, witnessed in the Calendar Rolls an order to the Sheriff of Devon instructing him to secure 12 shillings from John de Valletorta (Wyk) for yearly rent of land in Comewell near la Wyk. The land had been leased to Alured de la Porte but he had been hanged for felony and the king had learned from the Inquisition taken by the Sheriff into the felon's affairs that the land had been returned to the king's hands for a year and a day. Since the hanged man had held the land of the said John de Wyk, the king correctly considered that John de Wyk ought answer to him for a year and a day's rent; and instructed the Sheriff to collect it.

Some family names keep recurring in cases, which opens another avenue of investigation for anyone inclined to consider local conflicts further. The following relates to a case of 1798 described as being 'on behalf of Mr John Damerel':

Mr. John Steere in his lifetime was seized in his demesne as of fee simple of & in the manor of South Tawton, holden of the king, in free socage, To which there belongs a court Baron, though not annually kept. There are also belonging to this manor 32 tenants who hold their tenements to them & their heirs forever, paying out of each tenemt a certain yearly chief-rent, & the best beast for an heriot for each tenement on the death of a free tenant dying seized.

By his last will (26th Aug. 1789) the sd J. Steere devised all his manors, mess. lands, tenmts etc. (of which the manor of S. T. is parcel) unto James Lethbridge & John Lillisant... in trust (subject to certain annuities) to the use of the testator's grandson, John Damerel... etc. (proved 13 Aug, 1792) and the sd J. Damerel as the first tenant for years is now in "perception" of the rent & profits of this manor. Mr. John Codrington, one of the free tenants, died seized in fee of two tenemts belonging, to this manor, called Higher-Cessland & Lower Cessland & by will devised same in trust to W son of W. Nation of Exeter, banker, & Bartholomew Parr, as tenants (in common?). That on the death of Mr. Codrington one best beast of each of the two tenemts were seized... [because the trustees were seized of both moieties in common].

Question: Ought one or two heriots to have been claimed? If anyone has any idea how long the lawyers took to settle the case, and what the eventual result was, we should be pleased to hear from them.

In the year 1815:

William Long Oxenham was seized in fee of six estates of belonging to this manor, which paid certain annual chief rents thereto viz: For West Nymph 8s. Trendlebeer 10s., Taw Green 5s., Itton 4s.4d., Woodland 4s., Amlyn Taw 2s. On the death of Mr Oxenham, Mr Damerel ordered six best beast to be seized for heriot, of which five beasts (then on the s'd premises, the property of the occupiers) were seized, but the seizure of the sixth beast was resisted by the occupier of Taw Green. On application being made to Genl Acland's solicitor... he stated that in his opinion Mr D. was justified in seizing the beast only of the tenant dying seized, and not of the occupier.

From the *Western Times* on 26 July 1845 we read of an:

Action brought by Wm. Damerell Esq., the holder of the Manor of S. Tawton, against the Executors of Mr. Palmer Ackland to recover six beast as heriots on the death of Mr. Ackland, who held six tenements in that manor as a free tenant.

The following 'recipes' were written on the flyleaf of the St Andrew's Church 1739-1778 Register:

A RECIPE FOR KILLING RATTS
One quart of oatmeal; Four drops of Rhodium One Grain of Musk; Two Nutts of Nux Vomica finely rasp'd.
The whole reduced very fine and to be continued while they eat it.

An infallible cure for the Bite of a Mad Dog
A large handful of Rue, Sage and Wormwood
Three large handfuls of Garlic
Bruise them together in a Mortar
Half a pound of Stone Brimstone pounded
One pound of scrap'd Pewter
Two ounces of Assafoetida
One pound of Treacle
Boyl the ingredients over a gentle fire in Eight Quarts of Strong Beer till half is consumed, close stop'd in an earthen vessel.
To a man, half a Qtr of a Pint 3 mornings immediately after ye Bite if long before ye full moon and Quantity 3 days before and after full Moon in ye morning fasting.
For Horse of Bullock a Qtr. of a Pint.
To a Dog, 3 spoonfuls.

There's still doubt today about the parish's mystery milestone at Prospect.

THE HOLMANS AND THE DARTMOORS

The securing of the future of traditional dances is not the only clearly seen value that confirms the dedication of local individuals in the area. The secure future of precious livestock achieved through dedicated work is something the district can also take pride in.

Records show that the Holmans of South Zeal, near Okehampton, have been breeding Dartmoors since at least 1877. Several of the Stud Book's foundation stock were either bred or owned by members of the family and great care has always been taken to keep the lines pure and direct. Members of the family are still breeding ponies at top level from those descended from the mare, Queenie VII (Foundation Mare No.6). Queenie was bred by Mr John Cottle, their great-uncle, also of South Zeal, by the iron grey, Cannon Ball, the last stallion owned by the SouthTawton Commoners Society (which bought good stallions to run on this part of the moor, lying on the east side of Cawsand Beacon).

Top: *Breeders Betty and Jim Holman with Cosdon May and her foal, Cosdon Velvet, at the Royal Cornwall Show in 1975 (courtesy Western Times).*

Right: *Johnny Gillard, a parishioner of the 'old school' and one that knew a thing or two about healing horses; or even people.*

BEATING THE BOUNDS

Fortunately, there is still time devoted today to the old traditions, beating the bounds being one of the most popular, and the new millennium will be given a good start in 2001 when South Tawton bounds were beaten once again. The Belstone marker may no longer be moved by parishioners in turn and almost a century of change is recorded in two following newspaper reports, the first in 1933 and the second just over half a century later:

DARTMOOR MEN DISPUTE A BOUNDARY
Unexpected Meeting
By A Stream
THROWLEIGH BARS
THE WAY
South Tawton Halts,
But Passes On

There was an unprecedented incident at the ceremony of the beating of the bounds of the parish of South Tawton yesterday. Some 200 strong South Tawton parishioners had traversed almost two miles of their boundary, when upon arriving on the common land surrounding Payne's Bridge to Mill Farm, they were met by a small party of Throwleigh parishioners. These under the leadership of the lord of the manor of Throwleigh (Mr James Dunning, of Moor Cottage, Gidleigh), eagerly protested against their neighbouring villagers taking a certain boundary line in that particular locality. It was the contention of the Throwleigh commoners that the land in dispute belonged to their parish, but the South Tawtonians took a contrary view. SouthTawton bounds on the Dartmoor side of the village are beaten every seven years. No such argument arose on the last occasion, but following the observance of the ceremony 14 years ago, there was an inter Parish Council discussion on the matter.

CLAIM TO LAND
'Stream Ran in Another Direction'
Apparently the question of the legal ownership of this plot of ground was brought to a head comparatively recently. About 18 months ago, so it is stated, South Tawton parishioners began carrying away loads of stone and sound from the area in question, and had since continued this practice.

As Throwleigh claim the land as theirs the subject is being reopened and the first move was made yesterday. Through this area of more land bubbles a rivulet known as the Blackaton. The solution to the whole trouble lies in its noisy yet dumb meanderings. Could the stream but talk the hatchet could be buried. It has been generally regarded the dividing line between Throwleigh and South Tawton parishes around Payne's Bridge. Throwleigh adhere to the present course of Blackaton as being its primitive route, whereas parishioners of South Tawton aver that many years previous the stream ran in another direction, and that its course was diverted. The original course they take as their boundary mark. And so yesterday, amid the grey stones and undulating land of Dartmoor, inhabitants of both Throwleigh and South Tawton fought a verbal tussle over the affair. Mr H. C. Brown, solicitor, and of Okehampton, who represented the lord of the manor of Throwleigh, debated the situation with those gathered around, cross-examining the oldest of the old inhabitants who were on horseback. Mr Brown produced a plan of the vicinity and carried signed depositions giving details of the spot.

BEATING THE BOUNDS (1987)

With a spirit that has survived two thousand years and more, parishioners of South Tawton took to the moors on May 7th to mark their boundaries, much as the ancient tribal Dumnonii did before the Roman legions arrived. They set out from South Zeal, accompanied by visitors from across the county and far beyond, with almost St Crispian day thoughts that those "now abed, shall think themselves accurs'd they were not here", to march on Mill Farm, where Mr & Mrs Clarke continued tradition by letting one, representing all, walk through their home to mark the boundary line within. Onwards to Raybarrow stone, above Shelley Pool, where Hannah Tudor Wilson, the youngest babe present, and Megan Pillar the youngest walker, aged four, were each seated on the stone and 'bounced' seven times upon it to ensure that they would know the place in future years. Septuagenarian villager, Mr Gerald Jeffrey, was similarly ceremonially seated to remind all present that traditions pass from age to age. From stone to stone the boundary marks of the past were renewed once more as ancient settlements, and a circle of standing stones, placed on the moor by those long gone, reminded perhaps near two hundred walkers of the ancient rites being honoured and preserved, as our ancestors intended, by this trek around Cosdon Hill. Possible intruders from Throwleigh were warned off, passing mire and marshland miles of moorland were crossed to remind Belstone of our 'rights', before walkers wended their way through Skaigh Cleave to Sticklepath. Their lands secured, many possibly thought that "from my weary limbs Honour is cudgell'd", while many others mused, "and patches will I get unto these cudgell'd sores" as they returned to South Zeal, triumphant in having preserved a piece of England in just a few short hours.

Right: *Mr Jeffrey, senior parishioner, participating in the 1987 beating of the bounds, takes the traditional seat on a marker and instructs the 'tribe' on the necessity of regularly marking out their region.*

Below: *In accordance with tradition, as the youngest person present, Megan Pillar was shown the boundary markers during the beating of the bounds in 1987.*

Below: *A regular contributor, Ursula discusses folklore with popular presenter Douglas Mounce during one of his Radio Devon programmes.*

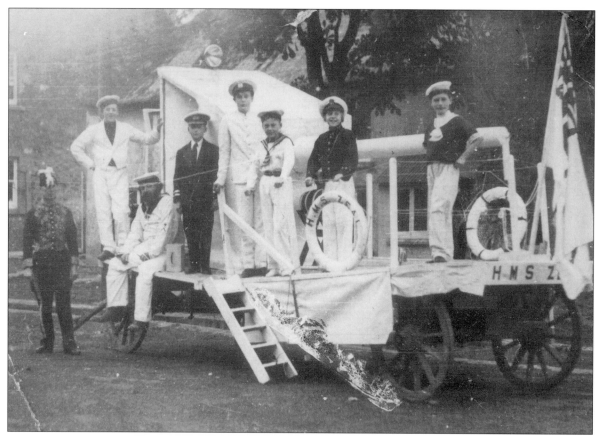

Local mariners on board HMS Zeal at the 1936 Carnival.

Will Wonnacott, driver, with Endacotts' (the bakers) first motor delivery van.

Chapter 12
Conversations on...

As part of our continuing, and much broader, project of recording area history on film, mini disc, tape and photographically, we have been meeting local people and previous residents. Personal memories of their past drawn from recordings are included in the following 'conversations' on many subjects.

FARMING

That 'farmers are an endangered species' is the worry of many of those with whom we have recorded conversations. Farming is their inheritance, a fourteen-hour day, seven-days-a-week job and they've seen it decimated during recent years. Less that 20 years ago Tim Argles' home at the bottom of the village was a shippen. Maurice and David Wonnacott were milking in barns down there twice a day before bulk business methods took them to Dishcombe. Maurice hasn't missed a day's milking in 24 years and his brother, David, has a record almost as long. They're the only ones still milking cows in a village where living memory recalls John White – Clarence's father; Jim Abbot, Jim Crocker, Tom Wright, Bill Dymont, Will Wedlake, John Knapman, Bert Wonnacott, Will Wonnacott at Shelly; Jim Lenthern, Tom Braughton and Clifford White's family – all milking cows.

At threshing time, farmers helped each other, especially when labour was scarce during the war; they'd contract the machine from North Tawton – from Alf Potter at Lousytown (who it is though was to be found along the Whiddon Down – North Tawton road).

'Saturday was market day' recalled one, 'in Okehampton, with cattle and sheep sales and pens for young cattle fortnightly but Joe Vick came into conflict with the Council, and took his market to Hatherleigh.' 'There was Spreyton market too,' another told us, 'held in a field; father walked cattle there

Les and Vera Wonnacott, with sons Maurice and David, are the last dairy farmers in the village selling 'green top' unpasteurised milk locally.

from Dishcombe, in the depression, the first depression, and sold an $8\frac{1}{2}$ cwt bullock for £12, he had to go... and sell... to pay the rent.'

A return to natural methods has been welcomed by some: 'Farming is getting back to what it was, in my youth there were no chemicals', said one farmer. 'It was about 1955 or '56 we started spraying... gradually got more stock... used more fertiliser, previously weeding between corn was done by hand - with a special tool for cutting thistles.'

There are fond memories of the harvest: 'The corn was stacked up, then built into ricks, eight or nine ricks per season, the regular helpers often worked for cider or rabbits.' And from another senior citizen of the parish:

Catching rabbits was almost an occupation at one time... we took them to Okehampton Station, or Sampford, to send them off to Sainsbury's. They used to take them... put them in hampers... a brace of rabbits.... Very popular, and farmers were glad to have rabbits caught.

There are memories of when 'the American laundry at Owlsfoot polluted the stream at bottom of village - sludge from washing - it was years before animals would drink [the] water.' We were asked by one person: 'Did you know the farm near Gidleigh Mill had a double privy outside - and the stream ran underneath?' Then we also had an illuminating conversation regarding a missing 'public' seat... outside 'Riverside':

There was a bit of fuss about the bit of ground at the front. There was a seat there... put round the back for collection; I put it out the back. I built the wall. Course, there was a lot of fuss at the time... [from a lady Councillor]. I had orders from the

143

Commander and his solicitor, which was Cann and Hallet, to go and move the seat at 6 o'clock in the morning. Of course, I did that, I moved the seat out the back. I left and I hadn't got home very long, I'd only come in and (she) was on the doorstep. "You're in trouble now," she said, "shifting that seat." I said I was only working under instructions, solicitor's instructions. "Oh you haven't heard the last of this yet." There was never anything done about it. We put the wall up. When the Commander found out that the ground was his... he got it all done up legally. Others said it wasn't... they had a battle... and lost.

Top: *After a long hard day, Clifford White heads for home, but in 2000 is the sun setting on the industry that his family and other local families follow?*
Above: *Back in 1940, Mr Littlejohns sheared his sheep by hand in much the same manner that sheep had been sheared for centuries*
Inset: *Tools may change, but not the work; Maurice Wonnacott and Basil Madge hard at work, July 2000.*
Right: *Boots were once the footwear of the day, even with summer outfits; a studio photo, c.1922*

ABOUT SCHOOL

At South Zeal school, in the 1930s, there were, according to one local resident, three teachers, Mr Heard, Bet Mallet, and Miss Leach, 'and three classrooms in main building. There were 80-90 children attending school – I went to each class to tally them up and write it on the board.' The only heating, apparently, was 'an old, round, black stove.' One pupil remembers how the Stennaford's used 'to walk in from Halford manor in the mornings when it was dark, and walked home again in the dark.'

Mr Heard helped one grateful student get to grammar school and 'girls wore boots, laced up to the knee [and were] dressed in white pinafores.' Leaving school to work on the farm was commonplace:

I left school at 14 and had to go ploughing – it was the war... I learned ploughing with two old horses... my brother cut in and up through the field to start him for a round or two... I took over and the horses would go with the reign, but my brother finished off... I was hardly man enough to turn the plough at 14 and put out in the field. An acre a day was a day's work. It was all horses and carts back then.

Some memories are more unpleasant than others:

I was about 11 when I was in a nasty crash by Okehampton Motel, by Fatherford Bridge. Smoke

from a bonfire in field combined with fog [and] a lorry from Okehampton and the School bus crashed head on. The bus driver broke his leg and a girl in front seat suffered a broken nose; possibly... the lorry driver was killed.

Muriel Finnucane (née Endacott) used to run the family bakery at Shelly and remembers at five or six years of age the bakers coming in to make dough at night, putting it in wooden troughs; the troughs' wooden tops were later used for moulding and shaping the dough. She recalls:

There was a cottage on the corner by the chapel – then a block of stables, and two cottages... all with thatched roofs. Horses were last used in the late 1920s and the stables were converted to cottages around 1927. We bought motor vans. In my father's times he baked 1d. buns, rock buns, dough cake... some ordinary, some with all butter, ginger cakes and Madeira cakes nothing very fancy. Seed cake was popular.

Muriel married Ned Finnucane and they eventually were persuaded to take over the shop. She continues:

The after-war years were difficult but we made hot cross buns and simnel cake for Easter, and a lot of Christmas cakes... for a small village. Father had bought the Wesleyan Chapel at the bottom of the hill before the war; it had been closed since about 1932. Before that the Bible Christians at Shelly Chapel had held combined meetings with the Wesleyans, with alternate chapels were used, but when they united nationally to form the Methodist Church, they all only needed one chapel. It was thought that Shelly chapel was brighter so the bot-

tom chapel went up for sale but it was a long time before father risked buying it. It was used for all sorts of things, the scouts... a cinema, Kit and Peter Cornthwaite used it as a carpenter's shop. When the Dunkirk boys were in the village, room had to be found... it was used by soldiers sleeping on palliasses; the main difficulty was lack of sanitation.

Top right: *Grateful to have a restored roof over their heads again after the storm damage of the previous year, Methodist members and friends gather at the Shelly chapel in 1960.*
Centre: *Roof restoration again, South Zeal, 1990s.*
This image: *Shelly, South Zeal, c.1920s.*

The next generation; Pupils of South Tawton County Primary School, 2000.
Left to right, back row: Amelia Davies, Natasha Day, Christian Clark, Edward Harris, David White,
Christopher Miller, Charlotte Rice, Steven Howard, Rosanna Hignett, Emma Bass, Jane Spence, Felicity
Wedlake, Laurie Laybourn, Stuart Jarvis, Hannah Crackett, Victoria Medlyn, Jan Jachnik,
James Van der Steen, Charlotte Saunders, Emily Smith, Jessica Day;
8th row: Catherine Souness, Billie Sanderson, Anuska Pritchard, Helen Cooper, Hollie Sampson, Freedom
Van Riel, Freya Young, Katey Hale, Hannah Madders, Ben Parr, Craig Guscott, Gemma Henry,
Lynsey Connor, Luke Wonnacott, Gemma Vincent, Andrew Mallett, Tristan Lindsay,
Alex Wooldridge, Sally Young, Jonathan Spinks, Francesca Lane, Ashley Hutchison;
7th row: Thomas Hall, Christina Mallett, Cassie Hooper, Rebecca Jarvis, Lucy Almond, Sophie Herd,
Aaron Easterbrook, Chelsea Pleace, Megan Pillar, Emily Webster, Robert Hearn, Scott Hussey, Alice Glover,
Hayley Jansz, Tom Bristow, Jonty McPhee, Lydia Wade, Nicole Grainger, Finn Francis,
Michael Aylen, John Radnor, Hannah Counter, Christine Van Minnern, Rosie Goodman, Alex Vincent;
6th row: Amy Webber, Jack Phare, Gabriel Aguilera, Emily Sanderson, Robin Grey, Huw Draper, Jake
Crackett, Emily Clements, Gemma Lindsay, Adam Clark, Harriet Davies, Joshua Chadwick, David Binns,
Matthew Dennis, Alex Law, Paul Hookway, Daniel Pope, Graham Francis, Samuel Pritchard, Ruari Evershed,
Amy Cooper, Beth Gillbanks, Rebecca Smith, Laura Bass, Eliza Unwin, Sarah Graham, Lucinda Howard;
5th row: Hope Davey, Kaine Van Riel, Joshua Van Riel, Jason Van Minnen, Declan McCaffery, George Jones,
Danielle Williams, Kit Cornthwaite, Vashti Jewell, Sophie Hookway, Tom Counter, Danny Watkins,
Jonathan Trussler, Isobelle Tilley, Jeb Pleace, Elona Wonnacott, Aisling Evershed, Danielle Turner,
Simone Lane, Thomas Mallett, Jamie Hignett, Hannah Coombe, Kirsty Hale, Jennifer Howard,
Rebecca Hall, Joelle Henry;
4th row: Mr Ray Souness, Jake Chadwick, Charlotte Radnor, Sam Thomas, Gina Brint, Tom Aylen,
Jacob Law, Buster Francis, Abbie Webber, Danielle Hussey, Daniel Boulton, Daniel Curtis, Naomi Connor,
Michael Hearn, Haniell Laybourn, Hector Jourdan, Thomas White, Sam Vincent, Lily Davies, Laura Lee,
Emma Beacon, Ryan Street, Abbie Brint, Annabel Clark, Sara Liversidge, Ross Smale-Beech,
Joshua Hutchison, Clemency Tilley, Ryan Dennis, Jordan Blackmore;
3rd row: Roseanne Hookway, Henry Holmes, Mrs Sue Wonnacott, Mrs Sue Trussler, Mrs Thea Sampson,
Mrs Tracey Smith, Mrs Angela Herrod-Taylor, Mrs Margaret Tarvit, Mr Patrick Shaw, Mrs Liz Vachon,
Mr Martin Unwin, Mrs Bobby Sutton, Mr Chris Rolls, Miss Teresa Roberts, Mr James Norman, Mrs Caroline
Boother, Mrs Ceri Hoggins, Mrs Jenny Woods, Mrs Angela Love, Mrs Trish Glover, Mrs May Madders,
Ryan Turner, Jordan Cornthwaite;
2nd row: Tara Davidson, Isis Van Riel, Kasia Jewell, Rebecca Hussey, Amelia Conroy-Gerrnan,
Rebecca Trussle, Rachel Coombe, Ellern Pillar, Nicola Pope, Molly Hawker, Isabel Crackett, Abagail
Crackett, Lucy Sanderson, Lucy Henry, Lydia Francis, Rebecca Andrew, Jessica Jeffery, Grace Davey,
Lisa Hearn, Poppy Chadwick, Molly Bell, Maddy Weaver, Helena Marshall, Emily Boothe, Hayley Hale,
Luke Liversidge, Alice Clements, Hugh Clark, Ike Francis, Lewis Day;
front row: Alex Bass, Adele Starling, Louis Scott-Lawson, Edward Almond, Daniel Hearn, Thomas Boother,
William Saunders, Harry Smith, Sam Cooper, Daniel Mallett, Keiran Shilston, William Wimberley,
Max Goodman, Edmund Howard, Harley Hale, Luke Jefferies, Daniel Clinch, Jack Thomas,
Thomas Wood, Dominic Wooldridge, William Beacom, Joshua Punchard, Joshua Stratton, Luke Vincent,
Ben Conroy-German.

19TH- AND 20TH-CENTURY SHOPS

There were the Westaways at the corner shop by the chapel... back in the mid 1800s I'd say. Aunt Susie Westaway, my granny's sister, granny was Ellen Wright, and then my mother was born in 1901. Mother and Uncle Tom told me how Aunt Susie Westaway used to come down and sit with Granny and if anyone went in the shop she'd toddle off up the street, hell for leather, to sell a ha'penny sweets, or a ha'penny worth of anything - it was all ha'pennys and pennys of things then. She had hanging oil lamps, and weights... used to weigh out ½lb of butter; cold floors and slabs kept things cool, and the butter and goods were fresh in from farms.

In reply, one parishioner said:

I don't know about that far back but... in the 30s it might have been... when we were kids, directly opposite the Post Office, we used to watch Jim Wonnacott sitting in the window making shoes, I think it was three cottages at one time.

Another remembered that 'one behind the little church... was a shoemakers... Mr Madders.' There were also:

... tailors at Ducks Hill... Greenbank... and at Shelly - Tailor Vigers at Shelly... where John Candler lives, and a blacksmith next door; and a blacksmith at 'The Grove' in Ramsley, the Lenterns... in a shed off the road.

Tommy Wonnacott, at the Old Store in Ramsley, is remembered as having gone to Throwleigh every other Saturday by one whose father 'had three oz of tobacco'. Apparently there was the paraffin tank in the back of Tommy's van and his daughter took over the business.

Mrs Wright is recalled as one who sold groceries, at what is now Low Cottage, and there was also apparently a grocery shop where Raymond Souness' workshop was which was run by the Wiltons, who

Top: *The area attracts folklore investigators from afar. Boris and Myrna Klapwald from New York consider Whiddon Down's rebuilt toll-house may hold clues in the mystery surrounding Uncle Tom Cobley.*
Centre: *'... and along the lane there was the stonemason's yard at Prospect.' Photo, 1939.*
This image: *South Zeal, towards Zeal head.*

Detail from image on page 24 which shows more clearly Sticklepath Shop and the Taw River Hotel around the turn of the last century. Later (inset) the inn suffered considerable damage at the hands of a severe fire.

Into the era of motorised delivery. Pictured here are A.C. Wonnacott's shop and van in 1938.

previously had the Corner Shop before moving down the road. This was 'The Stores... where Helen Law is.'

'There was a shop', remembered another, 'before the war... between Martin White's bungalow at Ford Cross and Road.' Another little shop was run 'up Shelly [which] used to sell groceries - the Coopers... George and May... that was it.' There was another outlet 'down at Taw Green... very small it was, [sold] tobacco... I don't know whether they did groceries.'

Next down from the Oxenham Arms was a chemists shop thought to have been run by Mr Fry of the drama group. We 'used to take our prescriptions down there and he'd make up your medicine for you. Then it was Mr Lovell's... he lived up the lane to your place, where Jeanie lived... up between the Little Ox and... yes... poor old chap got killed... he was out with his dog.'

For refreshment there was 'Ivy Cottage, behind the chapel [where] Mrs Lamasky had tea rooms... then changed it into a general stores, with an iron-mongers and things... and sold it to Mr Stagg.'

The Dymonts were butchers, 'where Bill Cann lives' and 'they had a slaughterhouse at the rear and did all the cutting up there.'

Of butchers also, one parishioner remembered:

Wonnacotts too... they ran the butchers by Ramsley Lane... had their slaughterhouse behind the shop... and the Wedlakes' barn, behind where Joan and Charlie Curtis live by the post office, that was a slaughterhouse... milking was done in other outbuildings. Joan's father did a bit of butchering.

Les Wonnacott's mum had a shop in her house where she sold 'lovely home-made ice cream' and 'next to Ray Souness, by the bridge, Sandicott sold paraffin from sheds at back.'

There are memories of the occasional treat: 'We used to get fish and chips from Ernie Mortimore... by the playing field... 50p for a meal for five on a Saturday night' and 'there was another fish and chip shop first... over where I said that grocery shop was at one time, where Raymond used to have his workshop.' 'Alfie and Edna Kelly started that there... Sad to think they've all gone.'

There were two bakers: 'John Holman ran his in South Zeal and Tom... his brother... Tom Holman ran the one in Sticklepath.' 'Mr Hussey was the tailor at Sticklepath, up from Taw River Hotel.' Hot cross buns brought back particularly happy thoughts:

[They] were brought round by the bakers on Good Friday in big baskets. The Endcotts and Holmans raced to see who was first to go up through the village, door to door - it was fun... the children were given so much to go round with baskets. Sad to think the traditions have gone too.

Joyce Worthington had some clear memories of one tradition that has gone:

Sundays, before I went to school, I used to take Mum's Sunday dinner over - it always amazed me that there would be about 30 dinners... but they were all different. The different ways that the cooks [made them]... there was one old [cook] - she used to do the roly-poly pudding and that was laid long ways beside the beef... spotted dick then, long ways, with the meat in the middle and then with the potatoes all the way round then another woman would place it another way with pork or whatever, but it always used to amaze me the different ways you'd see the different dinners.

John Holman cooked the dinners for the villagers - can't remember what it cost, you paid... coppers. Then go over maybe ten to one and collect it - and you'd all be queuing up, but if you took your dinner over first, you knew your dinner would be right down the bottom of the oven. He took your dinner - it was such a long oven - he put your dinner on a long spoon - and I've yet to find out what that spoon was and he'd just slip it off and it would be placed just were he wanted it - and the same spoon would get the dinner out. Dinner on a dish - everybody varied - piece of pork - a leg of lamb - round of beef in the middle and then nearly everybody then made a pudding - and it was suet pudding - and the one that sticks out in my mind is one like a roly poly pudding but 'twas a suet spotted dick but that would be laid at the side and then the roast potatoes all the way round. Some, if they were doing lamb would have onion - all sliced up - it all smelt beautiful - it would be cooked to a 't', lovely brown potatoes. Then you'd have to run home with it. I did that one day - you know what a stickler poor old Mum was - I came along the cobbles and dropped it - slipped or something - this poor old Jim Weaver heard me crying and came out and said whatever's the matter my dear? - he picked it all up and put it back in the dish again and I was saying that Mum would... He said, 'Oh I'll go in with 'ee' - I can't exactly remember what mother said - 'oh its like you all over— you should have been more careful.'

From Mr Alfred Woods we learned about the village water supply:

Back in the very early days it was all wells and running streams through the village. I can remember when there used to be a stone trough opposite the Kings Arms... and there was a stream coming in there and the horses used to drink there... and people used to fill up there... the majority had wells in the village, then I suppose it got short and

Main picture: *Traditionally, some start 'riding out' with the hunt very early in life.*
Inset: *Master of the Hunt, and local resident, octogenarian Colonel Varwell, takes the traditional stirrup cup in South Zeal, c.1999.*

the Parish decided to bring down their own water, hence the reservoir was built... and the pipe work was taken down through the village but that was before my time. They had standpipes down through... you still had to go out to get water... eventually they began taking it into the homes, and that's when the problems started. When flush toilets came on the scene you see, it wasn't adequate. Father and I were self employed but used to work for the old Okehampton Rural District Council... doing maintenance work... going up yearly, in the summer when the supply was down low, to clean out the reservoir.... and we used to bring in more springs... by land drain pipe. We used to dig across and find a spring and then pipe it in... ordinary four-inch clay pipes. The reservoir supplied the entire village, but it wasn't very successful. We had to keep shutting the water off. They rang the bell in the little church to warn people when they were going to shut the water off. When supplies got low, Shelly wouldn't get any water, they were all right in the bottom of the village; they got it all the time. Cross Park, they couldn't get it there. Mr Kellaway, in Cross Park, he was in charge of it and he used to turn it off at

6 o'clock in the night and turn it on again at 8 in the morning, and of course the reservoir would replenish by that time.

Then the pressure would be enough to throw it to Shelly until they took it all away down at the bottom again. The end of the pipeline went up to the Rising Sun. It was a natural flow from the reservoir and the water would just reach the Rising Sun, except when the pressure went down and then it wouldn't.

How he and his father solved that problem is another story.

After the First World War Mr Wood's father and his brother learned their trade as masons with Counters at 'Moorlands,' once a Ramsley tucking mill but later the area centre for the building trade. That trade is continued today in the same premises by Mr Keith Redstone who, as a local undertaker, maintains also the continuity of this family business. Wendy, his wife, told us once that she was unaware of that inheritance when they married.

South Zeal Post Office moved to its present location in 1902, as Diana England the present post-mistress explained to us:

My Mother always told me that the PO was taken on, or opened in this house on the day that she was born. She was related to the Crockers, and Mary Crocker was postmistress until 1923 - James Henry Weaver was postmaster until 1945 - then my mother, Elsie Irene Endacott, became postmistress - her husband, George, was local postman around the village and up to West Week, delivering on foot - bag on back. Another postman delivered along Throwleigh road out to Clannaborough, by cycle, in all winds and weathers.

They had little torches clipped on to a buttonhole on the uniform that they wore. The post van arrived at twenty to seven - they had to sort their letters and be out of the office by ten past seven.

I would have been five when my mother took it on and can remember playing in the public telephone box situated in the middle of the office - the office has been enlarged three times since I took it on in 1963.

I remember going into the telephone box to play, obviously when no one was using it, it was like a little house to me.

I suppose I sold a stamp when I was five or six to somebody, I enjoyed it then and still enjoy it all these years later. The post used to come in a little van at twenty to seven, in sacks sealed with string and sealing wax, and taken into the office.

My father sorted the village letters and parcels from those along Throwleigh road by Mr Crocker who lived at the top of the village. After he retired Frank Hambly took the post along Throwleigh road. I had two years' experience of the old delivery system until it was motorised. Father had retired then. There were two deliveries in the village... the afternoon one coming from Sticklepath, taken round by Tom Stead... and as far out as Wood. After Frank Hambly retired, all the post was delivered from Okehampton by van.

Of bombing:

... one night this plane came over and it was said that some Italians that lived down at Wood Ball - opposite the main entrance to Wood estate, they were flashing to the pilot with lights. Anyway, he made his run up from Taw Green and dropped the bomb - just outside the church - as you go over to the Glebe - right in the road. The next one he

Postman Tom Stead served the community for many years and is seen here with Joyce Reddaway.

dropped up behind Shelly chapel... took off a lot of slates up there, and from where Will Wonnacott lived further up. Then he dropped one up behind Poltimore farm, on Ramsley... in amongst a herd of cattle there... he killed a lot - they had holes in the side of them with shrapnel - I went up and saw it. The next one he dropped - out Throwleigh road. Before you get out to the kiosk, before you turn up to West Week... house stands back. Right opposite, there's a house almost out to the road... and there was a fellow living there on his own - and the bomb dropped right in that little plantation - that little field opposite. The fellow got out of bed and he come around to see what was going on - and a piece of shrapnel went right through the window - cut the window bar right in half - and went in his chest and out his back. He was the only casualty. Didn't hit any of the lorries - missed all the lorries... on out Shilstone Tors, and then just down over... going towards Gidleigh - there was a bog - and they dropped a bomb in the bog. It was the beginning of the war ....

The games children played, and adults too:

[There was] cricket, in the street. Everyone that walked by would stop and join in - start off in the early evening with two or three perhaps no more than 20 minutes or half an hour there'd be 20 or 30 people playing - adults as well as children. Dennis Wonnacott would have come down to milk the cows and then he'd stop on his way in and do a bit of fielding - in the slips - the fronts of houses weren't enclosed then - there was a bigger stretch - we could play right up to the house - of course when a window got broken we all had to run and think where's Mr Redstone - he'll have to come before dark to mend this broken pane of glass.

[There was] arrow chasing [as well, and], following the chalk marks, we used to play hopscotch in the middle of the street - might have to stop if a car went by but most of the time you weren't interrupted, there weren't many cars then. I used a vehicle tyre as a hoop, with a stick. Coming down the steep hill from Zeal Head, mine was quicker than I could keep up with. By the Kings Arms, it hit a large lady in the behind... she was not pleased... I cried.

Above: *Coga and wheels Morris dancers recruiting bemused boy – Ben – a visitor from Cambridge.*
Inset: *Father Christmas fortunately found friends in South Zeal who knew where Victory Hall was, anf helped him get there to visit the Pre-school Play Group bazaar.*

Indian actor and artist, Moti Makan, enjoyed and appreciated Grimspound Border, traditionally black-faced Morris dancers when visiting Dartmoor Folk Festival in 1998.

One resident remembers that 'pushball' was sponsored by the *Daily Mail*:

I suppose it was six feet, seven feet high, the ball was... and seven feet in diameter - darn great thing - I remember seeing it. The team was something like five or six - big fellows from each village. The problem was that Tom Wright used to have the field and he used to put cows in there a day or two before - now you understand the mess. My father came home... Oh... the state he was in... they'd roll this ball in the cow pats... it would come all up the sides... and their hands... covered all over.

Some years ago, after discussions with the late Mr Percy Brooks we wrote to the *Daily Mail* to ask they would co-sponsor a revival of the game... the suggestion was declined. We were shown photos of the game, but does anyone know where they might be now?

Football was also popular and was played on occasion with German prisoners 'in the field, where Reddaways yard is'.

Cinema was enjoyed in the old Wesleyan chapel:

Presumably, as chapel, one half was Sunday School, the other was chapel, so when it was converted, one part was for scouts and cubs, and the other for the cinema. There were films every Friday - Leslie Bailey the Borough Surveyor ran it - he came along with a projector - I don't remember it breaking down - there was a proper projection room. We also had a serial each week. I was probably sitting in the front holding somebody's hand - 6d. entitled you to sit at the front seats - only they weren't seats down there - it was a form.

There was 'a very crude sort of screen, and some chairs - they might get 30 there... we liked the cowboy films, the detectives films - vivid things going on - hustle and bustle.'

CHILDHOOD JOBS

I have the vivid memory from the age of five of pans of milk placed in rows on the cement floor in the kitchen passageway, all stone floors then... there to be left for 24 hours until the creamy head formed. The next procedure was the pans of milk being slowly heated on two oil stoves, again in the kitchen. Whereupon a thicker surface formed, a crusty head. I never fell in any of these big pans of milk.

At this time the milk was not delivered or collected in bottles it was collected from the farm house or delivered to the customers in their own jugs. I might also add that the cream from the pans was also sold especially on a Sunday morning as a treat. The milk was around 1/2d. a pint for the skimmed, that's after the cream was skimmed off, the new milk as it was then called, 1d. a pint.

Fun was not something forgotten during the war, as the RASC appears to confirm as these warriors set off to play comic football at Zeal Head in the early 1940s.

Another child was paid by the road-sweeper:

Mr Pillavant looked after the sewer field and swept the roads. On Saturday morning I pushed his square wheelbarrow, waited when he stopped off for a drink, and sat with barrow... for 6d. a week.

LOCAL ENTERTAINMENT & SAYINGS

Around 1950, at Victory Hall, dances and concerts were not for the faint hearted:

[It] used to be a rough place back then though... always fighting down there... I remember the police was tough back then. You'd have one constable... and he'd stand on the door and if there was any nonsense, don't matter if it was half a dozen of 'em, they'd come down over they steps one after the other - and he'd chuck 'em down... yes... And they'd lie on the bottom of the steps there... out.

The Circus was:

... in a field... opposite the Kings Arms - sideshows, roundabouts, and swings they used to come every year [on an] annual visit. I remember the swings almost out to the road [where there were] no houses [and] no bungalows...

Local sayings included some gems. A very mean person, it was said 'would take out your eye and spit in the hole' and one to be afraid of was 'a long-headed fellow!'

GOING FOR A SONG

During the war I used to deliver the milk up Ramsley and Owlsfoot way there... and let the Americans have it instead, for nylons. My father used to go mad when I had no milk to give to people in the village.

The property market was rather different in times past:

All South Zeal, all the cottages at one time belonged to Squire Cann of Dishcombe... all sold off cheap... cottages for a hundred quid a cottage. My mother and her twin sister used to work for him... as servant girls... up where John and Theresa Christian lives... it was burnt down... it was thatched at one time... burnt down... Squire Cann owned all of it around here... it wasn't all belonging to the Oxenham.

Miss Elston - school teacher at Sticklepath - had a new bungalow at Zeal Head - cost £500. Martin White's went for £350. [Golly - sorry Martin]

And so were petrol prices:

... the garage... down Ford Cross... back in the younger days, petrol was 1s.6d. a gallon... a free house, there was Cleveland Discol - Shell - BP - Benzole - all the pumps were all lined up and you could take your pick... 1s.6d. a gallon... that was 1936... it belonged to Counters... Woods was there during the war... then the Cox's had it for years... Jenny and Keith.... with the children... the Simpsons; it was a tragedy, two children... they died in an accident... tragic... of course they moved, poor dears... I think there were others... before... But Chris Darken was there till it closed... and he moved his repair shop down the road.

South Tawton parishioners and visitors enjoyed a street party on 11 June 2000, to celebrate the millennium. Prayers were spoken in appreciation of the past as people looked towards the future. As the sun began to set on a memorable day, keyboard orchestras, quietly, again began to play and homeward drifting people paused, in appreciation of musicians who, having already played their part in entertaining people, had taken up their hand-held instruments again. Mark Bazeley, Richard Penny, Mike Palmer, Dave Denford and Mike Bond brought an end to the day with an impromptu music session. As ageless melodies were shared, out from a skin-stretched circle came the sound of the Celtic heartbeat that set centuries aside and made each player, and pleasured listener, ever more aware that an inheritance is at its best when shared. A parish isn't something politicians make... it's what we all allow it to become.

The musicians' impromptu 'session' was much appreciated at the close of the Millennium Street Party.

Glossary

ADVOWSON The right to appoint a vicar to a living.

BENEFICE Ecclesiastical living; property held by a rector, vicar or similar.

BOOR Lowly free peasant.

BORDAR Feud: Villein of lowest rank, who rendered menial service in return for a cottage. Smallholder or tenant farm labourer.

BOVATE An ox-gang, or as much land as one ox could plough in a year; varying from 10–18 acres.

BURGAGE Plot of land as held by a Burgess.

BURGESS Inhabitant of borough with full municipal rights.

CALENDAR List of documents chronologically arranged with summaries.

CALENDAR OF CLOSE ROLLS Register of dealings with grants of the Crown, relating to enclosure awards, deeds poll, provisioning of garrisons etc.

CALENDAR OF PATENT ROLLS Register of titles conferred by the Crown since 1201.

CARUCATE As much land as could be tilled with one plough (and 8 oxen) in one year. Often another name for a Hide.

CHANCERY PROCEEDINGS Reports of the High Court of Justice.

COTTAR Tenant farmer holding only about 3–5 acres.

COURT BARON Private court enforcing customs of the lord of the manor,

COURT LEET Manorial court for trying petty offences and electing minor officials.

CURTILAGE Yard and outbuildings of house.

DEMESNE Manorial reserve of the lord's own land, worked by serfs of vassals as a duty.

FEET OF FINES Records of agreements following disputes over land ownership taken as equivalent to title deeds.

FINE A money payment made by a tenant to his lord on the transfer of property to him.

GELD An extraordinary tax based on the amount of land possessed.

GLEBE Portion of land allocated within a clergyman's benefice.

GLEBE TERRIER Survey of church land and benefices compiled by the Incumbent or churchwarden.

HERIOT Originally arms, armour etc. given to Anglo-Saxon vassal for war service, but remaining the lord's property and so returnable by his heir(s); later a death duty (best beast or chattel, or money) given instead on decease of a tenant.

HIDE Area of ploughable land meant to support a family and its dependants (varying from 60–130 acres accord ing to locality).

HUNDRED Administrative division of a county having its own courts; theoretically enough land to support 100 families.

INDENTURE Originally a document divided roughly into two parts so that it could be authenticated by matching up the edges. Later, any sealed agreement or contract, especially between an apprentice and a master.

INDUCTIONS TO LIVINGS Formal introductions of clergymen to their posts.

INQUISITION POST MORTEN Inquiry into the possessions, services and succession of a deceased person who held land of the Crown.

LEAGUE Varying measure of distance (usually one and a half or three miles).

MARK Unit used in accountancy. A weight of metal originally valued at 128 silver pennies (10s.8d. – 53p); but later valued at 13s.4d. – 68p

MESSUAGE A house, complete with outbuildings and yard.

MOIETY Portion of an estate, supposedly half.

ORA Amount of weight equivalent to 16d. or 20d.

PERCH — Measure of length, especially for land (five and a half yards).

RECOVERY ROLLS — Similar to 'Feet of Fines'

REEVE — Chief magistrate of town or district; other similar officer.

RELIEF — Related to the conveyancing of property. A relief (a fee) was paid by the purchaser to the Crown or feudal tenant-in-chief.

ROD — Same as 'Perch'; often used as square measure of thirty and a quarter square yards.

ROLLS — Originally, official records in the form of scrolls or documents.

SERF — Labourer; peasant – whose services were tied to the land in a condition of servitude or modified slavery.

SESTER — Measure of weight (about 32oz possibly).

SOCAGE — Feudal tenure of land by payment of rent or by providing service, other than military.

SUBSIDY ROLLS — Various taxpayers lists (13th century – 1689).

SUMMA — Measure of weight (about 240lb possibly).

TALLAGE/TALLIAGE/TAILL — A form of taxation; up to the 14th century.

TENEMENT — Any kind of permanent property as lands, rent, held of a Superior.

TERRAE OCCUPATAE — Lands that had been held independently but were 'entered upon 'and made appurtenant to some manor under the Conqueror'.

TERRIER — Book recording site, boundaries etc. of land OR collection of acknowledgements of vassals or tenants of a lordship.

THANE — Member of the lowest rank of Anglo-Saxon aristocracy.

TITHE — One-tenth of yearly produce and income taken to support clergy and church; any similar tax.

UNION — A combination of parishes administering poor laws, usually maintaining a common workhouse.

VENVILLE — Special form of tenure obtaining to parishes adjoining Dartmoor by which the tenants enjoy certain privileges in the use of the moor.

VILLEIN — Tenant farmer worker of the lord of the manor.

VIRGATE — Quarter of a hide (usually about 30 acres).

Bibliography

BOOKS, ARTICLES, PERIODICALS & SURVEYS

Baring-Gould, Revd S., *A Book of Dartmoor* (1900)

Beresford, Maurice, *New Towns of the Middle Ages* (1967)

Billings Directory and Gazeteer of Devon (various)

Burton, C.K., *An Account of the Parish Church of St Andrew's, South Tawton and St Mary's, South Zeal* (1956 edition)

Butler, Jeremy, *Dartmoor Volume 2* (1991)

Crossing, William, *Guide to Dartmoor* (1912)

Crossing, William, *One Hundred Years on Dartmoor* (1901 and 1967 editions)

Greeves, T., *Tin Mines and Miners of Dartmoor* (1986)

Hoskins, W.G., *Devon and Its People* (1959)

Hutchinson, V.W., *A Village School Chronicle* (1979)

Kelly's Directories (various years)

Lega-Weekes, Ethel, 'Neighbours of North Wyke' in *TDA* 1903–05

Major, J.K., *Finch Brothers' Foundry*

Radford, Mrs G.H., *Nicholas Radford* (1903)

Reichel, Revd Oswald J., *Devonshire Domesday*

St Leger Gordon, D., *Devonshire*

St Leger Gordon, D., *Under Dartmoor Hills* (1954)

South Tawton Parish Registers & St Andrew's Church - Churchwarden's Accounts (various)

Sticklepath WI, *Story of Sticklepath* (1955 and 1993 editions)

Transactions of the Devonshire Association. (various volumes)

Varwell, Emmie, *Throwleigh, The story of A Dartmoor Village*

White, William, *History, Gazetteer & Directory of Devonshire* (various).

Williams, H. Fulford, *History of Sampford Courtenay Parish*

NEWSPAPERS

Express & Echo

Okehampton Times

Western Morning News

Subscribers

Bryan Ainslie, Fern Cottage, South Zeal, Devon

Mrs Wendy Ainslie, South Zeal, Devon

Anne Arscott, Watford, Herts

Michael J. V. Bailey, Okehampton, Devon

Michael and Shirley Bazeley, Sticklepath, Devon

Mark and Sarah Bazeley and Family, South Zeal, Devon

M. B. and M.P. Bending, South Zeal, Devon

Mr A. J. Berry, Horrabridge, Devon

Nora Bertram, South Zeal, Devon

John D. Bewsher, Paignton, Devon

Binns Family, South Zeal, Devon

George and Margaret Bird, Sticklepath, Devon

R. J. Bishop, Tonbridge, Kent

David R. Blezard, Devon

Mrs Patricia R. Blizzard, Bussage, Glos.

Louise and Roland Bol, South Zeal, Devon

Stephen Bolt, Okehampton, Devon

Michael, Caroline, Thomas and Emily Boother, South Zeal, Devon

C. Roger and Ann Bowden, Sticklepath, Devon

Michael Bowden, Sticklepath, Devon

Mrs Phyllis Bradley (née Madders), Forres, Scotland

Mr and Mrs E. J. Brint, South Zeal, Devon

The Brint Family

K. J. Burrow, Bucks Cross, Devon

Arlene L. Cann, Exeter, Devon

Ria-Jane Cann, London

Stewart J. Cann, Exeter, Devon

Bob and Kath Cann, Portsmouth

Julia F. Carne, Winkleigh, Devon

Carol and Richard, Guestling, East Sussex

Gill Carter, Dover, Kent

John and Teresa Christian, Dishcombe, South Tawton, Devon

Lt Col and Mrs A. H. Clark, Ford Farm, Sticklepath, Devon

Pamela M. Clarke, Chudleigh, Devon

D. E. and M. J. Clatworthy, South Tawton, Devon

A. June Clements, South Tawton, Devon

Geoffrey Clinch, Wyken, South Zeal, Devon

Mr M. J. Clinch, Hatherleigh, Devon

V. G. Cooper, South Zeal, Devon

Bobbie and Peter Cornish, Oxenham Manor

Mr and Mrs M. E. T. Cornish, Belstone, Devon

The Cornthwaite Family, South Zeal, Devon

Mr and Mrs Michael Counter, South Zeal, Devon

Mr and Mrs David Counter, South Tawton, Devon

Tom Courtney, Poltimore Hotel, South Zeal, Devon

William A. Cox

Clive and Alison Critcher, Riverside, South Zeal, Devon

Archie Crocker, Okehampton, Devon

Joan M. Curtis

Dr Jim and Mrs M. Daly, Adley Lane, Chagford, Devon

John and Jasmine Darch, South Tawton, Devon

Chris and Tricia Darken, Sticklepath Garage

Dartmoor National Park Authority

Dartmoor Press

Rob and Eileen Davey, Sticklepath, Devon

Murial K. Davies, Bush, Cornwall

Dr Jacquita Davies (née Newcombe), Histon, Cambridge

Barbara A. Day, Sticklepath, Okehampton, Devon

Dave and Shirley Denford, South Zeal, Devon

Susan Derges, South Tawton, Devon

Andy and Jan Easterbrook, Taw Green, Devon

Val and John Easterling, Hayling Island, Hants.

David and Diana England, South Zeal Post Office, Devon

Paul, Sharon and Jonathan England, South Zeal Post Office, Devon

Maureen and Edwin Finnamore, Prospect, Sticklepath, Devon

Ann C. Finucane, Belstone, Devon

Peter Franklin, South Zeal, Devon

Mrs B. Gerry (née Letheren), North Tawton, Devon

Mrs Anne Gibbons (née Bowden), North Tawton, Devon

The Glover Family, South Zeal, Devon

P. and V. Goodman, Sticklepath, Devon

G. Goodman, Swadlincote, Derbyshire

Vicky and Henry Graham, Cosdon Cottage, South Zeal, Devon

Leslie and Gladys Gratton, Okehampton, Devon

Ann Green, Okehampton, Devon

Mrs Patricia Green (née Madders), Forres, Scotland

Mrs Jackie Green (née Madders), Forres, Scotland

Dr Tom and Mrs Elisabeth Greeves, Tavistock, Devon

Mr and Mrs H. W. Grey and Family, Ramsley, South Zeal, Devon

Nick Groom, South Zeal, Devon

David and Rona Gundry, Belstone, Devon

Mr P. Hamilton Leggatt BSc, Tavistock, Devon

Peter and Angela Hammond, Belstone (formerly South Zeal), Devon

Mrs Nancy Hannaford (née John), Cullaford Manor, South Tawton, Devon

Lynda Hardie (née Sampson), Whiddon Down, Okehampton, Devon

Bob and Vicki Hardy, Dalkeith, Ontario, Canada

Mr and Mrs Harris, Okehampton, Devon

Mr and Mrs Harris, Okehampton, Devon

Colin A. Hawkins, Tilehurst, Berkshire

D. J. Hawkins and M. J. Thomas, Tawton Lane, South Zeal, Devon

Richard Haynes, South Zeal, Devon

Joyce Hedges, South Tawton, Devon

Bruce Hewett, Budleigh Salterton, Devon

Mr Jack F. and Mrs Susan J. Hirst, South Zeal, Devon

Mrs J. Hiscocks, Easter Compton, Bristol

John and Selina Hodge, Okehampton, Devon

Mrs R. M. Hole and Mrs J. Norman, Orchard Lea, Sticklepath, Devon

Alan Holmes, South Zeal, Devon

Mr Alan J. Hooper, formerly of S. Zeal, Devon

Ray Hopcraft, Weeley, Essex

David Horan, South Zeal, Devon

Dr David Hornbrook, descendant of the Sticklepath Hornbrooks

Maria Horsley (née Sampson), Okehampton, Devon

Helen and Ian Howard, South Zeal, Devon

Edgar and Frances Hucker, South Zeal, Devon

Joan and Vic Hutchison, Sticklepath, Okehampton, Devon

Katie Jecks, South Zeal, Devon

Alan G. Jeffery, South Zeal, Devon

Mr W. G. Jeffery DFC, formerly of South Tawton, Devon

J. Loveys Jervoise, Sampford Courtenay, Devon

Sara John and Rob Jeffries, South Zeal, Devon

Mr and Mrs L. Jones, South Tawton, Devon

Mr and Mrs E. A. P. Jourdan, Hector and Phoebe, South Zeal, Devon

Carol and Pete Kilgannon, Ivy Cottage, South Zeal, Devon

Colin C. Kilvington, Stoke, Plymouth, Devon

Boris and Myrna Klapwald, New York, USA

The Knowles Family, Ramsley

Roman Kozlowski, Taw Green, Devon

Brian Le Messurier, Exeter, Devon

Mark and Debbie Lewis, Dunstable, Massachusetts, USA

Violet F. Littlejohns

L. Luck, Escrick, Yorkshire

Mr Brian Madders, Forres, Scotland

Mrs Lucy Amy Madders, South Tawton, Devon

Mr Christopher Madders, Charminster, Dorset

Mr Fred Madders, Sticklepath, Devon

Mr George Madders, Okehampton, Devon

Mr Clive and Mr Colin Madders, South Tawton, Devon

Mr Arthur Madders, South Tawton, Devon

Moti Makan, Navsari, Gujarat, India

Christine Marsh, Okehampton, Devon

Henry Marshall, South Zeal, Devon

James Robert Mawle, Sticklepath, Devon

Elizabeth Maycock (née Lentern)

Meg McCourt, Sticklepath, Devon

Jeremy and Fiona McKnight, Langmead, South Zeal, Devon

Quentin and Helen Morgan Edwards, Glebe House, South Courtenay, Devon

Margaret Mortimore, South Tawton, Devon

Gordon and Tania Murrell, Sticklepath, Devon

Tracey A. Needham, South Tawton, Devon

John Newcombe, Gunnislake, Cornwall

Alfie Osborn, South Zeal, Devon

Derek O. Oxenham, South Zeal 1936–1945

The Padfield Family, South Zeal, Devon

Angela Pengelly, Okehampton, Devon

Ruth Penrose (née Shields), Sticklepath, Devon

John and Welmoed Perrin, South Tawton, Devon

Mr and Mrs Martin Perryman, Middle Drewston Farm

Milo J. Pitkin, Hoffman Estates, Ill 60195, USA

Mr and Mrs P. Powell, Petersfield

Janice A. Preston, Basingstoke, Hampshire

South Tawton Primary School

Audrey Prizeman, Plymouth, Devon

F. and D. J. Prouse, South Tawton, Devon

Mr and Mrs J. Reddaway, Taw Green, Sticklepath, Devon

Mrs Elizabeth Reddaway, Margaret and Mary, South Zeal, Devon

Keith Counter Redstone, South Zeal, Devon

Ann Reed, Hendon, London NW4

Ken Rickard, Lydford, Devon

Mrs W. Roberts, South Zeal, Devon

Mrs Olive Roberts (née Barkwell), South Zeal, Devon

Dr Mark Rutter, South Zeal, Devon

David and Thea Sampson, South Tawton, Devon

David and Wendy Seddon, South Zeal, Devon

Sheila Shaw (née Meardon), Formerly of South Tawton, Devon

Helen Shields (née Bowden), Sticklepath, Devon

Mrs Kathy Smith (formerly Letheren), South Zeal, Devon

Dr Lawrence S. Snell, South Zeal, Devon

Dr A. Stainer Smith, Sticklepath, Devon

Mr John M. Stanton, South Zeal, Devon

Albert F. Stead

Harold Stentiford, Mountain View, California, USA

Doreen Taylor (née Madders), South Tawton, Devon

Boyd Templeton, San Francisco, California, USA

R. S. Tilley, South Zeal, Devon

Mr Barrie Tombs, South Zeal, Devon

Cyril J. Trick, Sticklepath, Devon

Mr and Mrs R. A. Vane, Lincoln

Mrs Margaret Vickery (née Madders), Barnstaple, Devon

Ken and Sheila Vincent, Sticklepath

Lynne Vincent, Sticklepath, Devon

Jean P. Waddington, South Zeal, Devon

John F. W. Walling, Newton Abbot, Devon

Mr and Mrs Tony Warren, South Zeal, Devon

David and Patricia Watkins, Sticklepath, Devon

Alan and Sheila Watson, Exeter, Devon

Mr A. Watson, Exeter, Devon

Peter Watson, Okehayes Nursery

Mr Charles Westlake, Okehampton, Devon

Mr and Mrs W. J. Westlake, Okehampton, Devon

Charlie A. L. White, South Zeal, Devon

Mr and Mrs Clarence White, South Zeal, Devon

Clifford and Vera White, Barton Farm, South Zeal, Devon

Thomas R. J. White, South Zeal, Devon

Richard White and Family, Shebbear, Devon

Mr and Mrs James Whiteside, Droitwich

Evelyn and Peter Wilkens, Ramsley, South Zeal, Devon

Dennis A. Wilkins

Ken Williams, Folly Gate, Okehampton, Devon

Peter and Gill Williams, The Drying House, Sticklepath, Devon

Doris V. Wonnacott, South Zeal, Devon

Michael and Sue Wonnacott, South Zeal, Devon

Kezia Wonnacott, South Zeal, Devon

Mr C. H. R. Wood, Reading, Berkshire

Mr and Mrs A. J. Woods, South Zeal, Devon

Mr and Mrs Barry Woods, South Tawton, Devon

Joyce Worthington, South Zeal, Devon

Irene Worthington, South Zeal, Devon

Michael, Jacqueline and Wyatt Wright, Grand Cayman, British West Indies

Mr and Mrs Roger Yeates, South Tawton, Devon

K. E. Young, Wood, South Tawton, Devon

ALSO AVAILABLE IN THE SERIES

The Book of Addiscombe, In Celebration of a Croydon Parish • Various
Book of Bampton, A Pictorial History of a Devon Parish • Caroline Seward
Book of Bickington, From Moor to Shore • Stuart Hands
The Book of Brixham, Portrait of a Harbour Town • Frank Pearce
The Parish Book of Cerne Abbas, Abbey and After • Vivian and Patricia Vale
The Book of Chittlehampton, Celebrating a North Devon Parish • Various
The Book of Cornwood and Lutton, Photographs and Reminiscences • Compiled by the People of the Parish
The Book of Creech St Michael, The Parish and Its People • June Small
The Ellacombe Book, A Portrait of a Torquay Parish • Sydney R. Langmead
The Book of Grampound with Creed • Amy Bane and Mary Oliver
The Book of Hayling Island and Langstone • Peter Rogers
The Book of Helston, Ancient Borough and Market Town • Jenkin with Carter
The Book of High Bickington, A Devon Ridgeway Parish • Avril Stone
The Book of Ilsington, A Photographic History of the Parish • Dick Wills
Lanner, A Cornish Mining Parish • Scharron Schwartz and Roger Parker
The Book of Lamerton, A Photographic History • Ann Cole and Friends
The Book of Loddiswell, Heart of the South Hams • Various
The Book of Manaton, Portrait of a Dartmoor Parish • Compiled by the People of the Parish
The Book of Minehead with Alcombe • Binding and Stevens
The Book of Meavy, Dartmoor Parish, Village and River • Pauline Hemery
The Book of North Newton, In Celebration of a Somerset Parish • Robins & Robins
The Book of Pimperne, A Millennium Celebration • Compiled by Jean Coull
The Book of Plymtree, The Parish and its People • Tony Eames
The Book of Porlock, A Pictorial Celebration • Denis Corner
Postbridge - The Heart of Dartmoor • Reg Bellamy
The Book of Priddy, A Photographic Portrait of Mendip's Highest Village • Various
The Book of Torbay, A Century of Celebration • Frank Pearce
Widecombe-in-the-Moor, A Pictorial History of a Dartmoor Parish • Stephen Woods
Uncle Tom Cobley and All, Widecombe-in-the-Moor • Stephen Woods
Woodbury, The Twentieth Century Revisited • Roger Stokes

SOME OF THE MANY TITLES AVAILABLE IN 2001

The Book of Bickleigh • Barrie Spencer
The Book of Blandford Forum • Various
The Book of Constantine • Various
The Book of Hemyock • Various
The Lustleigh Book • Joe Crowdy and Tim Hall
The Book of Rattery • Various
The Book of Publow with Pensford • Various
The Book of South Stoke • Various
The Book of Sparkwell • Pam James
The Book of Watchet • Compiled by David Banks
The Book of West Huntspill • Various

For details of any of the above titles or if you are interested in writing your own community history, please contact: Community Histories Editor, Halsgrove House, Lower Moor Way, Tiverton Business Park, Tiverton, Devon EX16 6SS, England, e-mail:sales@halsgrove.com If you are particularly interested in any of the images in this volume, it may be possible to supply a copy. Please telephone 01884 243242 for details.